Planning and Place in the City

e industrial-
hat define a
lanners and
ace without

d enhance-
tory of the
of analysis
lentity. This
eMaker' to
es appropri-

Asia, which
alytical and
ep in iden-
should be
sidents and
. The case
ured maps.
lays out an
ltural herit-

 Research
joined the
Department of Architecture of the University of Naples Federico II in 2003,
where she serves as a professor and as a member of the Research Doctorate
Committee in Urban Design and Planning. Sepe is on the Steering Committee
of the Italian National Institute of Urban Planning (Inu), and is a member of the
Urban Design Group (UDG) and European Urban Research Association (EURA).

Planning and Place in the City

Mapping place identity

Marichela Sepe

Routledge
Taylor & Francis Group

LONDON AND NEW YORK

First published 2013
by Routledge
2 Park Square, Milton Park, Abingdon, Oxon OX14 4RN

Simultaneously published in the USA and Canada
by Routledge
711 Third Avenue, New York, NY 10017

Routledge is an imprint of the Taylor & Francis Group, an informa business

British Library Cataloguing in Publication Data
A catalogue record for this book is available from the British Library

Library of Congress Cataloging-in-Publication Data
Sepe, Marichela.
  Planning the city : mapping place identity / Marichela Sepe. – 1 [edition].
  pages cm
  Includes bibliographical references and index.
  1. City planning–Social aspects. 2. Architecture–Human factors. 3. Cultural
    landscapes. I. Title.
  NA9053.H76S47 2013
  307.1'216–dc23
  2012025850

ISBN13: 978-0-415-66475-2 (hbk)
ISBN13: 978-0-415-66476-9 (pbk)
ISBN13: 978-0-203-07614-9 (ebk)

Typeset in 9pt Univers by GreenGate Publishing Services, Tonbridge, Kent

Printed and bound by Ashford Colour Press Ltd, Gosport, Hampshire

To my parents
To my family

Contents

Acknowledgements

I am grateful to all the people who in different ways and at different times have contributed to the updating and deepening of this work. Special thanks to: Professor Taner Oc for his accurate and sensitive foreword; the referees and Routledge staff for their useful suggestions and for having made possible the publication of my project; and the owners of images for their kind permission to reproduction.

I would also like to thank my students, whose stimulating questions have contributed to enrich the book with different points of view and perspectives.

Last but not least, I am grateful to the places, which, with their life, people and movements, constantly give me new stimuli and the occasion for *urban thinking*.

Foreword

The re-emergence of Urban Design in the early 1960s with the seminal contributions of Lynch and Jacobs has gained a significant momentum over the past two decades. This book is an important contribution to our understanding of place-making by introducing and developing PlaceMaker – a tool for understanding place identity. A questioning and inquisitive approach to Urban Design is now dynamic and evolving, as illustrated by this book.

Over the recent decades, Urban Design has evolved from an initial – predominantly aesthetic – concern with the distribution of building masses and the space between buildings, to become primarily concerned with the quality of the public realm – both social and physical – and the making of places for people to enjoy and respect. Earlier and narrower understanding of Urban Design was predominantly product oriented, tending to concentrate on the visual qualities and experience of urban spaces rather than on the myriad of cultural, social, economic, political and spatial factors and processes that are the ingredients of successful urban places.

Although the aesthetic experience and appreciation of urban design is important – and certainly not to be neglected or diminished – contemporary approaches to Urban Design also recognize the importance of the development and design process. Contemporary Urban Design is therefore simultaneously concerned with the design of space as an aesthetic entity and as a behavioural setting. Accordingly, it places greater emphasis on understanding how spaces function and on what cultural meanings and values are expressed. This book with its clear focus on mapping place identity – which is under threat in our globalising world – is a valuable contribution to our understanding of the city.

As Marichela Sepe notes, urban places change continuously in terms of the rhythms and exploitations of the city, the modalities of living, working and moving around, and the opportunities for enjoying leisure. The emergence of new typologies of place and changes in the patterns of usage for the existing typologies has given rise to whole new cityscapes. In the age of internet shopping, Facebook socialising and Twitter, identity of place may prove to be increasingly more important and placemaking – the art of making places for people – is essential to retaining and enhancing place identity.

The concept of place, in the sense of a space endowed with unique features (which are) fundamental to establishing the identity of the contemporary city, is key to Part I of this book. Part I concludes with an analysis of the main sites that define the contemporary city: new spaces for living, urban containers, networks and infrastructures, new places of perception, and monitored places.

The ongoing changes in places have prompted us to extend and innovate the tools of enquiry used for placemaking. Hence the endeavour to develop a 'complex-sensitive' approach retaining both the tangible and intangible aspects of the environment. The PlaceMaker method presented in Section II of Part II is a tool based on dialogue with local people to support professionals in the sustainable transformation of the city.

The case studies, which are wide ranging, are a major strength of this book. The focus on preserving place identity; reconstructing place identity; and enhancing place identity. The focus of the Trevi–Pantheon case study in Rome is understanding anthropic risk. The South Broadway in Los Angeles case study explores the loss of traditional functions, with an aim of identifying the resources in place for design interventions that can enable the historical tradition to re-emerge and be reinterpreted for current needs. The Kobe and San Francisco case studies assert the value of place identity as a reference point in the reconstruction process, both in terms of the wishes of the stakeholders and in safeguarding the urban image.

Oxford Street in London and Las Ramblas in Barcelona, where the process of globalization is underway, and the Esplanade area in Helsinki are case studies located in areas which are dimensionally and geographically different, but that share a central position and proximity to the historical core, and represent symbolic places for citizens as well as visitors to those cities. These case studies were designed to help understand whether the present identity of those places, while they are changing as a result of globalization, is sustainable with their walkability and if there are critical points where it might be possible to think in terms of urban redesign enhancing identity, the quality of its image, walkability and urban safety.

Understanding how well the physical milieu supports the multitude of functions and activities that take place in the urban environment/urban places, and how such spaces interact with and shape the lives of the city's inhabitants, is enhanced by the tools developed by Sepe and illustrated by the case studies discussed in this book. Such understanding is fundamental to the activity of Urban Design. When animated by the presence of people – as illustrated in the case studies of Oxford Street and Las Ramblas – spaces become meaningful places with their valued identities. This volume underlines the importance of design for human experience of urban space.

This book continues the tradition, which has developed over the past decades, of applying social sciences research, including environmental psychology and perception, to studying how the built environment functions for people of different cultures and subcultures at various stages of their life cycles and through major threats to their environment and well-being, as was the case in Kobe and San Francisco.

Synthesizing and integrating ideas, theories and techniques from a wide range of sources, PlaceMaker is a valuable tool and with this clearly argued and well presented/illustrated book it will gain a greater exposure which is much deserved. Urban Design will be enriched with this contribution, continuing the journey started by Kevin Lynch in 1960 with the publication of *Image of the City*.

Taner Oc, *Professor Emeritus*, University of Nottingham

Introduction
Planning the city – mapping place identity

This book talks about the identity of places and the issues connected with its identification, representation and shaping as a key element in planning the city of today.

The studies of Kevin Lynch on the image of the city and Taner Oc on public spaces, together with the approach to delineating the landscape developed by Bernard Lassus, are the chief coordinates for the topics dealt with in this volume, and in particular for the PlaceMaker method. We are operating at the intersection of two important and equally complex concepts: that of identity, full of nuances and interpretations; and that of city, for which a whole range of adjectives – porous, global, diffuse, virtual, hyper – have been employed in the attempt to account for the mutations we are witnessing in today's cities.

Places are termed 'places' and not just 'spaces' when they are endowed with identity (Hague and Jenkins, 2005). Such identity is related to the urban fabric and a series of morphological, natural, historical and cultural invariants. These invariants are closely interrelated to the life of the city and its inhabitants, and also to the perception the latter have of that place. At the same time, colours, materials, smells and sounds become an inseparable part of any one spot in the city, and thus emotional components of the urban image.

The identity of a place expresses a harmonious balance between variant and invariant components, people and urban events, which are intrinsically linked by a reciprocal relationship that makes a specific place unique and recognizable (Lynch, 1960). At the same time, globalization and technological development have contributed to accelerating the rates of change and transforming spaces in the contemporary city. The end result is that cities, places, itineraries, customs and behavioural patterns have all come to resemble one another, contributing to an increasing urban identity crisis (Bentley, 1999; Christensen, 1999; Forrester and Snell, 2007; Massey and Jess, 1995).

Many trends towards homogenisation of, and loss of meaning in, places relate to processes of globalization and the creation of global space, through improved communications (whether physical or electronic). Globalization is a multi-faceted process in which the world is becoming increasingly interconnected, with centralised decision-making exploiting economies of scale and standardisation. The changing, and problematising, of relationships between local and global has significant implications for what constitutes the meaning of place. Castells (1989, p.6) described the effects of information technology in the creation of a space of flow which dominates the histori-cally constructed space of places. ... With globalization has come 'mass' culture, emerging from the processes of mass production and consump-tion, which homogenises and standardises culture and places, transcending, crowding out, even destroying, local cultures. According to Crang (1998, p.115), much of the worry over 'placeness' can be interpreted as fear that local, supposedly 'authentic' forms of culture – made from, and making, local distinctiveness – are being displaced by mass-produced commercial forms imposed on the locality.

(Carmona *et al.*, 2010, pp.124–125)

The urban condition we experience today shows many changes in terms of the rhythms and exploitation of the city, the modalities of living, working and moving around, and the opportunities for enjoying leisure. The emergence of new typolo-gies of place and changes in the patterns of usage for the existing typologies have given rise to whole new cityscapes:

In practice the term 'the contemporary city' covers a very broad and diversi-fied series of transformations and situations. It is banal to point out that the urban condition today is very different to what it was in the past, and in any case this must not imply the existence of a homogeneous past. There has been a marked differentiation in the elements that generate urban organiza-tion: the ways inhabitants use their city, the mode of living and working, and the forms of production have all undergone radical changes. This has given rise to different cities, not so much in the form (*forma urbis* has always been declined in the singular) but in the modalities of realising and embodying the urban condition.

(Indovina, 2006, p.8)[1]

Striking juxtapositions and fragmentariness seem to predominate in the whole-sale dispersion with which subjects, things and habits coexist, characterized by boundaries which are transparent and yet at times unbreachable (Rowe and Koetter, 1978).

Interpreted often as a chaotic dispersion of things and subjects, practices and economies, the contemporary city, on the various scales of physical, social, economic, institutional, political and cultural space, appears to be characterized by the same degree of fragmentariness, the outcome of mul-tiple and legitimate rational approaches but often simply juxtaposed one to another, characterized by boundaries which are as invisible as they can be difficult to cross.

> The various pieces in the mosaic of the contemporary city, their dimen-
> sions, reciprocal distance, the period of construction and the inhabitants all
> show us a city that has been chopped up into pieces. In order to lay claim to
> being organized, recognizable and intelligible on each of the various scales,
> it relies on a variegated set of structures referring to different principles and
> prototypes.
>
> (Secchi, 2000, p.79)[2]

The contemporary city is the locus not only of complexity but also of simultaneity and instability, which give rise to situations of mutation and transitoriness
(Harvey, 1985, 1989; Hauptmann, 2001; Landrove, 1997). These are often predominantly motivated by economic gain, to the detriment of place identity which
becomes increasingly hybrid, compromised or unrecognizable. Railway stations
become shopping malls, libraries turn into shops selling books and gadgets or
even restaurants, houses are transformed into workshops, cinemas into supermarkets, residential streets into major highways. The extension of functions and
conversions of purpose become intertwined, giving rise to new cultural problems, namely 'the degree of tolerance, compatibility or incompatibility vis à vis
others, with their habits and activities, noises, smells, and overlapping and intersecting exploitation of time' (Secchi, 2000, pp.79–80)[3].

The lengthy periods of time required for the perception of the city that
Kevin Lynch[4] talks about have been altered by the acceleration of the new urban
rhythms. Nonetheless it still seems true that:

> City design is therefore a temporal art, but it can rarely use the controlled
> and limited sequences of other temporal arts like music. On different occa-
> sions and for different people, the sequences are reversed, interrupted,
> abandoned, cut across. It is seen in all lights and all weathers.
>
> At every instant, there is more than the eye can see, more than the ear
> can hear, a setting or a view waiting to be explored. Nothing is experience
> by itself, but always in relation to its surroundings, the sequences of events
> leading up to it, the memory of past experiences.
>
> (Lynch, 1960, p.1)

Undoubtedly the people and their activities are as important as the 'stationary physical parts', and we are part of the scenario together with the other protagonists.

> We are not simply observers of this spectacle, but ourselves a part of it, on
> the stage with the other participants. Most often, our perception of the city
> is not sustained, but rather partial, fragmentary, mixed with concerns. Nearly
> every sense is in operation, and the image is the composite of them all.
>
> (Lynch, 1960, p.2)

Figure 0.1
Simultaneity of urban events in a contemporary city

Placemaking, in the sense of 'the art of making places for people', to quote the definition given in *By Design: Urban Design in the Planning System* (CABE and DETR, 2000), 'includes the way places work and such matters as community safety, as well as how they look. It concerns the connections between people and places, movement and urban form, nature and the built fabric, and the processes for ensuring successful villages, towns and cities'.

The city thus becomes the outcome of complex intersections created by a number of operators who modify the system for different reasons. It becomes necessary to identify a microsystem within the macrosystem of the city able to make the urban variants intelligible: place is at once porous and resistant, a receptor for complex interactions (Bachelard, 1969; CABE, 2001; Chapman and Larkham, 1994; Dickens, 1990; Gandelsonas, 1991; Hayward and McGlynn, 1993; Hillman, 1990; Moughtin *et al.*, 1995; Norberg-Schulz, 1980; Orum and Chen, 2003; Pellegrino, 2000; Project for Public Spaces, 2001; Jacobs, 1993; Jacobs and Appleyard, 1987).

The concept of place, in the sense of a space endowed with unique features which is fundamental for establishing the identity of the contemporary city, is the key to the first of the three Parts which compose this book. I illustrate the environmental, historic, symbolic, urban, perceptive, anthropological, sociological and psychological characteristics, extending as far as virtual place and non-place. Place identity is considered 'not in the sense of equality with something else, but with the meaning of individuality or oneness' (Lynch, 1960, p.8). The concepts of both place and identity are illustrated with reference to texts produced by architects, urban planners, sociologists, geographers, environmental psychologists, anthropologists, historians and philosophers (Evans *et al.*, 2011).

Part I is enriched by an analysis of the main sites that go to define the contemporary city. These are both places – spaces for living, places of socialization, virtual and real infrastructures, places of perception and monitored areas – created by the effects of globalization and new habits of people, and existing places modified according to new needs. Some of these are difficult to perceive individually or to explain using the standard terminology, and may even be impossible to represent. Nonetheless, the interrelations between these places and their constituent elements can be deciphered by converting them in terms of place identity and recognizability.

In the last decades, the changes which were identified in contemporary places have been a strong stimuli to innovate the tools of placemaking, so as to contemplate a sustainable form of place able to encompass the transformations in progress. 'Good design can help create lively places with distinctive character; streets and public spaces that are safe, accessible, pleasant to use and human in scale; and places that inspire because of the imagination and sensitivity of their designers' (CABE and DETR, 2000).

There is a need to approach and represent the city using methods of transverse and multi-level analysis and planning of places. By bringing up to date the approaches to the city adopted by Cullen and Lynch, and also borrowing models from other disciplines for envisaging, investigating, explaining and representing the urban, natural, mental and virtual places in which we live, it becomes possible to decode their complexity and make it narratable and representable (Appleyard, 1976; Forrester, 1969; Gandelsonas, 1991; Middleton, 1996; Denis and Daniels, 1988; Miller, 2003; Russ, 2002; Tugnutt and Robertson, 1987; Whitehand and Larkham, 1992).

In Section I of Part II I illustrate the evolution of the concept of placemaking, starting from Lynch and Cullen and the current methodologies of analysis and planning, with the relative tools for representing places, presented according to typology: virtual (Mitchell, 1996); lateral (Boeri, 2003); people-oriented (Gehl, 2010); multi-scale (MVRDV, 2002); and configurational (Hillier, 2007). In evaluating these typologies of methodological approach I found it necessary to develop another type of approach, the 'complex-sensitive' (Sepe, 2006a–b), able to explore urban complexity by retaining both tangible and intangible aspects. The PlaceMaker method presented in Section II is collocated within this typology, and I illustrate the various phases of the method, together with the software and the sustainable place identity index. PlaceMaker is a method of urban analysis and design which both detects elements that do not feature in traditional mapping, constituting the contemporary identity of the places, and identifies appropriate project interventions. The main products are two complex maps; one of analysis and one of planning, which represent the identity of places and planning interventions with the dual aim of setting up a dialogue with local people and supporting planners and administrators in the sustainable construction and transformation of the city (Sepe, 2010b).

PlaceMaker was conceived in 2001 as a method of analysis and has been regularly updated during its pilot experiments which were started in 2002. The case studies, which were carried out in Europe, North America and Japan, led to the upgrade of PlaceMaker as a method of analysis and design and a test of its flexibility.

The PlaceMaker software – which was created during the updating of the method – provides useful support for everything concerning the application and visualization of the multimedia data and their updating, and facilitates inter-action with tablets and smartphones. Furthermore, the software is a support for calculating the index of sustainability for place identity, providing numerical values to be used in evaluating urban sustainability and paying more attention to intangible aspects.

The chief characteristics involve the method's flexibility and repro-duceability. Being flexible, it is possible on one hand to deal with different place typologies in order to achieve a variety of objectives, and on the other to adapt to the ongoing mutations in planning instruments. And the fact that it is reproduce-able means that, thanks to a specific investigative protocol, it can be accessed by a range of user types.

Numerous case studies have been carried out, some of which are presented in Part III of this volume, starting with the objectives and cultural back-ground and giving a broad explanation of the outputs. The phases of analysis and planning are described in detail, showing the different uses and diversity of places and the observations inferred during the experiments. The experiments made it possible to capture the complex identity of places and explore how interventions can be structured to contribute to preserving, reconstructing and enhancing a sustainable identity. The Trevi–Pantheon route in Rome and South Broadway in Los Angeles exemplify the preservation of identity; the Kitano-Cho area of Kobe and Market Street in San Francisco exemplify the reconstruction of identity; and Oxford Street in London, Las Ramblas in Barcelona and the Esplanadi area in Helsinki exemplify the enhancement of identity. These geographically and cul-turally different places were chosen as particularly representative of the cities they belong to. At the same time they can stimulate reflection on questions of a more general nature, not limited to the specific locations where the findings were made. The case studies carried out over the years have made it possible to define a number of principles for enhancing place identity. These are given at the end of this volume as a sort of check list that any urban project has to match in order to enhance the identity of place.

Part I
Definition of the field of investigation

Section I
Place and place identity as key concepts

Chapter 1

The concept of Place

The relationships linking the elements that make up the phenomenological world are complex and in many cases contradictory. As Norberg-Schulz has pointed out, phenomena may incorporate others, while some phenomena constitute the environment in which others manifest themselves. One term that can be used to define the environment in which phenomena manifest themselves is 'place' – the space in which events occur (or 'take place') (Norberg-Schulz, 1980, p.6).

Place is not evident: it should be sought, identified and gained.

> I would like there to exist places that are stable, unmoving, intangible, untouched and almost untouchable, unchanging, deep rooted; places that might be points of reference, of departure, of origin: My birthplace, the cradle of my family, the house where I may have been born, the tree I may have seen grow (that my father may have planted the day I was born), the attic of my childhood filled with intact memories … Such places don't exist, and it's because they don't exist that space becomes a question, ceases to be self evident, ceases to be incorporated, ceases to be appropriated. Space is a doubt: I have constantly to mark it, to designate it. It's never mine, never given to me, I have to conquer it.
>
> (Perec, 1997, p.91)[1]

Places are the element of the existential place and constitute the primary unit. Berque (1999) acknowledges the coexistence of two aspects in place, one quantitative and the other qualitative, which complement each other. Every place

> necessarily possesses a part which is both material – physical and ecological – and measurable, and therefore commensurable with other sites. This qualitative dimension is akin to the Aristotelian topos[2] and Heidegger's Stelle: as for the container, it is the external limit of a thing in the universal space of an objectified environment. On the other hand, place is related no less necessarily to an immaterial, phenomenal and semantic – non-measurable – dimension, and thus cannot be compared to other places. This qualitative and unique dimension makes it similar to Plato's Khora[3] and Heidegger's Ort[4]: it is the condition of existence of the thing within the sensitive world. These two aspects are combined trajectorively in the Ecumene[5] reality: every place is not only a topos, but also a khora, and vice versa.[6]

Specifically regarding the quality aspect, place – as Healey (2010, pp.33–34) asserts – is also related to the meaning that people give to their surroundings and their capacity to influence them. Places are not just a set of objects positioned on a site in order to make up a part of a city or of a territory. They assume a specific meaning in the moment in which we infuse them with a value. Indeed the term place – such as meant by Healey – does not concern the objective reality and their buildings, streets, landscapes and facilities, nor is it considered as necessarily coterminous with administrative jurisdiction. 'Things may be co-located, and relations may overlay each other in physical spaces when we feel that we have arrived somewhere, when we sense an ambiance, when we feel that we are at some kind of nodal space in the flows of our lives' (Healey 2010, pp.33–34).

Places and people possess, according to Norberg-Schulz, a *genius loci*, a sort of guardian *spirit* which accompanies them to their death and determines their character. The *genius* corresponds to what a thing is or what it wants to be. 'Since ancient times the Genius loci, or "spirit of place" has been recognized as the concrete reality man has to face and come to terms with in his daily life ... and the task of the architect is to create meaningful places, whereby he helps man to dwell' (Norberg-Schulz, 1980, p.5).

Aldo Rossi recognizes in the choice of place a strong value in the classical world both for a single building and a city.

> The 'situation' – the site – was governed by the genius loci, the local divinity, an intermediary who presided over all that was to unfold in it. ... To bring this idea into the domain of urban artifacts, we must return to the value of images, to the physical analysis of artifacts and their surroundings; and perhaps this will lead us to a pure and simple understanding of the value of the locus. For such an idea of place and time is seemingly capable of being expressed rationally, even if it embraces a series of values that are outside and beyond what we experience.
>
> (Rossi, 1984, p.103)

All places have a character which is the world's main mode of 'supply' *a priori*.

> 'Character' is at the same time a more general and a more concrete concept than 'space'. On the one hand it denotes a general comprehensive atmosphere, and on the other the concrete form and substance of the space-defining elements. Any presence is intimately linked with a character.
>
> (Norberg-Schulz, 1980, pp.13–14)

In place, we can recognize the infinite characters that it consists of (Sepe, 2007). Below, we will treat the environmental, historic, symbolic, urban, perceptive, anthropological, sociological, psychological character, until we reach the virtual and that of non-place, which is useful to provide a framework for the topics in this book.

Environmental character, as Norberg-Schulz (1980) affirms, is the essence of the place. It consists in shape, in concrete things, the atmosphere in which these live. The first operation 'to give life to a place' is to give it a name in order to make it recognizable to the rest of the world around it, or construct it, according to our own way of thinking and vision of the world.

According to an environmental-psychological approach, individual places should be treated by positioning them in a wider system of places in which they belong. As Bonnes and Secchiaroli (1995, pp.192–194) assert, the consideration with which to start is the existence of organizational modalities with which the individual experiences the place. Places are perceived as being interconnected at the individual or collective level.

Place is historical 'from the moment when – combining identity with relations – it is defined by a minimal stability. This is the case even though those who live in it may recognize landmarks there which do not have to be objects of knowledge' (Augé, 1995, p.44)[7].

Rossi (1984, p.106) refers to the study of Gallia by Eydoux on:

> places that have always been considered unique, and he suggested further analysis of such places, which seem to have been predestined by history. These places are real signs of space; and as such they have a relationship both to chance and to tradition. I often think of the piazzas depicted by the Renaissance painters, where the place of architecture, the human construction, takes on a general value of place and of memory because it is so strongly fixed in a single moment.

Rossi theorizes on the historical method for the study of the city which can be analysed from two different perspectives:

> In the first, the city was seen as a material artifact, a man-made object built over time and retaining the traces of time, even if in a discontinuous way. Studied from this point of view – archaeology, the history of architecture, and the histories of individual cities – the city yields very important information and documentation. Cities become historical texts; in fact, to study urban phenomena without the use of history is unimaginable, and perhaps this is the only practical method available for understanding specific urban artifacts whose historical aspect is predominant. ... The second point of view sees history as the study of the actual formation and structure of urban artifacts. It is complementary to the first and directly concerns not only the real structure of the city but also the idea that the city is a synthesis of a series of values. Thus it concerns the collective imagination. Clearly the first and second approaches are intimately linked, so much so that the facts they uncover may at times be confounded with each other.
>
> (Rossi, 1984, pp.127–128)

Historical places can also become symbolic. Urban environments contain not just meanings and values but also symbols which are the fields of investigation of semiotics.

> As Eco (1968, pp.56–57) explains, semiotics studies 'all cultural phenomena as if they were systems of signs'. The world is replete with 'signs', interpreted and understood as a function of society, culture and ideology. Following Ferdinand de Saussure, the process of creating meaning is called 'signification': 'signifields' are what are referred to, signifiers are things that refer to them, and signs establish the association between them.[8]

According to Magnaghi (2005, p.37):

> Place is a cultural entity speaking to its contemporaries in the long process of anthropization of the landscape, creating identity, memory, language, material culture, and symbolic and affective messages. As long as we treat places – in the wake of mass industrial culture – as beast of burden (without loading them to death, making them carry a sustainable weight), we will still have no idea of their deep riches and we will hardly be able to reverse permanently the planetary catastrophe caused through our lack of knowledge about local places and the environment.

Through the analysis of places, a more detailed and qualitative interpretation of the city is carried out. This is not circumscribed to its aesthetic essence, nor even to its physical geometry. The functional and symbolic interpretations of the elements of a place are the fundamental factors for understanding its meaning (Migliorini and Venini, 2001, p.129). 'And as society changes, so does signification. Meanings attached to the built environment become modified as social values evolve in response to changing patterns of socio-economic organization and lifestyles' (Knox, 1984)[9].

Mumford (1961, pp.9–10) states that the first urban nucleus was constituted when Palaeolithic hunters began to settle in some fixed gathering places which, as they became meeting places between groups that were no longer occasional, contributed to the formation of social groupings, the basis for proto-urban settlements in the Neolithic period.

> Thus even before the city is a place of fixed residence, it begins as a meeting place to which people periodically return: the magnet comes before the container, and this ability to attract non-residents to it for intercourse and spiritual stimulus no less than trade remains one of the essential criteria of the city, a witness to its inherent dynamism, as opposed to the more fixed and indrawn form of the village, hostile to the outsider. The first germ of the city, then, is in the ceremonial

meeting place that serves as the goal for pilgrimage: a site to which family or clan groups are drawn back, at seasonable intervals, because it concentrates, in addition to any natural advantages it may have, certain 'spiritual' or supernatural powers, powers of higher potency and greater duration, of wider cosmic significance, than the ordinary processes of life .... Some of the functions and purposes of the city, accordingly, existed in such simple structures long before the complex association of the city had come into existence and re-fashioned the whole environment to give them sustenance and support.

(Mumford, 1961, pp.9–10)

The urban character of a place changes in part with the change of time: the seasons, the passing of the day and the weather conditions, resulting in different light, contribute to changing its character. This character is also:

determined by the material and formal constitution of the place. We must therefore ask: how is the ground on which we talk, how is the sky above our heads, or in general; how are the boundaries which define the place. How a boundary is depends upon its formal articulation, which is again related to the way it is 'built'. Looking at a building from this point of view, we have to consider how it rests on the ground and how it rises towards the sky. Particular attention has to be given to its lateral boundaries, or walls, which also contribute decisively to determine the character of the urban environment.

(Norberg-Schulz, 1980, p.14)

Halbwachs in his studies on collective memory theorizes on the interrelationship that exists between a group and the space which it occupies:

The group not only transforms the space into which it has been inserted, but also yields and adapts to its physical surroundings. It becomes enclosed within the framework it has built. The group's image of its external milieu and its stable relationships with this environment becomes paramount in the idea it forms of itself, permeating every element of its consciousness, moderating and governing its evolution. ... Thus we understand why spatial images play so important a role in the collective memory. The place a group occupies is not like a blackboard, where one may write and erase figures at will. ... But place and group have each received the imprint of the other. Therefore every phase of the group can be translated into spatial terms, and its residence is but the juncture of all these terms. Each aspect, each detail, of this place has a meaning intelligent only to members of the group, for each portion of its space corresponds to various and different aspects of the structure and life of their society, at least of what is most stable in it.

(Halbwachs, 1992, p.54)

Expanding Halbwachs's thesis, Rossi (1984) states that the city itself is the collective memory of peoples, and that memory is linked with events and places. The city is therefore the 'locus' of collective memory. The value of history as collective memory, intended as society's relationship with place and the idea of it, helps us to understand the significance of the urban structure and the architecture of the city which is the shape of this individuality. The union between the past and the future is in the idea of the city that runs through it, and to become concrete it must take shape in reality, which remains in its unique events, in the idea that we have of them.[10]

The sensory quality of a place consists of all the elements that can be perceived by the senses: smell and noise, but also sensations of touch, sight and taste. All of these, both individually and in their overall perception, can influence our feelings, actions, general well-being and appraisal of what surrounds us. The perception of the city can be separate or partial and combined with other feelings: the overall image is the union of all stimuli.

According to Lynch (1960, p.3):

> Structuring and identifying the environment is a vital ability among all mobile animals. Many kinds of cues are used: the visual sensations of colour, shape, motion, or polarization of light, as well as other senses such as smell, sound, touch, kinaesthesia, sense of gravity, and perhaps of electric or magnetic fields.

Indeed, as Relph (1976, p.10) asserts:

> Perceptive space is a space of action centred on immediate needs and practices, and as such it has a clearly developed structure. ... This structure can clearly be in no way understood as objective or measurable – rather distances and directions are experienced as qualities of near or far, this way or that, and even when these are made explicit as paths or trails they are known with their special meaning. ... Perceptive space is also the realm of direct emotional encounters with the spaces of the earth, sea, and sky or with built and created spaces.

Migliorini and Venini (2001, p.129) observe that

> the factors which determine the description of a place are the visual, tactile, smell, sound perceptions which are felt. Place, unlike space, is described by objects which transmit specific cultural, historical or socially meaningful values which are different for each individual. As mentioned above, the dimension of a place is related to the way in which people live it. And the dimension can change following the measure that derives from the description of the events that can be played out.

The anthropological place defined by Augé (1995, p.42) has a variable scale and at the same time 'is a principle of meaning for the people who live in it, and also a principle of intelligibility for the person who observes it'. Anthropological places are identitary, relational and historical.

> Michel de Certeau perceives the place, of whatever sort, as containing the order 'in whose terms elements are distributed in relations of coexistence', and, although he rules out the possibility of two things occupying the same 'spot', he admits that every element of the place adjoins others, in a specific 'location', he defines the 'place' as an 'instantaneous configuration of positions', which boils down to saying that the elements coexisting in the same place may be distinct and singular, but that does not prevent us from thinking either about their interrelations, or about the shared identity conferred on them by their common occupancy of the place.
>
> (Augé, 1995, p.44)

The anthropological place is also geometric:

> It can be mapped in terms of three simple forms, which apply to different institutional arrangements and in a sense are the elementary forms of social space. In the geometric terms these are the line, the intersection of lines, and the point of intersection. Concretely, in the everyday geography more familiar to us, they correspond to routes, axes or path that lead from one place to another and have been traced by people; to crossroads and open spaces where people pass, meet and gather, and which sometimes (in the case of marketplace, for example) are made very large to satisfy the needs of economic exchange; and lastly, to centres of more or less monumental type, religious or political constructed by certain men and therefore defining as others, in relation with other centres and other spaces.
>
> (Augé, 1995, p.46)

Place also has sociological value:

> It is difficult to conceive of 'space' without social content and equally, to conceive of society without a spatial component. ... The relationship is best conceived as a continuous two-way process in which people (and societies) create and modify spaces while at the same time being influenced by them in various ways. Dear and Wolch (1989) argue that social relations can be: constituted through space (e.g. where site characteristics influence settlement form); constrained by space (e.g. where the physical environment facilitates or obstructs human activity); and mediated by space (e.g. where the 'friction of distance' facilitates or inhibits the development of various social practices). Hence, by shaping that built environment, urban designers influence patterns of human activity and social life.
>
> (Carmona et al., 2010, p.133)

As identified by Maslow (1968), it is possible to distinguish a five-stage hierarchy of human needs:

> Physiological needs: for warmth and comfort; safety and security needs – to feel safe from harm; affiliation needs: to belong – to a community, for example; esteem needs: to feel valued by others; self-actualisation needs: for artistic expression and fulfilment.

The needs – despite the existence of a hierarchy – are related in a complex series of inter-relationships (Carmona *et al.*, 2010, p.134). Specifically on the relationship between public and private places and their interchangeability, Goffman (1959, pp.22) notes that 'a place can be defined as an area bounded by barriers to perception' and that not all areas have the same types of obstacles (referring to the case of societies who live mainly in indoor environments). Futhermore, Goffman observes that performances take place in a well-defined territory in space and time, as if they were built inside a theatre. Representation of an individual on the front stage can be considered as a way to show that his/her actions in that area follow certain rules, which in turn are grouped into two categories: the way in which the actor treats the public while engaged with them in a conversation or an exchange of gestures, a substitute for the word; and the way in which the actor behaves when he/she can be seen or heard by the public, but is not necessarily committed to talking to them. Both contexts have temporal or historical qualities, of an everyday or exceptional nature.

Place in the psychological sense sees an active and central subject to its environment. The relationships established between the observer and place are reciprocal: a place can affect the person and his/her values and actions, in the same way that the intentions of the person and his/her actions can attribute meaning to a place.

As asserted by Healey (2010 p.34), 'A sense of place and of place quality can be understood as some kind of coming together of physical experiences (using, bumping into, looking at, hearing, breathing) and imaginative constructions (giving meanings and values) produced through individual activity and socially formed appreciations'.

Furthemore, Canter (1986) proposes a definition of place based on its components:

> (a) the activities which are understood to occur at a location and the reasons for them. Here we would add the consideration of the individuals – actors of these activities – as parts of the same component of activities; (b) the evaluative conceptualizations, or, better the representations which are held of the occurrence of those activities, and (c) the physical properties of the place, as they are evaluated – or better represents – in relation to the activities.

In this regard, Canter (1986 p.8) affirms that

> places can be readily distinguished from behaviour settings and situations. Unlike behaviour settings a) they are not created by the investigator on the basis of observing behaviour and b) they have distinct evaluative and physical components. Unlike situations, they have a distinct enduring existence as well as being inevitably intertwined with the physical properties of their location.[11]

Place also concerns an unconscious sense of place which is related to the association of it to somewhere:

> Place can be considered in terms of 'rootedeness' and a conscious sense of association or identity with a particular place. Rootedness refers to a generally unconscious sense of place. ... For Relph (1976, p.38) it meant having 'a secure point from which to look out on the world, a firm grasp of one's own position in the order of things, and a significant spiritual and psychological attachment to somewhere in particular'.
>
> (Carmona, 2010, p.120)

Extending the concept of place to a broader context, Castells (1989) refers to the place of flows as a real or virtual entity, which also includes electronic interconnections, where many temporalities, as well as many simultaneities – which become atemporal – are allowed. With new technologies, space is downsized to zero and, recreated in a virtual dimension, no longer constitutes an obstacle. These relationships are defined by Castells with the term cyberspace or virtual space, and are described by means of spatial language such as 'information highways', 'sites' and 'squares'.

In the informational economy for example – as Castells (1989, pp.169–170) asserts – the space of organizations is increasingly considered a space of flows:

> However, this does not imply that organizations are placeless. On the contrary, we have seen that decision-making continues to be dependent upon the milieu on which metropolitan dominance is based. ... Thus, each component of the information-processing structure is place-oriented. Nevertheless, the organizational logic of corporations and their satellite activities is fundamentally dependent upon the network of interaction among the different components of the system. ... While organizations are located in places, and their components are place-dependent, the organizational logic is placeless, being fundamentally dependent on the space of flows that characterizes information networks. But such flows are structured, not undetermined. They

possess directionality, conferred both by the hierarchical logic of the organization as reflected in instructions given, and by the material characteristics of the information system infrastructure. Organizations establish flows according to their hierarchy within the limits set by the telecommunications and computer infrastructure existing at a particular time in a particular place. The space of flows remains the fundamental spatial dimension of large-scale information-processing complexes.

In this regard, Soja (1996, p.278) notes the social meaning of these new kinds of places:

> A new mode of regulation seems to be emerging spontaneously from this diffusion of hyperreality, plugging us into the new economic machinery of virtual reality and cyberspace, protected by elaborately carceral system of social control and leading us to the promised lands of postmodern re-enchanment, where tax cuts for the rich magically benefit the poor and social spending for the poor is seen as hurting those that receive it.

The increasing loss of meaning of place as a recipient of social customs, histori-cal memories and symbolic contents has led to the emergence of places with provisional uses, linked to a contemporaneity which cares more about satisfy-ing immediate consumption than sedimenting traces of culture (Arefi, 1999). As Augé (1995, p.63) states, 'If a place can be defined as relational, historical and concerned with identity, then a space which cannot be defined as relational, or historical, or concerned with identity will be a non-place'. The word non-place identifies two different aspects of the reality: spaces created in relation to sites used for transport, transit, commerce or leisure, and the relation between people and those spaces.

> Non-places are the real measure of our time; one that could be quantified – with the aid of a few conversions between area, volume and distance – by totalling all the air, rail and motorways routes, the mobile cabins called 'means of transport' (aircraft, trains and road vehicles), the airports and airway stations, hotel chains, leisure parks, large retail outlets, and finally the complex skein of cable and wireless networks that mobilize extra-terrestrial space for the purposes of a communication so peculiar that it often puts the individual in contact only with another image of himself.
>
> (Augé, 1995, p.64)

Places and non-places often overlap and intertwine. In any place there is also the possibility of becoming a non-place and vice versa:

> Places and non-places are opposed (or attracted) like the words and notions that enable us to describe them. But the fashionable words are associated with non-places. Thus we can contrast the realities of transit (transit camps or passengers in transit) with those of residence or dwelling; the interchange (where nobody crosses anyone else's path) with the crossroads (where people meet); the passenger (defined by his destination) with the traveller (who strolls along his route), the housing estate ('group of new dwellings', Laurosse says), where people do not live together and which is never situated in the centre of anything (big estates characterize the so-called peripheral zones or outskirts), with the monument where people share and commemorate; communication (with its codes, images and strategies) with language (which is spoken).
>
> (Augè, 1995, p.86)

These characters were presented in order to understand the complexity of the concept of place. The place, although complex, is nonetheless a total phenomenon, a set of all the individual characteristics that make it up. Man receives the environment and focuses on buildings and things, things reveal the environment, and show their character, becoming in turn meaning (Norberg-Schulz, 1980).

The role of place, then, is to embody the world of life and its value lies in representing the general local essence, a space with unique characteristics. Recognizing the value of place as the key component of a city's identity becomes a basis of reference both for its design and the wishes of the community.

> Placemaking efforts need sensitivity towards 'who lives where, what they do, what they know, how they get on, how they relate to each other, what they care about and feel that they "need"'. This requires design at different dimensions both of relations and scale in order to imagine the future of a place. Such a sensibility will be achieved by taking into account a wider range of dynamics not necessarily contained within a determined territory boundary and able to grasp the contemporary urban complexity.
>
> (Healey 2010, p.35)

Chapter 2

Place identity

Places are termed places and not just spaces because they are endowed with identity. The identity of a person consists, for example, in a set of elements and patterns which determines the world he/she belongs to. On this point, Norberg-Schulz (1980, p.21) states that:

> This fact is confirmed by common linguistic usage. When a person wants to tell who he is, it is in fact usual to say: 'I am a New Yorker', or 'I am a Roman'. This means something much more concrete than to say: 'I am an architect', or perhaps: 'I am an optimist'. We understand that human identity is to a high extent a function of places and things. ... It is therefore not only important that our environment has a spatial structure which facilitates orientation, but that it consists of concrete objects of identification. Human identity presupposes the identity of place.

Definition

The notion of identity is a fundamental phenomenon which is difficult to define, although it is possible to recognize many of its characteristics. In order to frame this notion within the aims of this volume, we will report the definitions that are used in different ways in the placemaking practice and the relative components which contribute to their characterization.

The starting definition is that asserted by Relph who identifies the difference between 'identity of' and 'identity with', which is useful to gain a clearer idea of this concept:

> The identity of something refers to a persistent sameness and unity which allows that thing to be differentiated from others. Such inherent identity is inseparable from identity with other things; Erik Erikson (1959, p.1029), in a discussion of ego identity, writes: 'The term identity ... connotes both a persistent sameness with oneself ... and a persistent sharing of some kind of characteristic with others'. Thus identity is founded both in the individual person or object and in the culture to which they belong. It is not static and unchangeable, but varies as circumstances and attitudes change; and it is not uniform and undifferentiated, but has several components and forms.
>
> (Relph, 1976, p.45)

This is confirmed by Paul Gilroy, who claims: 'the sheer variety of ideas condensed into the concept of identity, and the wide range of issues to which it can be made to refer, foster creative links between themes and perspectives that are not conventionally associated'.[1] Indeed, Watson and Bentley (2007, p.6) observe that place identity matters to a wide range of people. This is easy to understand if we focus on the relationships between the identities related to humans and a different set of meanings which affect the cultural landscape: 'for us, place identity is the set of meanings associated with any particular cultural landscape which any particular person or group of people draws on in the construction of their own personal or social identities'.

Place identity is often viewed in relation to the definition of space. As Bauman notes (2004, p.13–14):

> There is always something to explain, to apologize for, to hide or on the contrary to boldly display, to negotiate, to bid for and to bargain for; there are differences to be smoothed or glossed over, or to be on the contrary made more salient and legible. 'Identities' float in the air, some of one's own choice but others inflated and launched by those around, and one needs to be constantly on the alert to defend the first against the second; there is a heightened likelihood of misunderstanding, and the outcome of the negotiation forever hangs in the balance. The more one practises and masters the difficult skills needed to get by in such an admittedly ambivalent condition, the less sharp and hurting the rough edges feel, the less overwhelming the challenges and the less irksome the effects. One can even begin to feel everywhere chez soi, 'at home' – but the price to be paid is to accept that nowhere will one be fully and truly at home.

Hague and Jenkins (2005, p.20) highlight the existence of both individual and collective definitions of place identity related to different ideas of the area within which one lives:

> in an increasingly complex society, overlapping definitions of place identity exist – again both individual and collective. The manifestation of these forms of social identity is what has been termed 'mind-maps' whereby we register physical space mentally. Thus if asked to describe, for instance, the area which they live within, members of the same household will define this area differently based on their perception and activities within it, and will use different physical attributes to describe this. More than this, an individual household member is quite likely to use different mind-map references when describing the same area to different people, and would probably describe the same place in different ways with the passage of time.

This is demonstrated by the fact that the experience of place assumes relational meanings rather than being merely subjective.

> This means that our capacity to identify a place as a place is shaped by what others tell us about the place, and filtered by our socialization, as shaped by class, age, gender, ethnicity, nationality, professional education, etc. As Rose (1995, p.88) commented: 'although sense of a place may be very personal, they are not entirely the result of one individual's feelings and meanings. It is this process of receiving, selectively reconstructing, and then re-communicating a narrative that constitutes identity and transforms a space into a place'.
>
> (Hague and Jenkins, 2005, p.5)

Furthermore, Proshansky *et al.* (1983) links the various kinds of relationships between people and their experiences: 'Thus, place identity is the result of a constant, and often subconscious negotiation between individuals and the potpourri of experiences, objects, and even idealized places they encounter during their lives'.[2]

Southworth and Ruggeri (2010) point out that Stokols and Schumaker (1981) coined the term 'social imageability', which derives from the shared meanings generated by the involvement of individuals with a place. This terms leads to the concept of place attachment.

> Researching the effects on identity of displacement and detachment from familiar places, sociologist Melinda Milligan has identified what she calls 'locational socialization,' through which one's active involvement with a place generates shared meanings (1998; 2003, p.383). These meanings are layered onto a place, and it is in the very act of embedding these meanings that place identity and place attachment emerge and are shared with others.
>
> (Southworth and Ruggeri, 2010)

Place identity can also be related to the concept of authenticity which Southworth and Ruggeri define as

> the quality of a place being unique, distinctive, and rooted in the local. Geographer Edward Relph describes authentic places as being generated unselfconsciously and without theoretical pretense by individuals working alone or in small community groups over long spans of time. 'The end result is places which fit their context and are in accord with the intentions of those who created them, yet have a distinct and profound identity that results from the total involvement of a unique group of place-makers with a particular setting' (Relph 1976, p.68). Ancient Italian hill towns and preindustrial English villages epitomize these qualities.
>
> (Southworth and Ruggeri, 2010)

The close link that interrelates place identity with the history of a place is identified by Lo Piccolo. Accordingly, the first definition which we can attribute to urban identity is that related to physical aspects of the city, making urban identity coincide with historical identity which is elaborated through continuous stratifications.

> Whilst acknowledging the prevalence of the physical and material dimension, similar importance is given to morphology of places, which contributes in no small way to the configuration of specific local characteristics, hence also to identity, in terms which must not be understood in the sense of rigid environmental determinism, since it is easy to observe that very different choices or interpretations can correspond to similar morphologies. … Therefore identity does not only refer to urban fabrics but to the whole area, whose morphological, natural and cultural invariants – in the most detailed analyses and the most sensitive up-to-date approaches – take on the role of 'strong', structuring, recognizable elements.
>
> (Lo Piccolo, 1995, p.15)[3]

On the other hand, as Magnaghi (2005, p. 46) pointed out, it is important not to confuse history with its evolutionary interpretation:

> The identifying structure of place also grows because of the breaks between different civilization cycles. In conclusion, recognizing permanence, structural invariance and landscape features defining the identity of places must not lead to interpreting place as the outcome of an unequivocal deterministic relationship between the settled society and environmental structures: each territorialization cycle is a cultural event affecting the same inherited environment, realizing, reifying and structuring in the territory specific differentiated forms of settlements in the complex universe of potential and random outcomes, but always shaping the process as the result of a symbiosis between human and natural elements.

Place identity is therefore the product of a continuous evolutionary process.

> It is not a static image of its state, but is rather the result of concrete development over time. This is due to the fact that identity is the outcome of the relationships established between people and their environments. By making their mark on a region's cultural heritage, they have made every regional context unique and different. The uniqueness of places, area identity and the stratifications of history cannot be represented without running the risk of abstraction and crystallization, of the extraneousness of the product with the space-time context. Area identity can only be shown and communicated through the history which has shaped it, requiring continuous interpretative mediation.
>
> (Carta, 1999, p.151)[4]

In continuity with this assertion, place identity also assumes significance in relation to its public meaning, which in turn influences and stimulates citizen participation. In this connection, Southworth and Ruggeri (2010) observe that:

> Place significance may also result from historic or political events. But places with strong public identity need not have strong visual identity. ... While strong visual form is not essential for identity, it can provide a framework for attaching meanings. Place identity has greatest power when visual form, individual and social meaning come together. According to Lynch (1960), '(S)ense of place in itself enhances every human activity that occurs there, and encourages the deposit of a memory trace'.

Castells (1997, p.60) proposes that urban movements are based on three factors combined in different ways:

> urban demands on living conditions and collective consumption; the affirmation of local cultural identity; and the conquest of local political autonomy and citizen participation. Different movements combined these three sets of goals in various proportions, and the outcomes of their efforts were equally diversified. Yet, in many instances, regardless of the explicit achievements of the movement's participants, but for the community at large. And not only during the lifespan of the movement (usually brief), but in the collective memory of the locality. Indeed, ... this production of meaning is an essential component of cities, throughout history, as the built environment, and its meaning, is constructed through a conflictive process between the interests and values of opposing social actors.

Components

The different definitions related to the concept of place identity reflect the many components which go into it and the innumerable possibilities of combining them. Relph (1976, p.61) identifies three interrelated components which can be expressed in any identifiable place, creating its specific identity: 'physical features or appearance, observable activities and functions, and meanings or symbols'. He observes:

> In terms of our experiences this sharing does display certain consistencies that make it possible to distinguish a number of types of identities of places.
> 1. From the individual perspective or sociality in communion of existential insideness places are lived and dynamic, full with meanings for us that are known and experienced without reflection.

2. For empathetic insiders, knowing places through sociality in community, places are records and expressions of the cultural values and experiences of those who create and live in them.
3. From the standpoint of behavioural insideness place is ambient environment, possessing qualities of landscape or townscape that constitute a primary basis for public or consensus knowledge of that place.
4. In terms of incidental outsideness it is usually selected functions of a place that are important and the identity of that place is little more than that of a background for these functions.
5. The attitude of the objective outsider effectively reduce places either to the single dimension of location or to a space of located objects and activities.
6. The mass identity of place is a consensus identity that is remote from direct experience for it is provided more or less ready-made by the mass media. It is a superficial identity, for it can be changed and manipulated like some trivial disguise so long as it maintains some minimum level of credibility. It is also pervasive, for it enters into and undermines individual experiences and the symbolic properties of the identities of places.
7. For existential outsiders the identity of places represents a lost and now unattainable involvement. Places are all and always incidental, for existence itself is incidental.

   … The identity of place is not a simple tag that can be summarised and presented in a brief factual description. Nor can it be argued that there is a real or true identity of a place that relates to existential insideness.

As was pointed out by Montgomery (1998, p.100), it is possible to distinguish

> between 'identity', what a place is actually like, and 'image', a combination of the identity with perception of the place by the individual with their own set of feelings about, and impressions of, it. Furthermore, Pocock and Hudson (1978, p.33) suggest that the overall mental image of an urban environment will be: Partial: not covering the whole city; Simplified: omitting a great deal of information; Idiosyncratic: every individual's urban image being unique: Distorted: based on subjective, rather than real, distance and direction.
>
> (Carmona et al., 2003, p.88)

The components used for analysing the environmental image are for Lynch (1960, p.8) identity, structure and meaning: they always appear contemporaneously and are studied separately only for the purposes of analysis.

It is useful to abstract these for analysis, if it is remembered that in reality they always appear together. A workable image requires first the identification of an object, which implies its distinction from other things, its recognition as a separable entity. This is called identity, not in the sense of equality with something else, but with the meaning of individuality or oneness. Second, the image must include the spatial or pattern relation of the object to the observer and to other objects. Finally, this object must have some meaning for the observer, whether practical or emotional. Meaning is also a relation, but quite a *different* one from spatial or pattern relation.

The structure of a place is also mentioned by Norberg-Schulz (1980). This, in the opinion of the author, even while changing, maintains its identity for a certain period of time.

Stabilitas loci is a necessary condition for human life. How then is the stability compatible with the dynamics of change? First of all we may point out that any place ought to have the 'capacity' of receiving different 'contents', naturally within certain limits. A place which is only fitted for one particular purpose would soon become useless. Secondly it is evident that a place may be 'interpreted' in different ways. To protect and conserve the genius loci in fact means to concretize its essence in ever new historical contexts.

(Norberg-Schulz, 1980, p.18)

According to lo Piccolo (1995, p.15), identity can be interpreted in its relationship between civitas and urbs, through which the social nature of the architecture and public spaces, concrete and symbolic expressions of the city, may be recognized.

In other words, it is the way in which the city, as a set of citizens, is able to express its own character through its physical forms, in the present historical moment, showing the relationship of mutual belonging between inhabitants and places within the respective cultural context, both present and past. ... And it is precisely in this evolving relationship of attribution of value to extremely different permanent elements, in this continuous 'tension between the long times of the stones and the so much briefer pace of social life', which the wider but maybe at the same time more precise notion of urban identity has to be identified.[5]

The territorialist approach defines the territorial heritage as the result of the historical process of territorialization, whose identity is determined by how its components are integrated. This approach is configured as a deposit of long duration which specifies its own identity and character in the way in which environmental components (neo-eco-systems produced by successive civilizations) are integrated with built components (monuments, historical cities and structural invariants of long duration: in particular, infrastructures, agriculture traces, building, urban and landscape types, and constructive and transformation rules) and with anthropic ones (socio-cultural and identity patterns, artistic, productive and political cultures). As a matter of fact, the process of territorialization, adding layers of territorializing acts determined by different patterns of civilization, increases during the time the complexity and richness of sedimented, stratified and interagent elements in the long term (territorial mass, material and cognitive sediments and identity of places). The territorial and landscape typology which characterizes identity of a place – as well as the existence of a milieu – is the result of that long process of co-evolution between settlement and environment.

(Magnaghi, 2005, pp.41–46)

In this respect, Carta (1999) asserts that communities change and transform, preserving certain invariants which are fundamental for recognizing place identity.

We need to find these invariants and adapt them to contemporary situations and conditions, and it is on this heritage of specificity and intrinsic values (history, culture, nature) that one can establish an effective, sustainable local innovation process, which can become a source of collective identity, a tool of communication between generations and a means of maximizing opportunities.

(Carta, 1999, p.112)[6]

Further components are identified by Amundsen. These, variously combined with each other, are present in the identity of a place:

spatial qualities that distinguish the place from others – e.g. location, but also infrastructure, communication and architecture; characteristics or qualities of the inhabitants that distinguish them from inhabitants of other places – e.g. values, customs, physical appearance; social conditions and social relations between inhabitants; culture and/or history, seen as a unifying element that again connects the inhabitants to tradition and distinguishes them from 'the other'.[7]

On the other hand, Barbara and Perliss (2006) argue that issues related to the concept of identity cannot nowadays only rely on local characteristics. The issue of identity may refer to the local scale for elements which are an expression of the materials, the feelings that make one city different from another or bring them together.[8] 'In fact, the identity of a work may play on the "iconic language" that no longer concerns the form, plants, gables, columns and decorations, but the colours, materials, smells and sounds which are recognized and shared emotional heritage' (Barbara and Perliss, 2006).

The various components which contribute to the definition of place identity suggest, as was observed by Southworth and Ruggeri (2010), that this concept 'should be thought of as a gradient that includes several dimensions and should be as complex as the processes at play in every neighbourhood. It should account for aesthetic appeal and imageability, but be expanded to include social considerations, the discourses and meanings that are shared by community members'. This means that other more nuanced definitions of place identity may be identified.

> It can be found by looking at a range of places, from the historic downtowns of our cities to the everyday landscapes of suburbia, using a variety of methods, including physical form analysis, observations, interviews and other sociological methods. This new definition should consider the need for memorable and imageable environments, expressions of shared social values, new forms of non-place communities, and the multiple mechanisms by which meanings are embedded and communicated in the landscape.
>
> (Southworth and Ruggeri, 2010)

Indeed, in order for identity to be captured it needs to establish a deep engagement with place and local life in order to affect its natural evolution.

> As a result, design integrity is seen as a sign of a healthy identity, while changes and adaptations are interpreted as signs of an unhealthy, degraded place identity. Maintaining a gradient of identity is a much more complex endeavour, as it cannot rely purely on the maintenance of an original form. It must include considerations of the social, economic and cultural processes needed to successfully manage the evolution of the cities and neighbourhoods we design, allowing them to change and adapt to future conditions, while maintaining their essence. Only this can insure that the place identity resulting from our designs will be stronger, more imageable, and ultimately more sustainable.
>
> (Southworth and Ruggeri, 2010)

Finally, based on these interpretations the role of identity should be understood within the project of transforming the city, assessing the potential of design and planning tools as regards urban identity, and integrating them (Neil, 2004).

Part I

Definition of the field of investigation

Section II

New places in the contemporary city

Chapter 3

New spaces for living

Living can no longer simply be identified with dwelling because, with the opportunities offered by global organization, people have begun to inhabit the world in a more diversified way: the place where you live is no longer automatically a house, just as the city is no longer represented by a physical form (Krier, 1984; Lawrence, 1987). The differences regarding the past do not merely derive from the redistribution of complex functions over greater areas but are also due to the continuous evolution in lifestyle and modalities of settlement.

The mutation of the typical family and the rise of new forms of cohabitation, together with technological development and climate change are the main developments that have produced a reconfiguration of living spaces. These mutations led to the arising of new spaces for living where different needs and habits emerged (Sepe, 2005b).

Developments in living spaces

In the city of today we can identify different types of cohabitation, including the single young person, the couple without children, the elderly single person, the elderly couple, the long family and the enlarged family, and groups of immigrants. Within the new households we find people cohabiting with various cultures, levels of instruction and professional profiles, and different attitudes towards consumption and how to employ their time (Secchi, 2000). A young person, an adult, an old person, an immigrant, or a family including the elderly or handicapped each have their own necessities with respect to the living space, which the public and private offer of housing is trying to satisfy. Above all, the increase in the numbers of single and elderly people[1] – which is noted in different European countries, in America and in Asia – is requiring a new configuration of housing. In particular, as observed in recent field studies (Belsky et al. 2007), growth of the population in older age groups influences the household formation more than does the younger age group growth. However, in the USA, 'growth of the population aged 20 and over as a whole is the single most important factor determining the change in the number of households due to population growth'.[2]

Another phenomenon which is determining a transformation in the living space is linked to the residential insertion of immigrant populations. There is a diversification of places for interrelation in order to find room for new customs and traditions. In this way, the space, in the sense of a fundamental component of the cultural identification of each ethnic group, varies both inside and outside. The dimension of such transformations constitutes an important element in the changing face of housing and identifies the characters of a new, 'multi-ethnic' condition. One further phenomenon which is contributing to transform the territorial configuration is that of bi-residentiality, due to a growing mobility in sectors of the population which work, live and consume in different places and congregate in still other places of socialization and entertainment. In these cases, the second home becomes increasingly a complementary place of residence, so that bi-residentiality is having a great impact on living space (Lanzani, 2003; Ohnmacht *et al.*, 2009).

With the use of the internet, different actions that can be carried out in a specifically designated room can be carried out in others. The main use that is modifying the living space is that of work and study which, with the advent of the internet, may be satisfied in any space of the home. The place of the house acquires in this way a multiple value, moving also outside it. The urban space becomes an extension of private space, creating new boundaries between public and private sectors (Farè, 2003) .

Climate change is causing different kinds of urban transformation, housing included. If on one hand the green agenda requires arriving at a proper balance between energy consumption and capacity of the environment, on the other hand the demands for new housing to satisfy the new needs are imposing an unsustainable strain on resources such as land, materials and traditional fuels (Towers, 2005).

'Each group of people is characterized by a way of inhabiting the house and occupying the itineraries and places of socialization that change during the individual's life cycle. In this way the house becomes a place with a multiple identity whose modalities of habitation can change several times in the course of a day, juxtaposing work, privacy, socialization and free time' (Viganò, 1999)[3]. As observed by Stanek (2011, p.86):

> the research of the city by means of concepts initially employed to analyse the domestic interior was facilitated by rethinking dwelling in a broader perspective, both scalar and historical. Already in the introduction to *L'habitat pavillonaire*, Lefebvre related dwelling to scales larger than the apartment or a building and qualified the practices of habitation by various societies and modes of production, in spite of a transhistorical persistence of some of their features. By relating the specific research procedures applied in the pavillon study – the examination of words and objects – to a broad 'anthropological' understanding of dwelling ('the earth is the dwelling of men'), he redefined dwelling as consisting of practices that relate to multiple scales of social processes rather than being confined to an individual dwelling.[4]

New demands and solutions

According to different needs, new requirements concerning housing are emerging. The increase in the total number of families corresponds on one hand to a growing demand for single-family housing and on the other to a certain rigidity in the amount of middle- to large-sized housing available.

The demand for new homes is mainly related to three themes: 'the demand for additional units to accommodate household growth; the demand for new units to replace existing units lost on net from the stock; and the demand for additional second homes and vacant units for rent or sale that accommodate the normal turnover of a larger housing stock' (Belsky *et al.* 2007).

Experimentation at international level, aimed at finding a solution to these requirements, is investigating the construction of flexible models of residence through the organization of housing units in buildings with complementary spaces which may be added to or removed from the inhabited area. As declared in the CABE and DETR (2000, pp.29–32) Ministerial guide *By Design: Urban Design in the Planning System – Towards Better Practice*, adaptability and diversity are the two key concepts. Adaptibility (p.29) applies at every scale:

> A household makes different demands on a house as children are born and grow up. Towns and cities as a whole have to adapt as industries rise and decline, demand for housing and the nature of workplaces changes, and buildings and infrastructure age. Distinctive buildings help people find their way around. Something memorable is worth a hundred signs thinking about urban design. Simple, robust building forms, not tightly designed to a very particular use, allow for the greatest variety of possible future uses to be accommodated.

Diversity too is to be considered on a variety of scales:

> The mix of uses (whether within a building, a street or an area) can help to determine how well-used a place is, and what economic and social activities it will support. A mix of uses may be appropriate at a variety of scales: within a village, town or city; within a neighbourhood or a street; or even in a particular building. In a town centre, for example, housing can provide customers for shops, make use of empty space above them and generate activity when they are closed. In residential areas, workplaces, shops and other facilities can make the place more than just a dormitory.
>
> (p.31)

And mixed use is meant in a functional as well as a social sense:

> To promote social inclusion, in well-designed places social housing is not distinguishable from private housing by its design, nor is it banished to the least attractive site.
>
> (p.32)

The flexibility of the apartment is obtained in different ways, with the aim of conserving as much surface area as possible for a variety of uses (Gausa, 2002). This solution makes it possible to create differentiation in the common spaces, fulfilling the needs of various kinds of users. Contemporary research into residence has come up with a further working hypothesis: the passage from the traditional single-family house to the urban house, in opposition to living in isolation and autonomy, where the concept of flexibility is applied not only to the lodging but to the building as a whole.

As pointed out by Sinai (2008), this demand reflects the desire to live in urban areas. People need to live close to their jobs, but they also wish to take advantage of the greater availability and quality of goods and services. Even the rise of the internet has not diminished the desire to live in cities.

In fact, Sinai and Waldfogel (2004) have observed 'that the number and variety of websites focused on a city increases with the city's population. By enhancing the welfare benefits of living in cities – perhaps by mitigating the effects of congestion or facilitating communication and connection among city residents – these sites have an offsetting positive effect on urban housing demand'. Furthermore, Towers (2005, p.103) affirms that:

> The pressures to reduce travel coupled with the shortcomings of the transport system are likely to make home working an increasingly attractive proposition. For many activities, working at home requires no special provision. For most desk-based activities the use of a spare bedroom or, at most, the conversion of a dining room, makes a more than adequate work environment. Such changes should be welcome since they intensify the use of urban housing. This increases effective density and supports a wider range of local services.

Indeed, the model for the urban house guarantees some of the qualities of the single-family house while making for greater density and possibilities of alternative modalities according to new social and multicultural needs.

Various projects aiming to satisfy new housing requirements have been undertaken in recent years. These experiments offer new combinations of the housing units, new assemblages and juxtapositions, with the chief goal being to combine privacy with a responsible densification of the construct. These buildings for residence allow multiple combinations and connections between levels and hence different sizes; an architecture which takes care not to be rigid in determining the lifestyle, in organizational and functional terms, but limits itself to accurately defining relationships with the exterior (Carmona, 2001; Gausa, 2002; Losasso, 1997, 2011).

As regards the ecological issues, there are various issues that new housing is trying to address. The first is conserving energy, also achieving a higher level of insulation, improving the efficiency of insulation and obtaining the benefits of solar gain. Then, to use the renewable sources in order to generate energy and to use more collected and recycled water. Furthermore, to select suitable materials in order to conserve the scarce resources and safeguard the wider environment.

Finally, to realize houses following a good design, which improves quality and healthy places (Towers, 2005, p.111).

With respect to the new solutions, the Borneo Sporenburg houses in Amsterdam – in the framework of an urban plan designed by Adrian Geuze and the West 8 group – feature 60 plots designed by different architects for individual houses. Here, each building owner could express their preference for both internal and external appearance. The Mirador at Sanchinarro is a residential tower on 22 floors implemented by MVRDV in collaboration with Blanca Lleò Asociados. The houses provide a wide range of lodgings, based on the requisites of different households (couples without children, young people sharing one apartment, users who are only passing through or need a lodging for a brief period, evolving family structures undergoing transformations, the elderly, residents who work at home or stay out all day, etc.) in order to both ensure an extensive range of possibilities for residents and a high standard of living space (Costanzo, 2006).

The Bercy area in Paris consists of a regeneration project which includes both a park with recreational and community facilities and housing. The housing was built in order to allow a considerable possibility of choice in variation and diversity within each development (Towers, 2005, p.168). The Ferencvaros area in Budapest (Towers, 2005, p.282) involved a renewal programme devoted to regeneration, creating a more socially mixed community and improving the environment and local economy. To the existing building renovations and new housing construction other improvements were added in order to guarantee the success of operation. The existing green squares were renovated and improvements were carried out to the local shopping streets. This has made the area more attractive to locals, businesses and visitors, encouraging commercial developers and generating new employment.

Finally, the Bedzed, Beddington Zero Energy Development, in the London Borough of Sutton, is a prototype for sustainable urban housing which combines housing and workplaces and uses many green features, including: insulation, recycled materials, materials from local sources, passive ventilation, rainwater and grey water recycling, and green roofs (Towers, 2005, p.251).

The question of living is one of the more complex among the new spaces in the contemporary city because many issues overlap and a lot of possible kinds of changes may influence the modalities of inhabiting the space of residence. The different demands – generated by new households and different questions related to technology development and climate change – and the relative answers – have produced a wide range of new housing. On one hand, we can observe good examples of urban housing and residence design or zero energy projects, on the other it is more difficult to find good examples that combine all these issues. To the aspects of flexibility and quality there must be added the collective spaces, spaces for socialization and connections with the network of infrastructures; new normative approaches must go hand in hand with new solutions able to combine the traditional typologies, aggregative possibilities, styles and habits of life, and the total quality within the urban context.

Figure 3.1
**Geuze West 8: Borneo
Sporenburg housing in
Amsterdam**
(© Jeroen Musch)

Indeed, mutations in housing assume a fundamental role in the urban transformation process. The new needs are translated into different ways of requesting and designing dwellings, neighbourhoods and cities because all the changes that are carried out at the housing level are reflected in different ways and modalities at the urban scale.

Chapter 4

Urban containers

Changes in habits have led to a lot of activities taking place outside the house that used to go on inside, which in turn has led to an increasing need for new containers. People no longer feel they have to stay inside their homes, and are increasingly looking for other places that can satisfy their demands, places able to receive them. It is a question of moving from one container to another (Sepe, 2007b).

Common daily activities have become actions that are performed everywhere and at every moment. In the contemporary city, traditional places of socialization have been replaced by urban structures which are generally built outside the city and enriched by functions that simulate urban values suitable to the rhythm of fast traffic. Urban containers are private places and spaces intended to attract a large number of persons for the purposes of consumption.

Figure 4.1
Detail of highway edge with billboards indicating globalized malls

Urban containers vary in dimension, quality and shape, but have in common the aim of favouring a prolonged use, substitutive of that of public spaces. Indeed, the predominant characteristic of these large containers is that they are able to expand the time devoted to their use and to connect different places through the distracted perception of the surrounding environment, relegating the city to a backdrop to be consumed fleetingly, like all the other images offered by our 'communication culture' (Koolhaas *et al.*, 2001).

The widespread use of urban and extra-urban containers hasn't completely substituted traditional public places in the city. The changes that we can observe regard the social typology of people that use them, the times and ways the spaces are used and how they are perceived.

There are multiple containers in the contemporary city, reflecting the new combinations of functions that are arising to satisfy the needs of different categories of users. Among these, three main categories can be identified. The first covers shopping malls, multi-screen cinemas and multicontainers, where the functions – including entertainment – are mainly connected with shopping. The second includes airports, railway stations and motorways. This group is characterized by mobility and transport functions which prevail over all others. The third category, which includes amusement parks, waterfronts and theme parks devoted to leisure and entertainment, is the one which is most evolving.

Shopping malls, multi-screen cinemas and multi-containers

Shopping malls are containers where function is more important than shape. The prevalent scheme that characterizes these places is constituted by the shopping structure, a huge parking facility and other connected amenities (Mello, 2002).

Parking, allowing people to arrive easily and stop for a long time, plays a fundamental role in the success of these structures. No urban character informs these buildings, no fragments of the city are transposed onto the territory or onto the background of inter-personal relationships. The strongly recognizable image characterizing these 'no-places' makes it possible to identify them even without knowing what they are, because the image is not related to any particular type of architecture (Augé, 1995; Bauman, 1998, 1999; Dawson and Lord, 1985). As Dovey (1999, p.24) points out:

> the deep ringy structure of the private shopping mall is conductive to certain forms of pseudo-solidarity framed by the instrumental imperatives of consumption. The deterministic conflation of physical enclosures with social constraint, or of open space with liberty, is a dangerous move. An open syntax can operate as a powerful signifier of solidarity and democracy in the absence of the practice.

The urban landscape drawn by the shopping malls has a character which is difficult to describe. As Zukin (1991, p.20) reports with respect to the American landscapes:

> Economic power provides the structured coherence behind America's shifting landscapes.[1] The replicas of smokestack America, their dispersal and eventual abandonment, precede another historical phase, one marked by supermarkets, shopping malls, office towers. This leads in turn to their replication, dispersal, and abandonment. The simultaneous combinations of concentrations and dispersal, of growth and decline, make it difficult to grasp the character of American landscape today. … It takes an effort of imagination to distinguish among the 'non place places' in such landscape. Yet in the quest for an image of distinction, local business and political leaders continue to build and rebuild as a sign of economic growth. Their blueprint for growth is often limited to constructing a microcosm of the past or a panorama of the future, and presenting this landscape by techniques of historic preservation or futuristic new construction that are completely detached from specific places. Without a specific social and material context, the organizing principle in these landscapes is simply a visual theme.

Furthermore some shopping malls are taking over more and more elements from theme parks, giving rise to a new mix which is both scenic and functional. As Mills (2008) has said, 'The Mall of America in Minnesota already seems to have taken the shopping experience to levels that could have embarrassed even Walt Disney. Is this shopping with entertainment or a theme park with massive purchasing opportunities?'

In addition to shopping malls, multi-screen cinemas have become prevalent, replacing the single-screen cinema. As in the case of the shopping mall, function prevails over shape, and the presence of parking, even though not observable in all these structures, is an important element of success. Most of the multi-screen cinemas are located within shopping centres or villages created by the big film production companies.

A more recent generation of multicontainers is emerging. These are above all commercial or tourist-commercial extra-urban spaces equipped with large-capacity parking areas and where several functions – which include cinema – are able to satisfy a lot of needs at the same time and are linked, but without representing anyone in particular (Torres, 2000). Referring to the phenomenon of 'bundled' urban environments, Graham and Marvin (2001, p.264)[2] have pointed out 'invented street systems within shopping malls, theme parks and urban resorts, often with strong tie-ins to leading sports, media and entertainment multi-nationals (Disney, Time-Warner, Sony, Nike, etc...),' which have been created in order to 'exploit merchandising spin-offs. Such developments cover increasingly large footprints and developers attempt to bundle together the maximum number of "synergisitic" uses within a single complex – retailing, cinemas, IMAX screens, sports facilities, restaurants, hotels, entertainment facilities, casinos, simulated historic scenes, virtual reality complexes, museums, zoos, bowling alleys, artificial ski slopes, etc...'

Fainstein (1994, p.232) observes that the popularity of many out-of-centre shopping complexes and revitalized areas appears to drive 'the cultural critics into paroxysms of annoyance as they attempt to show that people ought to be continually exposed to the realities of life at the lower depths'. It is people who give meaning and value to a place. 'Furthermore, most places are discretionary environments and people must actively choose to use them for them to be successful'.[3]

Airports, railway stations and motorways

Airports and railway stations have become places where people spend time not only waiting for departure but shopping, meeting people and working, among other activities. These places are increasingly being designed to offer a variety of facilities in order to attract people.

In line with these places, motorways have also become new places of socialization, where the public role of the motorway restaurant is enforced because it represents one of the places where the maximum density of users is concentrated. The idea of the service station as a monument to the velocity myth acquires less sense; its use and market value increases as a place for breaks, sales and relaxation, through a grid which connects everything as well as everybody. The bar and the little restaurant close to the petrol station pump are transformed into a big commercial machine, while providing petrol becomes an accessory function, a necessary occasion for other services (Ciorra, 1997).

The no-places are also defined with text or words which are displayed to indicate the way we have to use them. These are provided with prescriptive, prohibitive or informative inscriptions that sometimes resort to more or less explicit and codified ideograms and sometimes to natural language (Augé, 1995). These structures represent spaces, all characterized by size, which are established on autonomous aggregative rules, facilitated by the possibility of use of different connections: vertical, by means of elevators; horizontal, with cars and other means of transport.

Through size, a city which can be defined as generic is affirmed (Koolhaas, 1994). Here, motorways are an evolved version of avenues and squares, and occupy larger and larger spaces; airports, hotels, galleries and bridges characterize a development which is isolated from any urban or sector planning.

Furthermore, as reported by Dovey (1999, p.24), Markus observes that in the airport terminal, buildings are increasingly called upon to produce an illusion of freedom, solidarity and liberation, coupled with the reality of control, manipulation and surveillance. And the ring syntax of the open-plan office and school can be interpreted as a new form of control (Hillier and Hanson, 1984, p.195).

Amusement parks, waterfronts and theme parks

The increasingly frequent, large-scale use of spaces where fleeting consumption takes place in the context of greatly increased flows of people has caused a process of global competition among cities, which involves concentration and specialization in enhancing attractiveness to large masses of people. The artificial collective places that are affirmed in this process are represented not only by shopping centres but also by waterfronts, amusement parks and theme parks, which simulate the spaces of collective memory and imitate experience through intensification of sensory perceptions. These represent the places where competition among cities as well as economic and social interests will be increasingly focused (Sorkin, 1999; Torres, 2000). As Crang (1998, p.128) pointed out, 'although enclosed environments have multiplied, there has also been a renaissance of the city in all parts of the city itself as an arena of consumption'. One of the reasons is a process of urban regeneration which is transforming de-industrialized areas into new spaces of consumption. Different kinds of places have emerged including new waterfronts – such as Hafencity in Hamburg, the Albert Dock in Liverpool, Arabianranta in Helsinki and Abondaibarra in Bilbao, to cite some examples in European cities (Sepe, 2009a). In these cases the waterfront transformation was the starting point in order to revitalize not only the image of the area in question but the whole city. In other cases the transformation was more focused on the regeneration area:

> What were once landscapes of labour become landscapes of leisure; former docks and factory sites become arts centres, are renovated for accommodation or form the sites for new festivals ... In Manhattan, Zukin (1982) identified this with the return to the city by 'professionals', often in creative or media industries, taking up living in the lofts of SoHo. Conflicts can emerge over the different meanings groups ascribe to urban areas – over both residential and commercial development. Thus London's Spitalfields market redevelopment produced diverging views on whether the market should be kept as a local facility, an updated national market or as a tourist attraction.
>
> (Crang, 1998, p.128)

As regards theme parks, Hannigan (1998) offers a general framework for the features which define what he identifies as urban entertainment destination (UED), or 'fantasy city'. The urban entertainment destination is Theme-o-centre, 'everything from individual entertainment venues to the image of the city itself conforms to a scripted theme, normally drawn from sports, history or popular entertainment'. Then it is branded, which means that urban entertainment destinations could be both financed 'on the basis of their ability to deliver a high degree of consumer satisfaction and fun' and 'on their potential for selling licensed merchandise on site'.[4]

Fantasy city operates day and night, reflecting 'its intended market of "baby boomers" and "Generation X" adults in search of leisure, sociability and entertainment centers'. It is also modular, 'mixing and matching an increasingly standard array of components in various configurations'[5] and solipsistic, 'isolated from surrounding neighborhoods physically, economically and culturally'. Finally, Hannigan defines the urban entertainment destination as postmodern, 'insomuch as it is constructed around technologies of simulation, virtual reality and the thrill of the spectacle', where the Disney model has served as a strong source of inspiration.[6]

Sircus (2001) defines 'Invented places', which 'may be themed as an authentic or symbolic recreation of a past time and place', as 'the quintessential invented place'. He affirms that places such as Disneyland offer visitors a 'safe environment' in which they can experience 'safe adventures'.[7] He identifies some principles which, over the years, 'Imagineers' have used in order to successfully generate an invented place. These include 'structure and theme (organization of ideas and people flow), sequence experience (telling of story or purpose), visual communication (details, symbols, and magnets), and participation (through the senses, action, and memory)'. But the indispensable ingredient is a design that is evidently amalgamated with the story put in place. In this connection, Augé (1999) noted some characteristics which denote the typical user of amusement parks, but which can be extended to the typical user of all other collective artificial touristy places. He observed that everyone who films or takes pictures is at the same time filmed and photographed while filming or taking pictures. 'Going to Disneyland is a visit to the future that will fully make sense later, when we show to friends and relatives the photos that our child took of this while his father was filming him, followed by the father's film as proof'. Furthermore, Augé notes that 'we live in an age that puts history on stage and transforms it into a show, undoing reality. This kind of spectacularization is never so sensitively realized as in the tourist advertisements which propose travel tours, a series of instantaneous images which will only assume a sense of reality when the photos we have taken are watched by a resigned public of friends and family'[8] (Augé, 1999).[9]

The new urban containers are aimed at obtaining profits through the use of collective places transformed into public spaces of consumption. As Mills (2008) observes:

> It is hardly surprising that other developers, promoters and cities have increasingly sought to duplicate Disney's profitability by providing all-weather, secure shopping, commercial and entertainment facilities. ... Shoppers too can be safely sheltered from inclement weather, as most cities now have all season, totally enclosed shopping malls, where old people jog and youngsters court, families visit the multiplex and artists exhibit. But though many members of the general public treat such enclosed spaces as public space they are most definitely private, and can exclude groups or individuals deemed likely to disrupt the ambience of painless shopping and recreation.

Some of these containers, which apparently seem to be external to the city, such as multi-screen cinemas or huge shopping malls, have arisen alongside freeways, but are now tending to be increasingly located inside urban centres, modifying spaces and habits. In almost all the new urban structures what is consumed above all is the sense of place. These new structures are aimed at capturing the attention of the visitor for as long as possible, with the risk of confounding him inside a generic and indefinite space able to generate a sense of confusion and transience. The danger represented by this kind of space of consumption is to make the sense of local belonging disappear. Torres (2000) observes that this happens when efficient alternatives to the values expressed by the consumer culture are not proposed on the political and cultural agenda and when the traditional spaces of socialization – such as piazzas, parks and streets – are absent or degraded or not renewed.[10] Indeed, while some containers make suitable use of the history and place identity in order to reinforce the cultural tradition for the specific place, for the majority, the lack of authenticity and the supremacy of the consumption laws are evident. The risk is the loss of a feeling of identity with collective places, perceived more and more as places with weak and provisional identities to be used and then abandoned.

Chapter 5
Networks and infrastructures

It is no longer necessary to stay in specific places in order to exercise communicative, productive and organizational actions. The internet, in its current evolution, is not just a technology for communication, but an authentic informative and economic ecosystem, a complex system constituted by subsystems in which no codified laws interact and where communication and market laws constantly overlap and intersect. The contemporary city is increasingly dominated by networks, meaning the set of virtual and physical connections which intersect territories, creating both overlaps of routes and links, and new temporal modalities and habits of living the places. As Mitchell (1996, p.107) asserts:

> In a world of ubiquitous computation and telecommunication, electronically augmented bodies, postinfobahn architecture, and big-time bit business, the very idea of a city is challenged and must be eventually reconceived. Computer networks become as fundamental to urban life as street system. Memory and screen space become valuable, sought-after sorts of real estate. Much of the economic, social, political, and cultural action shifts into cyberspace. As a result, familiar urban design issues are up for radical reformulation.

The nomadism[1] of the information technology era we are living in does not depend on an anthropological transformation but instead relies mainly on the continued and rapid transformation of the scientific, technical, economic, mental landscapes (Levy, 1999). Indeed:

> mobile technology users take the nomadic concept one step further, because not only their paths are mobile but also the nodes. With the fixed Internet, and fixed landlines, computers and telephones were primarily connected to places. Conversely, cell phones represent movable connection points, accompanying their users' movements in physical spaces.
>
> (De Souza e Silva, 2006)

Virtual networks

Hypertext, interactive multimedia, videogames, simulation, virtual reality, hyper-reality, artificial life and expert systems are only some of the terms that nowadays designate new forms of real-virtual interactions which lead to new possibilities of connections. The increasing use of the internet and new technological tools has given rise to an erroneous idea about distance and time. To a typical internet user it seems more natural to communicate with his email friends living in another part of the world than with a colleague sitting in front of him. New technologies, by creating an artificial nearness and simultaneity between people, things and events, have destroyed the idea of proximity which was the base of urban construction and have produced a constant search for stability and appropriate distance.[2]

> Because of these dynamics, and the intensifying uneven development of infrastructures, physically close spaces can, in effect, be relationally severed (Graham and Healey, 1999). At the same time, globally distant places can be relationally connected very intimately. This undermines the notion of infrastructure networks as binding and connecting territorially cohesive urban spaces. It erodes the notion that cities, regions and nations necessarily have any degree of internal coherence at all. And it forces us to think about how space and scale are being refashioned in new ways that we can literally see crystallising before us in the changing configurations of infrastructure networks and the landscapes of urban spaces all around us.
> (Graham and Marvin, 2001, pp.15–16)

Buildings, rather than just relating to natural and urban contexts, also widen their connections to include structures created in cyberspace,[3] through electronic processors able to permit such interactions. As noted by Mitchell (1996), building these programmable places is not only a question of installing cables within walls and electronic boxes within rooms. With the development of new technologies, smaller and smaller electronic devices are already tending to disappear within the structures of buildings.

Among the products of the new temporal modalities and living habits, virtual cities are the most evident. These are electronic places inhabited by thousands of citizens and visited everyday by many tourists where it is possible to address questions to administrators and carry out many kinds of actions as in real life. De Souza e Silva (2006) notes that:

> Internet has been studied as a social immersive space in which users develop communities and construct worlds (Dibbell, 1999; Donath, 1997; Kim, 2000; Rheingold, 2002; Smith and Kollock, 1999), multiuser domains (MUDs); MUDs, object oriented; and recently MMORPGs are examples of such online social spaces. Multiuser environments, constructed metaphorically as public social places, have attracted many people willing to socialize with others outside their situated geographical boundaries .... Unlike traditional social public places, such as bars,

squares, and automobiles, these new communities are reconfigured in hybrid spaces, because their users are simultaneously moving through physical space while connected in real time to other users via digital technology depending on their relative positions in physical space.[4]

Physical infrastructures

Internet spaces present several points in common with the motorway network. Neither has a centre, nor is it possible to define them by indicating a starting or finishing point of the network, the space of relationship is expressed above all horizontally, and their value is affirmed by the number of access points to which it is possible to connect.[5]

(Ciorra, 1997, p.43)

High-speed trains, superhighways and motorways have been changing the appearance of the contemporary city. Increasingly, articulate hubs and infrastructure corridors bring into connection larger and larger territories and urban landscapes at different scales and, with them, different cultures and traditions.

In several cases these networks represent the only element of continuity of heterogeneous territories, even if they also contribute to the crumbling of urban space due to the same network logic which aims to optimize functionality. Their capacity to serve as a reference point for less urbanized contexts results in infrastructure spaces which have created new urban centralities. These places can be distinguished by their generic images which make them recognizable due to their similarity in indefiniteness.

Figure 5.1
Tokyo: detail of the highway infrastructure

Furthermore, infrastructures have become:

> not only centres where goods are distributed and services are offered, but also – and above all – places for entertainment and spending free time. The city has been transferring to infrastructure spaces all those activities favoured by better accessibility, either in terms of time and space or – above all – of economic advantages. Large buildings, viaducts, motorway exits and car parks configure huge spatial events even if extraneous to any intentional relationship. In contrast to those present in the city, often these non-integrated spaces – hugely out of scale – remain indifferent to characters and intentions of place.[6]
>
> (Desideri, 2001, pp.60–61)

New connections

The relationships between old and new routes and links give rise to new kinds of networks, due to the demands for increasingly complex connections among places and temporalities and with the urban space which they cross. According to Graham and Marvin:

> Contemporary urban life is revealed as a ceaseless and mobile interplay between many different scales, from the body to the globe. Such mobile interactions across distances and between scales, mediated by telecommunications, transport, energy and water networks, are the driving connective forces of the much-debated processes of 'globalization' …. Much of the history of modern urbanism can be understood, at least in part, as a series of attempts to 'roll out' extending and multiplying road, rail, airline, water, energy and telecommunications grids, both within and between cities and metropolitan regions. These vast lattices of technological and material connections have been necessary to sustain the ever-expanding demands of contemporary societies for increasing levels of exchange, movement and transaction across distance.
>
> (Graham and Marvin, 2001, pp.8–10)

In this way old borders open and new walls and thresholds are created, making the limits between private and public spaces not always clear.

> In the built fabric of a city, the enclosing surfaces of the constituent spaces – walls, floors, ceilings, and roofs – provide not only shelter, but also privacy. … Spatial divisions and access-control devices are carefully deployed to organize places into hierarchies grading from completely public to utterly private.[7]
>
> (Mitchell, 1996, p.121)

Graham and Marvin (2001, pp.10–12) identify four typologies of connection between infrastructure networks and contemporary urbanism. The first connection can be defined as 'sociotechnical' due to the relationships between people and institutions in order to carry out the actions of everyday life. 'Technological networks (water, gas, electricity, information, etc…) are constitutive parts of the urban. They are mediators through which the perpetual process of transformation of Nature into City takes place' (Kaika and Swyngedouw, 2010, p.1). As Hall and Preston (1988, p.273) put it, in modern society, 'much innovation proves to depend for its exploitation on the creation of an infrastructural network (railways; telegraph and telephone; electricity grids; highways; airports and air traffic control; telecommunications systems)'.

    The second concerns the relationships between the system of production with that of consumption. Infrastructure networks create dynamic relationships among places, people, buildings and urban elements with heterogeneous characteristics.

> They unevenly bind spaces together across cities, regions, nations and international boundaries whilst helping also to define the material and social dynamics, and divisions, within and between urban spaces. Infrastructure networks interconnect parts of cities across global time zones and also mediate the multiple connections and disconnections within and between contemporary cities.
>
> (Amin and Graham, 1997, pp.411–429)

The third kind of connection is responsible for significant parts of the economic and geopolitical fabric of cities and system of cities. 'As capital that is literally "sunk" and embedded within and between the fabric of cities, they represent long-term accumulations of finance, technology, know-how, and organizational and geopolitical power. New infrastructure networks "have to be immobilised in space, in order to facilitate greater movement for the remainder"' (Harvey, 1985, p.49). This means that they can 'only liberate activities from their embeddedness in space by producing new territorial configurations, by harnessing the social process in a new geography of places and connecting flows' (Swyngedouw, 1993, p.306).

    The fourth connection is involved in defining the 'structure of feeling' of modern urban life (Williams, 1973). 'Networked technologies of heat, power, water, light, speed and communications have thus been intrinsic to all urban cultures of modernity and mobility' (Thrift, 1995): they are invariably invoked in images, representations and ideologies of urban 'progress' and the modern city by all sorts of actors – developers, planners, state officials, politicians, regulators, operators, engineers, real-estate developers and appliance manufacturers, as well as artists, journalists, social scientists, futurists and philosophers (see Kaika and Swyngedouw, 2000).

The new complex system of virtual and infrastructure networks is increasingly growing with no specific rules. The system of empty spaces and infrastructures nowadays appears as a counterbalance to the transformation into full spaces, a sort of emptiness that seems to resist every kind of planning and transfiguration. A system of empty spaces conceived as a place of conflicts, or a network of empty places in which city and architecture live together: a network generated from the transformation of the city into a metropolis. In this scenario it is possible to observe on one hand the apparently imperceptible virtual network, and on the other the physical network, result of the new fluxes of paths due to the infrastructures, of the new spaces of socialization, etc. (Desideri, 2001).

> The normally invisible quality of working infrastructure becomes visible when it breaks: the server is down, the bridge washes out, there is a power blackout. ... Catastrophic failures, on the other hand, serve to reveal fleetingly the utter reliance of contemporary urban life on networked infrastructure.
>
> (Graham and Marvin, 2001, pp.22–23)

> This apparent conflictuality of the contemporary metropolis leads to an idea of space able to integrate the old connections with the empty spaces, to transform the network into physical and conceptual structures capable to connect the metropolitan territories and to compose the thread of the complex looms of the metropolitan infrastructures. The contemporary infrastructure has been tending to give physical and conceptual simultaneity to the whole network system: a part of urban space where the various networks and their different logics, constituting the metropolitan territories, coexist. The new infrastructural building is not a simple addition of many concurrent cables: the empty space corresponding to the cavities also takes part in determining the eventual shape. The resulting space, which is going to configure in the contemporary city, is a place where the specific morphologies utilized for the connections do not appear anymore as opposing and incomplete realities, but as complete entities which overlap, sharing common functions and parts of territory with borders.
>
> (Desideri, 2001, p.31)[8]

Chapter 6

New places of perceptions

The elements of human perception have an essential link to cities and places. Cities are perceived by the senses as networks of symbolic significants that can influence human behaviour. As Augé (1999, p.94) puts it:

> The city has a fictional potential, in the sense that it has provided a setting for the leading 19th and 20th century novelists. While perhaps this is to state the obvious, it can make us think about two complementary and inverse movements, two interlocking perspectives: the author is seen through the cities he has depicted, just as the cities are seen in the work of those who have celebrated them. ... Conversely, mere mention of the name of the authors suffices to conjure up an image, perhaps a little indistinct but nonetheless persistent, of the cities they have evoked, with the noises, colours, vistas and above all the secret alchemy which, in the eyes of the promeneur, can transpose places into moods and sensibility into a landscape.[1]

Indeed, the perceptions are influenced by our sense organs, which can vary from one person to another, and our preconceptions, shaped by socio-cultural conditioning.

> In this formulation perception is grounded in sensations which are a series of environmental stimuli and involves cumulative, analytical and synthetic, processes of the brain, each working together to give use a sense of a world, or geographical understanding. Perception is therefore a relationship to the world and a decision-making process with respect to that world.
>
> (Rodaway, 1994, p.11)

The senses contribute to a primary knowledge of the world. Sensory landscapes are created by the senses – hearing, smell, sight, touch and taste – as classified by Aristotle. This list does not include the perception of pain or balance or others produced by two or more senses. As Landry points out: 'Depending on classification, somewhere between 9 and 21 human senses have so far been identified, more (up to 53) if you include those recognized by metaphysicians' (Landry, 2006, p.40).[2]

The sensory stimuli are generally perceived as a whole: people may experience them individually in specific actions or by paying attention to a particular perception.

> The individual dimension can only be separated out by deliberate actions (closing one's eyes, blocking one's nose or ears) or by selective attention. While vision is the dominant sense, the urban environment is not perceived visually. Bacon (1974, p.20), for example, argued that the 'changing visual picture' was 'only the beginning of the sensory experience; the changes from light to shade, from hot to cold, from noise to silence, the flow of smells associated with open space, and the tactile quality of the surface under foot, are all important in the cumulative effect'.[3]
>
> (Carmona et al., 2003, p.87)

Usually perceptions are the expression of local, religious and political identities, but there may be other cultural motivations which, by imposing new modes of behaviour and tastes, have an influence on the overall perceptions of the environment we live in. In spite of a general tendency in the contemporary city for perceptions to be blunted, it is still possible to identify their origins.[4]

Visual perception

Whether or not a place is recognizable is largely a matter of visual images: colours, architectural typology, natural elements. As Porteous (1996, p.31) observes, 'Psychologists, urban designers, landscape architects, and advertisers all stress vision as the chief mode of knowing about the world. So much so, indeed, that when we use the term perception we almost always mean visual perception.' Vision is not the same in every culture:

> Orientation in space is chiefly achieved visually except in cultures such as the Inuit (Carpenter 1973). Visual perception relies on space, distance, light quality, colour, shape, textural and contrast gradients, and the like. It is a highly complex phenomenon. ... The perceived environment, then, is largely a visual one, and most science is 'eye science' (Cunningham 1975).
>
> (Porteous 1996, p.32)

But vision is not enough to form a comprehensive idea of a place. Our eyes do not allow us to see in the back of our heads and our arc of vision is limited to what is before us. This determines a sort of 'psychological distance' between whoever observes and what is observed. (Porteous, p.31). Furthermore,

> our sense and our locomotor apparatus paint a clear picture of an extremely alert pedestrian who looks ahead and down, but has a limited

field of upward vision. ... This whole account of the horizontal sensory apparatus is the key to how we experience space, for example, how much of buildings pedestrians experience when walking along streets. Naturally that also impacts on the experience of low-rise and tall buildings in cities.

In general, the upper floors of tall buildings can only be seen at a distance and never close up in the cityscape.[5]

(Gehl, 2010, p.41)

The most apparent elements of vision nowadays are those of advertising; the image of the city and its elements have changed, and publicity has become the discriminating factor, bringing about changes in behaviour (routes taken, objects purchased, etc.), so that places have been turned into one long commercial. In this way, street lighting is increasingly acquiring a private advertising function, promoting a product, event or supermarket chain and thus losing its original function as a public utility, becoming increasingly individualistic. Particularly in streets with a prevalently commercial function, whether urban or extra-urban, as well as in the main squares of cities, the lighting used for publicity logos and shop windows is much stronger than that for buildings, parks and streets.[6] The immediate effect is that urban spaces and architecture are largely concealed behind the glare of neon lights.

Figure 6.1
Time Square in New York: a strong visual perception

As has also been pointed out by Landry (2006, p.73):

> Advertising hoardings increasingly shape the look of the city as they expand in size and impact. Less discreet than a decade ago, they can be immense – the largest billboard in the world, erected in Manila in 2005, was 50m long and 50m high. Occasionally beautiful and often intrusive, it is Eastern Europe that sets new standards of garishness, impact and boldness, and the Far East has always been visually wild to Western eyes. Think of Tokyo's electric city, Hong Kong's Nathan Road or Delhi's Chandri Chowk – you choke in colour and sign overload. The city is increasingly a sign system and a message board. It is a staging set communicating products and images to you. But it all depends where you are. The colours and materials used in commercial districts vary. In the upscale parts things are more discreet and materials obviously better. The hues in modern settings, in part because of the mass of glass, have a light blue, light yellow translucent overlay. Think here of the new 101 district in Taipei, where the world's largest skyscraper stands.

The advertisers' messages can also be concentrated inside consumer venues, through the spectacular exploitation of visual perception. Shopping malls are commonly perceived as vivid environments full of people and bright lights. This is a golden opportunity for advertisers, able to give vent to all their creativity thanks to the large scale exhibition of goods, lighting effects, and images and videos thrown up on maxi-screens fostering cheerfulness and reckless purchasing (Torres, 2000, p.117).

Another important element of great visual suggestion is represented by some contemporary architecture, whose shape is created independently by the context and whose main objective is aesthetic. These kinds of buildings, which generally are replicable in any part of the city and in any city in the world, have the main function of capturing the attention of observers. The risk is that the cities are increasingly characterized by these symbols of globalization with a resulting homogenization of places.

The grey colour of streets also characterizes many places in the contemporary city:

> Overriding everything – and again we cannot avoid the greys and blacks – is the colour of roads on which the buildings sit as if bedded in a sea of asphalt. Grey is the canvas on top of which the city plays itself out. The buildings do not feel independent. Asphalt's homogenizing feel shrouds the city at ground level in a veil interspersed by signage and yellow and red traffic lines.
> (Landry, 2006, p.73)

And within the streets, the sheer volume of means of transport and in particular cars affects the vision of the city, often obscuring the overall vistas.

Cars are a very real danger that both pedestrians and motorists have to be aware of in order to survive. If we're careful, we look sharply left and right at junctions and crossings to check for oncoming traffic. Thus, by necessity in such situations, we are attuned to an entire lexicography of signs dedicated to communicating conduct in relation to motor vehicles. But the interpretation of greens, reds and ambers at traffic lights and crossings can preclude an even-paced, reflective urban experience.

(Landry, 2006, p.46–47)

Sound perception

Each town has its own sound. Barbara (2000, p.127) shows that cities can be distinguished according to the predominant musical note underlying the buzz of everyday activity. Porteous (1996, p.33) observes that, unlike the space created by visual perception which is 'sectoral', the acoustic space is 'all surrounding':

It has no obvious boundaries, and, in contrast with vision, tends to emphasize space itself rather than objects in space. Sounds, compared with things seen, are more transitory, more fluid, more unfocused, more lacking in context, less precise in terms of orientation and localization, and less capturable. Audition is a fairly passive sense; one cannot close one's earlids. Sound, therefore, is ubiquitous; there is no end to traffic roar, building and machine hum, the rustling of leaves. Sudden silence can be extremely disconcerting.

If one were to record urban soundtracks one would find that the historical centre of Barcelona would bear a considerable resemblance to that of Naples, for instance; or downtown Milan to New York; or the metropolitan area of Paris to Tokyo. This is not to say that they are comparable in geometric or topological terms, but that certain urban features intersect, such as superstores or infrastructure nodes.[7]

The materials used for streets, urban furniture and buildings determine the new sound of the contemporary city:

Concrete, glass and steel create a 'canyon effect' that loudens the growls and honks of traffic, sirens and exhaust from big buildings. The sound artist and urban observer Hildegard Westerkamp sums up parallel developments in modern architecture, as exemplified by the Bauhaus movement, and sound. She points out that the new international architecture that is homogenizing our visual urban environment is also homogenizing our soundscape.

(Landry, 2006, p.52)[8]

In general one can observe an overall homogenization of the urban soundscape, making it more and more difficult to recognize a specific sound quality from city to city. This is due in part to the increasing noise pollution produced by transport, traffic, music played at a high volume to attract clientele into shops, and also to new patterns of cultural behaviour that have gradually modified the prevailing soundscape. As pointed out by Landry (2006, p.52):

> Transport vehicles are the worst: large trucks, buses, cars, aircraft, trains, and motorcycles all produce excessive noise. As does construction equipment such as jackhammers, bulldozers, drills, grinding machines, dumper trucks, pile drivers and cranes. Air conditioning provides a constant background whirr and computers an electrical hum. So the noise of global transactions is a broadband hum. Shops have foreground and background music. Even in the suburbs we have lost the art of silence; gardening equipment grinds, grates and whirrs. Overwhelming everything is the big petrochemical roar of the car, but we do not notice it anymore.

Smell perception

The sense of smell provokes emotive sensations, and, unlike sight, directly involves thought and cognition. Porteous (1996) states, 'We feel we belong to a totality partly through the sounds around us', while

> sight clearly distances us from the object; thus we tend to structure 'visions' as we do pictures, using outsider schemes. In terms of a visual landscape, we are very likely to come up with a conceptual response, as a function of culture. Whereas smells envelop us, penetrating our bodies and permeating all the immediate environment: this means that the response is likely to be emotive, linked with strong affectivity.

The sense of smell has a direct, almost subconscious relationship to the emotions: a smell can recall a situation, place or city better than an image. It is of great importance for the human psyche and behaviour, and has had a considerable influence on the construction and evolution of the city; the cultural diversity of smells becomes an environmental component of the difference between places.

Each place features a set of smells which varies as the seasons and time of day change, although not everybody is able to identify this characteristic: 'cities with the smell of curry, or on the sea with a mixture of brine and rust, cities with a stale, mouldy smell, and others with the acrid smell of burnt out cables' (Barbara and Perliss, 2006, p.125).

> The relationship between smell and the material from which it emanates is iconic: the scent of bergamot, jasmine, vanilla … of frying from the fast-food opposite. In reality, although this relationship is intrinsically iconic, it is surely extraordinary that at 'Toku hands', one of the largest supermarket chains in Japan, one can buy small cones of incense called

> Aroma Trip with the specification Rome, London, Istanbul etc., com-
> plete with a guide to the fragrances on the back. This is indeed a bizarre
> commercialisation of some 'iconic', or merely allusive, syntheses of the
> smells of desirable cities.
>
> (Barbara and Perliss, 2006, p.125)

Indeed, as Porteous (1996, p.34) notes, it is possible to identify cities and countries by their smells:

> from Hershey, Pennsylvania (chocolate) through Tadcaster, England
> (brewing) and Uji, Japan (green tea) to the sour gas smells of oilfields and
> the sulphite smell of pulpmills in Western Canada. Old-fashioned cheese,
> hardware, tobacco or chocolate stores can be an olfactory delight. Yet
> North American cities have become increasingly smell impoverished.
> Unlike their counterparts in Mediterranean Europe, North Americans
> rarely relish smells. Most environmental smells have been designed out
> of existence by means of personal and public deodorants, air condition-
> ing, air cleaners, and plastic packaging. The keynote smell in our cities
> has become, like the keynote sound, that of the motor vehicle. Sensory
> impoverishment rules in a world selectively 'sanitized for your protection'.[9]

According to Pergola (1997) the current shift in the perception of smells is due
to the difficulty of disposing of rubbish (which is increasing as population grows),
atmospheric pollution caused by car exhaust fumes, and the lack of any official
policy concerning smells. Another element which is contributing to the homogenization of smells is the fast-food chain:

> The fast-food chains have a smell of their own. McDonald's, KFC,
> Wendy's, Subway, Burger King. They mush into one. They are almost
> sweet, crusty, a slight smell of cardboard, dry. Grease and ketchup liber-
> ates and heightens the papery cardboard smell from which you eat the
> chips and chicken nuggets.[10]

Pergola relates his experience of how smells may characterize the perception of
a city:

> I first went to North America aged 20, and in Toronto I was struck by
> the smell of frying that filled all the eating places in the mornings: I can
> still recall it. I went in to have breakfast, ready for my cappuccino and
> pastry in true Italian style, and I was met by the smell of fried egg and
> sausages. That smell went with me for the whole of the holiday, in
> supermarkets (hamburger and chips) and in the streets (fish and chips).
> The cultural difference in eating struck me through smell even before
> taste, and became an environmental component of that difference.

Without wishing to offend anyone, I thought, and still think, that the Italian culture of eating was properly represented by the smells it produced. I was delighted to rediscover those smells on returning home. Just a few days ago, more than 20 years on, in a street in the centre of Florence I was assailed once again by that 'American' smell. I have never gone along with those who railed against 'the invasion of fast food take-aways in the heart of Florence', but I must say that this particular smell was at odds with the austerity of this city of the Renaissance!'[11, 12]

Taste perception

The sense of taste represents a contact linked with the survival of human beings (one cannot live without eating), but also with pleasure, or disgust, and like the sense of smell it is closely bound up with the subconscious. Food is connected with local traditions and also habits, and is able to evoke places, situations and people. Current market trends have fostered two different attitudes: on one hand, the proliferation of supermarkets, hypermarkets and fast-food takeaways etc., selling standard products, and on the other, the creation or conversion of delicatessens, patisseries and small restaurants featuring choice products and typical local fare. In terms of the relationship with the city, this trend has had a considerable influence, introducing changes which, as we have seen in the case of the sense of smell, have involved other perceptive aspects. In addition to the different tastes, in the street one is struck by glaring advertisements for businesses, you hear background noise and various types of music played at full volume inside the shops, you are assailed by odours from the kitchens, and you come into contact with food containers increasingly made of plastic, cardboard or aluminium.

Furthermore, Barbara (2000), referring to a story by Italo Calvino (1995), attempts to place food in relation to architecture, drawing various parallels, for example, between the Mediterranean diet and Mediterranean architecture.

> ... the true journey, involving the interiorization of a setting which is different from the one we are accustomed to, implies a total change in what we eat, as if it was a matter of ingesting the country we are visiting, its fauna and flora but also its culture (not only the different habits in cooking and seasoning but also the use of different instruments for grinding the flour or stirring the dough), taking them in as it were through the lips and the gullet. This is the only way to travel in this day and age, when everything you can set eyes on is there in front of you on television, without you having to move from your armchair. (Please let me hear no talk of achieving the same result by going to exotic restaurants in our metropolises: they falsify the reality of the cuisine they claim to reproduce to such an extent that, in terms of cognitive experience, they are not so much a documentary as an environmental reconstruction in a film studio.)[13]

Tactile perception

Unlike the other senses which have a demonstrable link with the spatial dimension of the city, tactile sensations involve perception in close-up, requiring you to recognize the material quality of objects. We touch the setting around us in various ways, and the perception deriving from the use of one material rather than another is able to bring about a significant change in the overall perception of a place. The paving beneath our feet, the handrail we use when going up or down steps, the handle on a door, the seat we use to pause and admire a monument or wait for a bus, have all gone through many variations with the passage of time. As Porteous (p.38) notes: 'Textural experience, just as with sound and smell, is thereby eliminated or severely reduced. An increased use of textured sidewalks (gravel, tile, metal, glass, brick, wood) and Portuguese-style mosaics would greatly enhance the sensuous pleasure of city walking'.[14]

As Pergola (1997) remarks:

> If paving using flagstones ... was once beguiling, this was connected above all with the fact that getting somewhere on foot involved a whole amount of information and sensations concerning time and route that are obviously lost in a mechanised transfer. ... The perception of levelling out, of removing all irregularities, is commensurate with the need for speed but also for non-permanence in a specific place and with a neutralised environment.

The industrial production of objects in everyday use has begun to show a great interest in the tactile message of electronic gadgets and the materials available for paving, walls, furniture, etc. In the same way there is a diversification in the production of handles, concerning form and materials, with particular attention to the tactile properties of the material used:

> when it comes down to it, the handle, however small, has a key role to play in the context of a door, wall or overall architecture, bestowing a touch of vitality: a handle immediately tells us whether a door is being used or not: if it was used recently it may even still be warm to the touch. But what can we expect of an automatic door in a supermarket or airport, which is not even touched?[15]
>
> (Pergola, 1997, p.52

In consumer venues today there is all too little contact with the street, or possibility of seeing the goods on offer from outside. The spaces are strictly turned in on themselves, to be traversed using standard routes; by eliminating shop windows, the products can be seen and picked up easily, creating an illusion of an open-air market with wares set out on stalls. At the same time there is a parallel trend involving a re-evaluation of the sense of touch: electronic and domestic gadgets which are made soft to the touch, creating a user-friendly feel; while machines able to create virtual sensations and artificial environments also impinge on tactile sensations.

One further contemporary strategy includes the use of all five senses for commercialization in public venues by simulating places through the perceptive involvement of visitors, creating hyper-places that simulate the concept of place. As we mentioned above, since the current trend in favour of digitalized communication seeks to do without buildings and people, eliminating public perceptions, the simulation of a place in a hyper-place tends to ripristinate these sensations artificially to encourage people to consume and purchase products and goods (Torres, 2000).

The recognition of a place is strongly determined by the sense stimuli, and one of the main components of place identity is our perceptions:

> The identity of places is multisensory, but in some cases one or more sense perceptions may be dominant. Sensory interaction is vital; people who hear more, for example, also see more (Southworth 1969). Kinaesthesia (motion by foot or vehicle) is the sense which most readily helps integrate the other senses over time.
>
> (Porteous, p.41)

The pleasure related to experiencing a place through the senses is hence considerable. Adequate attention should be paid to sensory quality, and specific policies designed to safeguard or enhance the perceptions as a whole have to be carried out in design and planning processes. Otherwise, as Porteous (1996, p.41) has warned, 'urbanites will continue to regard cities as sensory blackspots and seek sensory pleasure chiefly indoors, in private gardens, public parks, and nonurban rural and wilderness areas'.

Chapter 7

Monitored places

Nowadays, public spaces, including streets, places for breaks, transport hubs and surrounding areas, and urban containers are increasingly equipped with control systems. Among the various transformations to have affected territory, one of the main ones is represented by the compartmentalization of spaces. Surveillance video cameras, metal detectors and new technologies create monitored places where it is possible to pilot masses of people, potentially limiting individual freedom. Indeed, video camera surveillance systems are not comparable to traditional security and control devices, because rather than simply observing potential thefts or security problems, they also have the function of monitoring consumer behaviour. They constitute tools for safety, as well as for violating privacy, providing guidance, changing habits, and limiting possibilities of encounter and choice of where to take a break (Carmona *et al.*, 2003, p.119).[1]

Figure 7.1
Monitored private open space

As has been observed by Agre and Rotenberg (2001, p.8):

> Goffman (1957) argued that people construct their identities through a
> negotiation of boundaries in which the parties reveal personal informa-
> tion selectively according to a tacit moral code that he called the 'right
> and duty of partial display'. Goffman developed this theory in settings
> (e.g. public places) where participants could see one another face to
> face, but it has obvious implications for technology-mediated interac-
> tions. In particular, to the extent that a technology shapes individuals'
> abilities to negotiate their identities, Goffman's theories have implica-
> tions for that technology's design. … As Goffman's theory wants to
> demonstrate, technology cannot, of course, guarantee fairness in
> human relationships, but it can create conditions under which fairness
> is at least possible.

There are various reasons which lead to the installation of video surveillance,
several related to the prevention of crimes and preservation of heritage. Marcus
(2000) identifies the following motivations:

> The prevention of technical incidents is the predominant reason for the
> installation of cameras, the images from which are both looked at directly
> and also, increasingly often, analysed using software. Preserving the
> integrity of these facilities is the second priority of these installations;
> misuse and intentional damage require rapid interventions for certain
> equipment, the functioning of which might affect thousands of people.
> The third motivation behind these installations is compensating for the
> reduction in the human workforce responsible for operating the equip-
> ment. It is for all of these reasons that our cities have become consumers
> of video surveillance images. The users of these images belong to both
> the private and public spheres. But a fourth motive has become apparent,
> and it brings a political twist to the debate. Thanks to CCTV cameras we
> can stop criminals from operating in the streets, in public spaces.

Traditional safe places

The problem with creating places in which people can move around safely has
been faced by many urban designers and planners. Jane Jacobs in *The Death and
Life of Great American Cities* (1961) identifies the qualities which a space has to
possess in order to ensure safety:

> A city street equipped to handle strangers, and to make a safety asset, in
> itself, out of the presence of strangers, as the streets of successful city
> neighborhoods always do, must have three main qualities: First, there
> must be a clear demarcation between what is public space and what is

private space. Public and private spaces cannot ooze into each other as they do typically in suburban settings or in projects. Second, there must be eyes upon the street, eyes belonging to those we might call the natural proprietors of the street. The buildings on a street equipped to handle strangers and to insure the safety of both residents and strangers, must be oriented to the street. They cannot turn their backs or blank sides on it and leave it blind. And third, the sidewalk must have users on it fairly continuously, both to add to the number of effective eyes on the street and to induce the people in buildings along the street to watch the sidewalks in sufficient numbers.

As Gehl (2010, pp.97–99) pointed out, people from all socio-economic groups have to be able to move around in public spaces without problems. Together with other factors (respect for identity of place, good design, location, etc.) the sense of safety contributes to the livability of a place for all its users, which have to be taken into account in the design process. 'Barbed wire and iron bars fortify houses, security patrols cruise residential areas, security guards stand in front of shops and banks, signs threaten "armed response" outside houses in exclusive quarters, gated communities abound: all of these are examples of people's attempts to protect themselves against invasion and trespass of private property'. But, as Gehl (2010, p.98) noted, simple individual urban crime prevention is not always much help, and this raises a more general problem concerning city life:

> If we shift the focus from defending the private sphere to a general discussion about feeling safe while walking in public space, we will find a clear-cut connection between the goal to strengthen city life and the desire for safety. If we reinforce city life so that more people walk and spend time in common spaces, in almost every situation both real and perceived safety will increase.

Public spaces

Public spaces are places where any kind of modification may determine who can use them and who not, and thus also take on a political meaning. According to Patton (2000, p.183):

> Don Mitchell argues that public places function politically as 'spaces for representation.' They are places in which political movements – homeless activism in his study – make themselves visible. Negotiations over the behaviours allowed in public places are highly political because they legislate who counts as the public and who is allowed to be a part of the community. Public places thereby provide an important setting for the explicit civic life of political activists and the implicit civic life of the

homeless and other marginalized groups as legitimate members of the public.[2]

The question of the social aspect of controlled places is also highlighted by Nemeth (2004, p.19):

> Access for all individuals is the minimum condition of a truly public space. In publicly accessible spaces, humans should expect to interact with those maintaining diverse interests, opinions, and perspectives. True public spaces are vibrant sites of open communication and deliberation. Institutional powers desire to situate individuals in spaces that determine their physical interaction. Planners design the sites to facilitate these interactions, and these constructed spaces become the contexts of regulated social relations. So as truly public parks and plazas accommodate unconstrained social interaction, they lack the control necessary for governments to seamlessly advance policy agendas. ... By controlling the public spaces in which true human interaction occurs, planners and policymakers are challenging the fundamental desires of groups to forge social bonds and enhance their own sense of familiarity with the environment. Security is not merely achieved through an understanding of territory but through acknowledgement and confrontation with individuals or groups maintaining diverse perspectives on the world.

On the ambiguity of surveillance Patton (2000) cites Victoria Bellotti, in *Design for Privacy in Multimedia Computing and Communications Environments*. Bellotti describes the difficulties related to the design of public spaces which are both controlled and protective with respect to the privacy: 'Particularly if people are unaware of being watched, these circumstances raise serious privacy questions. In fact, making people aware of their observation is one technique for enabling people to protect their privacy'. Bellotti's proposed design solutions shift the burden onto the people being monitored to keep track of their own privacy. She advocates providing feedback to those being monitored on what monitoring is taking place and who has access to the information.[3]

Furthermore, Sætnan *et al.* (2004) investigate how social interaction can be encouraged in places by using closed-circuit television (CCTV) systems. In their study they start from the idea that public spaces should invite a broad range of activities, and identify different questions related to the use of CCTV.

> If the deployment and use of CCTV led to a space being safer, or perceived as safer, then that could lead to the space being used by a broader segment of the public for a wider range of activities. If so, then it could contribute to greater social integration. By contrast, if CCTV were used to categorically exclude members of the public from access to the space, or if CCTV were perceived as threatening to individuals or

as a signal that the space was dangerous, then that would detract from the space as a resource for social integration.

The issue of safety also has other kinds of implications for Sætnan *et al.* (2004), including economic and cultural aspects:

The safety and perceived safety of public spaces is an issue not only at the personal level (for victims of crime) but also at the social level, since spaces that are unsafe or are perceived as such will have reduced value as economic, cultural, and social capital.

Shopping centres and websites

The question of video surveillance does not only concern public spaces but also private places such as shopping centres. In this case the surveillance has the aim of both preventing crimes and studying consumer habits. With respect to the control in these places Kajalo and Lindblo (2010) pointed out that the sense of security is an important element for its design: 'The theory of Crime Prevention through Environmental Design (CPTED) provides a theoretical approach to preventing crime and feeling of insecurity in shopping centres'. The Data was analysed in four Nordic countries – Denmark, Finland, Norway and Sweden – and in 68 shopping centres.

The study revealed that informal surveillance (e.g. clean and well-lighted shopping environment) had positive impact on customers' or employees' feeling of security. Formal surveillance (e.g. security guards and surveillance cameras) had no impact on customers' or employees' feeling of security. However, formal surveillance had impact on competitiveness of the shopping center directly, and also through consumers' and employees' feeling of security. Overall, the study shows that both formal and informal surveillance are important for competitiveness of a shopping centre.

Finally, still another kind of monitored place can be observed in contemporary territories. Satellite images and the websites connected to them have become commonplace and are now used for many purposes.[4] For example, the Google Maps website is organized by geographic areas both on maps and for language selection, and shows cartography and satellite images, both separately and combined. One can even observe movements of people and objects via the internet, thanks to increasingly sophisticated websites which display high-resolution images. Again, the application of these technologies reveals a dual aspect: studying the habits of the unaware user and managing their actions, as well as trying to prevent damage and destruction.

There can be no single point of view on this question. Video surveillance has become a requisite not only for safety but also for social interaction, economic success and in general a factor which contributes to liveability. If, on the one hand, this technology has allowed more accurate control of spaces, on the other it has not always resulted in effective prevention of crimes, or indeed in positive perception of their safety and benefits. The study of its appropriate use in order to not compromise the freedom of people in living places becomes therefore a necessity rather than just a choice.

Part II

Making places for people

Section I

Place analysis and planning methods

Chapter 8

Placemaking
Origins and changes

Placemaking can be defined – using the definition of urban design reported in the UK government planning guide *By Design: Urban Design in the Planning System – Towards Better Practice* (CABE and DETR 2000) – as 'the art of making places for people. It includes the way places work and matters such as community safety, as well as how they look. It concerns the connections between people and places, movement and urban form, nature and the built fabric'.[1]

The importance of the relationship between places – in its wide meaning – and people was first mooted in the early 1960s, when new ways of interpreting the urban environment arose in the USA and the UK. The key figures in these studies are Kevin Lynch and Gordon Cullen, whose theories can be considered – for their particular attention to the perception and design of place and its identity – as the origin of placemaking.

In the USA, during a period in which there was a need to construct a common language in which all people could recognize themselves, Kevin Lynch, an American urban planner who taught at MIT in Cambridge, created a method for interpreting the city based on the mental image, meant as a form perceived by its citizens. The theoretical approach is based on what is termed by Lynch (1960, p.2) 'legibility', that is 'the ease with which its parts can be recognized and can be organized into a coherent pattern', which Lynch considers fundamental for understanding the urban scene.

In identifying a path within a city, what is important for Lynch is the construction of an environmental image, the result of the immediate perception which the observer has of that place and the memory of previous experiences, which contribute both to guide and orientate him/her. The environmental image is analysed by Lynch through three components: identity, structure and meaning; of which the first two – due to the considerable variety of individual meaning which can be attributed to a city – are considered independent variables useful to the study of physical qualities of an environment.

From this concept the idea of 'imageability' derives, defined by Lynch (1960, pp.9–10) as:

> that quality in a physical object which gives it a high probability of evoking a strong image in any given observer. It is that shape, colour, or

> arrangement which facilitates the making of vividly identified, power-
> fully structured, highly useful mental images of the environment. It
> might also be called legibility, or perhaps visibility in a heightened sense,
> where objects are not only able to be seen, but are presented sharply
> and intensely to the senses.

The method to apply the idea of imageability consists in interviews with open answers – administered to a sample of previously instructed observers about their image of the environment – and site inspections to understand the image which these places evoke in the interviewees.

The interview is carried out in an office and is based on the request to sketch a map of the urban area in question, describing both some routes within it and the elements which were considered mainly representative for the inter-viewee. At the end of the interview the observer is taken out into the study area and requested to walk along the route described previously and explain the motivations which lead him/her down that path, as well as indicate the elements observed during the itinerary and the points where he/she feels more or less ori-entated. For external verification, further interviews are conducted with people at street level. The final map with the image of the area in question is given by the overlay of the outputs produced from the interviews and site inspections.

The search for a symbolic language able to translate consistently the information collected and also to be used to produce design orientation leads to the identification of five categories of elements which are represented in the Lynch maps: paths, edges, districts, nodes and landmarks, none of which actu-ally exist in isolation, but which overlap. As defined by Lynch (pp.46–48), '[p]aths are the channels along which the observer customarily, occasionally, or poten-tially moves. They may be streets, walkways, transit lines, canals, railroads'.

As regards edges, these

> are the linear elements not used or considered as paths by the observer.
> They are the boundaries between two phases, linear breaks in continu-
> ity: shores, railroad cuts, edges development, walls. They are lateral
> references rather than coordinate axes. Such edges may be barriers,
> more or less penetrable, which close one region off from another; or
> they may be seams, lines along which two regions are related and
> joined together.
>
> Districts are the medium-to-large sections of the city, con-
> ceived of as having two-dimensional extent, which the observer
> mentally enters 'inside of', and which are recognizable as having some
> common, identifying character. Always identifiable from the inside, they
> are also used for exterior reference if visible from the outside.
>
> (Lynch, 1960, pp.46–48)

Figure 81
Kevin Lynch: The visual form of Los Angeles as seen in the field
(Source: Banerjee, T. and Southworth, M. (eds) (1990), *City Sense and City
Design: Writings and Projects of Kevin Lynch*, Cambridge, MA: The MIT Press.
© MIT 1990)

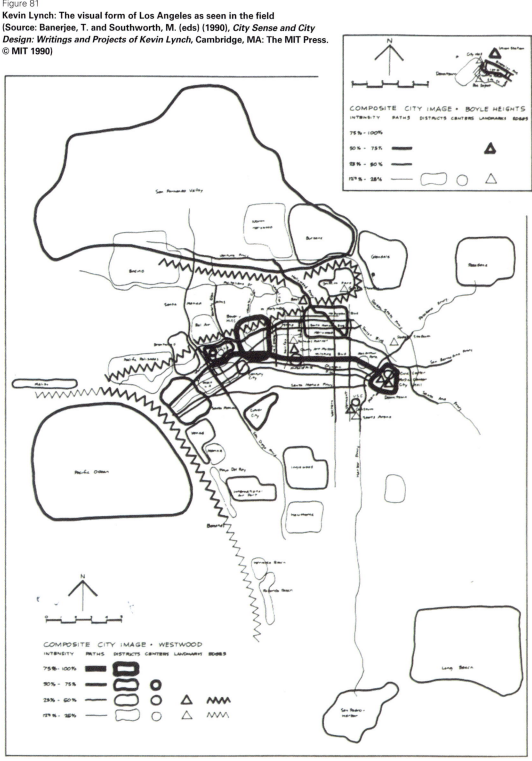

With respect to the fourth element, nodes, Lynch (1960, pp.46–48) says:

> they are points, the strategic spots in a city into which an observer can enter, and which are the intensive foci to and from which he is travelling. They may be primarily junctions, places of a break in transportation, a crossing of convergence of paths, moments of shift from one structure to another. Or the nodes may be simply concentrations, which gain their importance from being the condensation of some use or physical character, as a street-corner hangout or an enclosed square.

Then there are landmarks, which are defined by Lynch (1960, pp.46–48) as:

> another type of point-reference, but in this case the observer does not enter within them, they are external. They are usually a rather simply defined physical object: building, sign, store, or mountain. Their use involves the singling out of one element from a host of possibilities. Some landmarks are distant ones, typically seen from many angles and distances, over the tops of smaller elements, and used as radial references. They may be within the city or at such a distance that for all practical purposes they symbolize a constant direction. Such are isolated towers, golden domes, great hills.

The choice of the map as a way to describe the area and the five elements as representing the new symbolic language constitute an integrated part of his method.

Development of the image has to be accompanied, as asserted by Lynch, by an education to see, so as to form a sort of circular process, 'the visual education impelling the citizen to act upon his visual world, and this action causing him to see even more acutely'. Clarity of structure and vividness of identity are characteristics able to develop symbolic meanings and enrich the memory of places which the observer will be more able to fully enjoy and sediment.

The visual impact of the city is also, for Gordon Cullen, a fundamental factor for its reading and interpretation. Cullen, an English urban designer who initiated the Townscape movement theme, theorizes on what he defines the art of relationship:

> Suppose that we are just looking at the temple by itself, it would stand in front of us and all its qualities, size, colour and intricacy, would be evident. But put the temple back amongst the small houses and immediately its size is made more real and more obvious by the comparison between the two sales. Instead of being a big temple it TOWERS.
>
> The difference in meaning between bigness and towering is the measure of the relationship. In fact there is an art of relationship as there is an art of architecture. Its purpose is to take all the elements that go to create the environment: buildings, trees, nature, water, traffic,

> advertisement and so on, and to weave them together in such a way
> that drama is released. For a city is dramatic event in the environment.
>
> (Cullen, 1961, p.10)

The aim of Cullen's theory

> is not to dictate the shape of the town or environment, but is a modest
> one: simply to manipulate within the tolerances. This means that we can
> get no further help from the scientific attitude and that we must there-
> fore turn to other values and other standards. Vision is not only useful
> but it evokes our memories and experiences, those responsive emotions
> inside us which have the power to disturb the mind when aroused. It is
> this unlooked-for surplus that we are dealing with, for clearly if the envi-
> ronment is going to produce an emotional reaction, with or without our
> volition, it is up to us to try three ways in which it happens.
>
> (Cullen, 1961, pp.8–9)

Vision is also able to evoke our memories, if the environment is able to produce emotions. This can happen in three ways: optics, place and content.

Optics are meant by Cullen as emotions which an urban scene provokes through the visual sense. 'The scenery of towns is often revealed in a series of jerks or revelations. This we call Serial Vision' (p.11). Serial visions are revealed through 'the drama of juxtaposition' which can happen when we walk along a road and are attracted by different images that compose it. 'The human mind reacts to a contrast, to the difference between things, and when two pictures (the street and the courtyard) are in the mind at the same time, a vivid contrast is felt and the town becomes visible in a deeper sense'. In this respect, Cullen identifies two kinds of views, which from the optic point of view we can have in the city: the 'existing view', which exists and remains, and the 'emerging view', which can be unexpected.

Place concerns our reactions stemming from the position of the body in the environment. The kinds of reactions deriving from entering in a place are 'I am outside it, I am entering it, I am in the middle of it'. The experiences which we can live with a space concern the range between 'the major impacts of exposure and enclosure (which if taken to their morbid extremes result in the symptoms of agoraphobia and claustrophobia)'. The position of the body in a context is therefore considered by Cullen an important factor of environmental design.

> Arising out of this sense of identity or sympathy with the environment,
> this feeling of a person in street or square that he is in it or entering IT
> or leaving IT, we discover that no sooner do we postulate a HERE than
> automatically we must create a THERE, for you cannot have one with-
> out the other.
>
> (Cullen, 1961, p.12)

Figure 8.2
Gordon Cullen: serial vision
(Source: Cullen, G. (1971), *The Concise Townscape*, Oxford: Architectural Press)

Content concerns 'the fabric of towns: colour, texture, scale, style, character, personality and uniqueness' (p.13). The fabric of towns shows the different periods of construction and style and many towns show the mix and irregularity of styles and materials. Nevertheless – Cullen asserts – if we were to create a new urban scene, we would create an ordinary road with symmetry and balance.

Within a commonly accepted framework – one that produces lucidity and not anarchy – we can manipulate the nuances of scale and style, of texture and colour and of character and individuality, juxtaposing them in order to create collective benefits. In fact the environment thus resolves itself into not conformity but the interplay of This and That. It is a matter of observation that in a successful contrast of colours not only do we experience the harmony released but, equally, the colours become more truly themselves.

(Cullen, 1961, p.14)

At this point all that remains is to combine the different information with the imagination and create the 'home of man'.

Lynch and Cullen's new ways to interpret the city have been implemented over the years. Research carried out by Robert Venturi (1966, 1972), Marc Augé (1995), Rem Koolhaas (2001) and many others variously involved in the study of urban issues is grounded in the findings made by Lynch and Cullen.

Indeed, nowadays, changes in the contemporary city are extremely rapid. The urban image referred to by Gordon Cullen is no longer a typical example of the urban landscape.

Simultaneity and fragmentation characterize the city, with the resulting difficulty in deciphering the components that are part of it and the extent to which each component contributes to the urban scene. People with their different modes of living and perceiving space are essential in the interpretation and design of the contemporary urban landscape. New technologies, 'augmenting' the perceptions, have accelerated urban changes and opened people up to different possibilities of living in the world. Furthermore, the types of 'urban containers' are increasingly growing and the kind of entertainment is diversifying, which is mostly but not wholly devoted to satisfying shopping needs.

'The art of making places for people' has updated its theory and has added representational tools in order to become suitable to illustrate more complex urban scenes. In this respect, new ways of mapping the city have arisen, with the main purpose of identifying the urban dynamicity using direct observation or *ad hoc* electronic devices. What are shown in this section are new approaches to placemaking, including: virtual, lateral, people-oriented, multi-scale, configurational and complex-sensitive approaches. The selection does not aim to be exhaustive but sets out to illustrate various possibilities, both to approach the study of contemporary places and to seek the way to represent them accordingly (Sepe, 2002, 2006a, 2007a–c).

The different ways of collecting information are translated into specific display modes which cover a wide range of schemes, maps and virtual tools, often using combinations of data to obtain new kinds of information.

Chapter 9

The virtual approach

The virtual approach to analysing the urban landscape is an approach that finds its expression in the myriad of places created through the use of the internet. These are spaces, squares, architecture, platforms and gateways which, despite borrowing terms from the constructed world, are not physical places, but are able to influence movement, behaviour and habits. The resulting map is a sort of virtual architecture whose concrete meaning lies in the virtual paths that we habitually take (Abrams and Hall, 2006; Horan, 2000; Mitchell, 1996, 1999, 2002).

In his *City of Bits*, W.J. Mitchell (1996) analyses the single components of the system of new virtual spaces, the superhighway of information, of social, work, cultural places, internet meeting rooms and the various virtual communities that are being created, each with different attitudes, uses and needs, but joined by the virtual distance that divides them at the same time. The analysis proposed by Mitchell is a sociological and cultural example of a reality dominated by the internet that we have experienced in the last two decades. This reality is profoundly changing people's lives and the space in which they circulate.

> The Net negates geometry. While it does have a definite topology of computational nodes and radiating boulevards for bits, and while the locations of the nodes and links can be plotted on plans to produce surprisingly Haussmann-like diagrams, it is fundamentally and profoundly antispatial. It is nothing like the Piazza Navona or Copley Square. You cannot say where it is or describe its memorable shape and proportions or tell a stranger how to get there. But you can find things in it without knowing where they are. The Net is ambient – nowhere in particular but everywhere at once. You do not go to it; you log in from wherever you physically happen to be.
>
> (Mitchell, 1996, p.8)

The cities of physical space are concentrations of activities aimed at developing and improving accessibility and interaction 'face to face'. At the same time, cities have structures devoted to controlling access, which are realized through the creation of neighbourhoods, districts, green areas and jurisdictional and ownership boundaries. In the real world, to go from one threshold to another is for the inhabitants a rite of passage and there is a difference between being a native, on one's own land, feeling at home or being a stranger.

However, when you live in the internet the rules change even though the same things may happen. Access from one place to another does not happen in physical terms, but as logical connections: I connect to a site, I visit a site, I go to see a site are some of the access modes which are used by a common internet navigator on a daily basis.

> Some virtual places, like hermits' huts, can be occupied by only one person at a time. But others are designed to serve as shared-access, multiuser locations for joint activities – electronic calendars that can be updated by several staff members, CAD files that can be accessed simultaneously by several participants in a design session, or virtual chat and conference rooms. Sharing a virtual place is not quite the same thing, of course, as sharing a physical place like a room, a bed, or an umbrella in the rain. Bodies need not be in close proximity, and they need not to be enclosed by the same architectural or natural boundaries. The crucial thing is simultaneous electronic access to the same information. At their simplest, shared places are created by displaying the same scrolling text on multiple personal computer screens. In more sophisticated places, inhabitants share the same two-dimensional graphic display or even the same immersive, multisensory virtual reality.
>
> (Mitchell, 1996, p.22)

Mitchell entrusts to the sensitivity of the professionals who are involved in the organization of the city the task of becoming aware of what is happening and rethinking the territory as a 'bitsphere', considering not only spaces and individuals, but also places and the way of thinking, and new rules of thinking, law and economics associated with them.

The main types of spaces, activities and persons identified are: the 'electronic agoras', 'cyborg citizens', 'recombinant architecture', 'soft cities' and 'websites', in the dual and opposite meaning of both physical and tangible and virtual and intangible place.

A suitable example is the 'electronic agora', which contains some opposing features including spatial/antispatial, corporeal/incorporeal, focused/fragmented, synchronous/asynchronous, counterposing the antispatial, incorporeal, asynchronous nature of *City of Bits* with the spatial, corporeal and synchronous nature of the physical city.

The final result is a picture of the transformation of architectural and urban space/place and their users/residents as an effect of technological innovations introduced by the internet in its present and future state. A sort of platform on which virtual urban identities are constructed through reference to films, cities, famous people, architecture, museums, libraries, theatres, hospitals, banks, professionals and business types. Through this construct the future of the city can be imagined.

The virtual approach has led to different ways of reading the urban landscape from which useful data can be drawn to understand urban dynamics and movements, people's everyday activities and behaviour.

Carlo Ratti, for example, maps the area created by the radio networks using GIS techniques, overlapping the complex ways in which the landscape of the radio spectrum intersects with the built-up and urban areas[1] (Ratti et al., 2005).

The results obtained by means of graphic conventions and transformation of sets of points which represent the data in the form of maps provide information on places where calls are being made at different times of the day.

In the 'Real Time Rome' experiment, use was made of LocHNESs, the Localizing and Handling Network Event Systems platform of Telecom Italia. With this platform it was possible to evaluate the urban dynamics using anonymous monitoring of mobile cellular networks.

Figure 9.1
Carlo Ratti and Senseable City Lab, Live Singapore, HUB OF THE WORLD 2011: a project by MIT Senseable City Lab (Source: senseable.mit.edu/livesingapore)

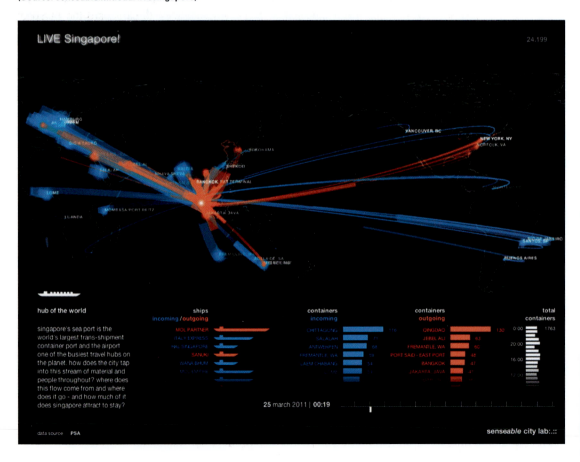

With the data from mobile phones and other wireless devices the city was mapped in real time, displaying vehicle traffic, bus and taxi positions, the flow of people during major events, thereby offering new possibilities for research in designing cities (Calabrese *et al.*, 2010).

A further example is the Amsterdam Real Time project to construct a dynamic map of Amsterdam and the Netherlands, monitoring the movement in real time of a selected number of people with GPS receivers. With these data, information can also be obtained on the location of the largest concentrations of people at various times of the day, the daily flows of pedestrians on the city's streets and in its buildings (Ratti *et al.* 2005).

In LIVE Singapore!, a platform designed to be a toolbox for real-time data collecting able to describe urban dynamics, is carried out. Thanks to this platform, people can access the wide range of real-time information about their city. In this way people can take their decisions in synchrony with what is happening around them which is increasingly characterized by the simultaneity of events.

Using the data that can be obtained from this system, Mitchell asserts it is possible to get information of a very different type, that is on data related to navigation, or the network behaviour at work and at leisure. The range of possible results may be extended for many topics concerning city research and planning. At the same time, given the possible confidentiality of certain information, appropriate legislation must be established to safeguard the personal sphere (Mitchell, 1996).

Chapter 10

The lateral approach

The lateral approach is an approach to interpreting the urban landscape that presupposes a cross-sectional analytical approach to studying an area from different points of view and at different scales of interpretation. Such an approach is also based on perceptual, sociological or anthropological aspects, or on all three together. It is a method whose foundations lie in the urban studies of Lynch and Cullen but whose results, in addition to visual-perceptual images and maps, also comprise eclectic atlases, installations, and any tool considered useful for the representation of the observed elements (Banerjee and Southworth 1990; Barajas, 2003; Harvey, 1989; Lassus, 1977).

With the USE – Uncertain States of Europe[1] – a research programme on contemporary Europe, Stefano Boeri studies the change in real time of contemporary space and investigates elements testifying to changes in people's behaviour and the flows of goods and ideas (Boeri, 2003, 2011; Koolhaas *et al.*, 2001). The aim is to construct a network consisting of people with various skills applied to observing the contemporary urban condition.

The landscape is investigated, focusing on the physical and spatial signs of the social and cultural change that is now underway, offering a kind of reversal of the gaze, and recognizing that physical space is the place where processes are visible and comparable. It is recognized that the living behaviours have a faster pace of change than spatial mutations, and between them there forms a sort of friction in which the traces and indicators of new lifestyles can be explored.

European urban space under investigation is meant, more in an anthropological than architectural sense, as an intersection of levels of truth, rather than a simple summary of elements. European cities are analysed horizontally, vertically and cross-sectionally in order to comprehend the dynamics, desires and idiosyncrasies of the inhabitants, and the economic and cultural energies that run through them.

The assumption is that urban space is nowadays a metaphor for society, full of signs of contemporary life; history, in this perspective, is not considered an independent field of study but as manifested in the contemporaneity of urban conditions.

History is in this sense seen as a material inheritance, through the observation of concrete spaces, and its intangible manifestations, through research into the invisible structures of customs and traditions.

Boeri proposes to interpret the changes in society with the attitude of an investigator, starting from indications which do not appear significant, observing places, people and cultures from many standpoints. The aim is to convert the complexity of contemporary changes into comprehensible language, offering new interpretational keys for surveying the urban landscape. The city derives not only from an urban stratification of levels of truth, but also as a collective way of conceiving space, that requires a proper form of representation.

The experiments carried out are formalized through a representation of information in the format which is considered most appropriate for the specific case study, collecting different evidence of the same analysed condition:

> The texts are heterogeneous (reports, photographic surveys, geographic and literary descriptions, classifications, research reports, qualitative investigations, essays and articles, anthologies and monographs, collections of plans or projects…), but they are similar in their visual approach. They tend to take on the form of an 'atlas' because they seek new logical correspondences between spatial things, the words we use to name them, and the mental images we project upon them …. They produce provisional and inconsequential maps in which the territory is not represented as a continuous mineral substrate or as a layering of stable 'states of things', but as the interweaving of sinuous and multiple configurations which are reversible and which never share the same time-frame.
>
> (Boeri, 1997)

The changes in the contemporary city are observed in the case studies with dynamics from the 'bottom', noting the innovations produced in the spaces left free to live outside of the general policies and forms of traditional planning and programming.

To investigate the urban phenomenon of rave parties and trends, for example, video and photographic survey techniques were chosen in order to adequately gather mobile and unforeseen events. The sites where raves are held are located in public places that are both mobile and temporary, and which do not leave tracks except during the event.

The study reveals that these phenomena arise mostly in marginal areas which affirm their centrality in the imagination of some European population groups, expanding instantaneously to then disappear once again, opposed to the closed space of the large shopping containers: rave parties represent an extreme version of a trend in the construction of Europe for temporary public places, unable to deposit lasting traces on the region (Boeri, 2003, p.102).

In another case study on the doubling of the A4 autobahn in Germany, the observation 'from below' noted the possibility of observing the outcome of the transformations that act on parallel levels of reality and at the same time, the effects produced. Hence the widening of the A4 autobahn is currently unable to interact with the dynamics that surround it:

We are dealing with the tough urban marketing policy of the cities of Leipsig and Dresden, the unexpected increase in value of agricultural production, the birth of new leisure time areas, or the siting of new firms and manufacturers close to the freeways. At the same time, with the widening of the A4 Poland has become closer to Germany but with regard to its infrastructural endowment, it has grown further away from other EU countries.[2]

(Boeri, 2003, p.112)

Figure 10.1
**TuttoEuropa, edited by Maddalena De Ferrari and Giovanni La Varra/Multiplicity
(Source: Boeri, S. (2003),** *USE: Uncertain State of Europe,* **Milano: Skira Editore.)**

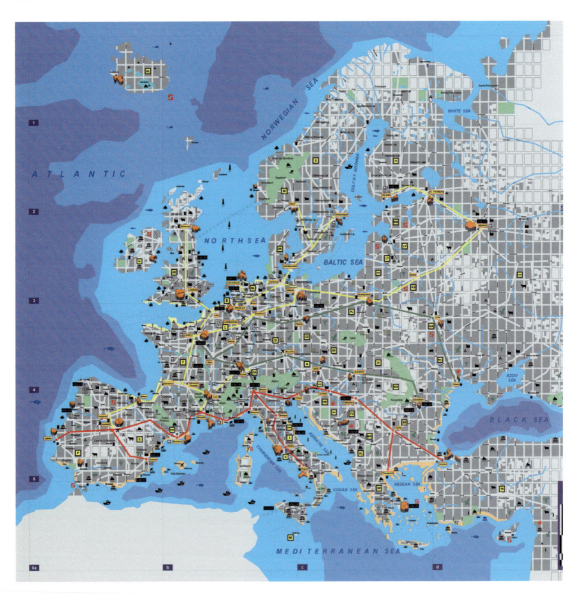

The final product of the lateral method consists of *eclectic atlases*, containing a variety of texts such as photographic campaigns, geographical descriptions, classifications, research reports, investigations and different ways of representing urban society, which all share the same visual approach. The atlases represent the urban condition from different initial starting points, focusing on places sideways on, while moving between both physical and mental space.

The maps produced are temporary and the area which is represented is the intertwining of multi-dimensional, reversible configurations. These maps are produced simultaneously from several angles: from high up, from below and within, replacing the eyes of those who 'live' the space, in other words from new experimental perspectives.

In this way, new ways of viewing and representing the urban landscape and its identity are experimented, producing local maps and biographies of places, narrating an individual path in space and using the representation to establish contact with the landscape.

According to Boeri, the use of an evidential paradigm and interpretation of the traces of the new behaviours do not only stem from the need to raise the question of how the enquiry is organized; it is the slowness with which the physical space reflects the change in such behaviours that makes the landscape a set of clues, which do not arrive simultaneously to shape the space, but mark it with transient and intermittent traces, evidence of an ongoing process.

Chapter 11

The people-oriented approach

The people-oriented approach is based on the observation of places from the pedestrian's point of view. Jan Gehl begins his study on public space with the observation that in many contemporary cities the opportunity for 'pedestrianism' has been reduced to a form of transport, increasingly losing its social and cultural function. This is due to many factors, chiefly the lack of suitable public spaces and the presence of noise and pollution caused by the intensive use of cars.

In order to allow the creation of lively, safe, sustainable and healthy cities, Gehl (1996, 2010) proposes to strengthen the social function of public spaces, favouring their role as meeting places.

The term 'lively city' is used to mean a city where there are spaces where people are encouraged to perform actions such as walking, cycling and staying. A 'safe city' is a city where there are short walking distances, various urban functions and services, and public spaces which are attractive. In this way the feeling of security increases because there are more eyes along the street and people are incentivized to participate in events in the city. A 'sustainable city' is a city where a broad system of green mobility is used, including not only public transport but also pedestrianism and cycling. A 'healthy city' is a city where people can easily walk or cycle to reach their place for daily activities instead of taking a car or riding a motorbike, whose increasing use is becoming a problem for diseases connected to a sedentary lifestyle (Gehl, 2010, pp.3–8).

The necessary requisite for lively, safe, sustainable and healthy cities is, hence, walking, meant in its widest meaning: having conversations, meeting people, experiencing street entertainment, shopping and so on.

In this respect, Jan Gehl recognizes three main types of pedestrian activities in public spaces: necessary activities, optional activities and social activities (Gehl, 1971, pp.11–16).

> Necessary activities include those that are more or less compulsory – going to school or to work, shopping, waiting for a bus or a person, running errands, distributing mail – in other words, all activities in which those involved are to a greater or lesser degree required to participate. …

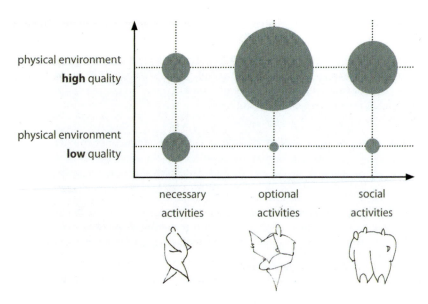

Figure 11.1
Jan Gehl: diagram of the activities that generate a good-quality public space (Source: Gehl, J. (2010) *Cities For People,* **Washington: Island Press)**

Because the activities in this group are necessary, their incidence is influenced only slightly by the physical framework. These activities will take place throughout the year, under nearly all conditions, and are more or less independent of the exterior environment. The participants have no choice.

Optional activities – that is, those pursuits that are participated in if there is a wish to do so and if time and place make it possible – are quite another matter. This category includes such activities as taking a walk to get a breath of fresh air, standing around enjoying life, or sitting and sunbathing.

These activities take place only when exterior conditions are optimal, when weather and place invite them. ... These activities are especially dependent on exterior physical conditions.

Social activities are all activities that depend on the presence of others in public spaces. Social activities include children at play, greetings and conversations, communal activities of various kinds, and finally – as the most widespread social activity – passive contacts, that is, simply seeing and hearing other people. ... These activities could also be termed 'resultant' activities, because in nearly all instances they evolve from activities linked to the other two activity categories. They develop in connection with the other activities because people are in the same space, meet, pass by one another, or are merely within view.

Quality of public spaces, as shown in the diagram used by Gehl (2010) (Figure 11.1), occurs when there is a good presence of optional and social activities. The presence of only necessary activities denotes an outdoor area of poor quality. However, when the public space is of a high quality the necessary activities continue to take place with similar frequency but the time that people spend there is longer due to the better conditions.

The method used by Gehl in order to improve the quality of public spaces consists in observation of both public spaces and behaviour of pedestrians within these. Based on this observation, the problems or potentials of the public space are highlighted and the strategies for quality improvement are outlined.

Pedestrian activities are surveyed by counting the number of people who walk in public spaces and by identifying how these are used, people's activities and the kinds of facilities that are offered for walking and staying. In particular, the data for behavioural mapping are collected through counts of pedestrian traffic and surveys of stationary activities at specific times, days and periods of the year.

In this regard, an emblematic case study exists in the city of Adelaide, Australia, in which the above observation of public spaces identified different kinds of places and use modes to be developed or enhanced, which include the following. The first observation is that in Adelaide's city centre, despite efforts being made to increase the number of outdoor cafés, a more diverse range of activities has to be introduced to encourage people to walk and stay. The presence of heavy traffic due to the intensive use of private transport does not improve the overall quality of the spaces. The squares cover a large area but are poor quality and suffer from a lack of an overall plan with indications as to how they might be used. Another observation is that the wide streets offer many opportunities to develop not only recreational activities but also suitable spaces for pedestrians and cyclists as well as bus lanes.

With respect to the conditions of pedestrians, the study indicated low priority in the city centre. The public spaces are not too densely populated because urban conditions show pedestrians as an obstacle. A lack of dedicated safe lanes for cyclists is also observed. Outdoor seating is sufficient but not always well placed, and in some case there is the lack of view, shade or suitable public access.

Finally, the survey identified a city mainly inhabited by young people, with a low presence of children and elderly people. In this case, interventions which were identified target the following principles:

> Capitalize on the unique qualities, Create a better city for walking, Create a better city for staying, Reduce through traffic, Create a beautiful city, Create a diverse, safe and lively city. Each of these indications are proposed with different measures mainly based on: reducing traffic, both by establishing a ringroad to redirect the traffic out of the city centre and introducing traffic calming measures; developing a suitable pedestrian network and creating a strategy to differentiate and improve

the squares; developing a design program for urban furniture, signs, lighting – both daily and nightly – and city colours; improving north-south connections; developing a good public transport network; create more accommodation in the city centre for a lively 24-hour city.

(Gehl, 2002, pp.69–83)

This method has been applied in many cities including Melbourne, Oslo, Perth, Portland and Copenhagen. Development of the main streets of these cities follows a similar process of transformation: the 'car-oriented' phase, the cars occupy the street, leaving limited space to pedestrian circulation; the 'shopping-phase', where the street is pedestrianized but the main pedestrian purpose is shopping; the 'cultural phase', in which people use public spaces in order to stay and recreate thanks to the presence of new activities. Finally, the 'spatial identity phase' where public spaces are interconnected, creating a network and assuming a new meaning (Gehl, 2002, 2010).

In the different cases in which the people-oriented approach was carried out, the observations which concern public space included the composition, size, sitting of the place, the traffic situation and the conflicts for pedestrian flows. Protection, comfort and enjoyment are the main criteria which are identified in order to obtain a '100 per cent place'.

Chapter 12

The multi-scale approach

The multi-scale approach is a complex approach that presupposes knowledge and attainment of a very large body of data from different sources able to interact and supply the answers required to interpret an area. It is a type of approach that from some points of view may be described as the completion and extension of a GIS (Geographic Information System) into a more dynamic and flexible form (Gausa, Guallart and Muller, 2003; Hall, 1988).

The Dutch MVRDV design team (2002) developed a method of analysis and design of the area starting from some assumptions. According to MVRDV, cities must be able to ensure the coexistence of a set of diversified functions and facilities that entail enormous economic benefits. Smaller urban areas cannot offer the same complexity of facilities as cities, which have the edge in terms of supply. In order to make the former competitive, the MVRDV solution lies in networks, in the creation of complex systems of towns, cities and regions.

Combining hard and soft resources intelligently, multi-centre cities can be competitive because they combine the variety of resources of large centres with better quality of life. Hard resources consist of nature, commercial structures, cultural attractions, architecture, museums and monuments, while soft resources are the population, culture and the heritage of traditions. In order to successfully network the multi-centre urban areas and the cities, the two types of resources must be connected by a combination of physical and IT networks.

MVRDV tested the multi-scale approach in various contexts. In the RhineRuhrCity research project developed for the North Rhine-Ruhr region of Germany, the idea was based again on the belief that cities are complex organisms and full of internal connections.

The Rhine-Ruhr region of Germany has lost its identity: it is now best known for the presence of heavy industry. It is very populous, but not high-density and each area can be easily accessed in the same way due to the presence of a very efficient road network. The purpose of this study was, first, to define the region as a new urban dimension and, second, to draw up a development hypothesis for the North Rhine-Ruhr region and suitable tools for visualization.

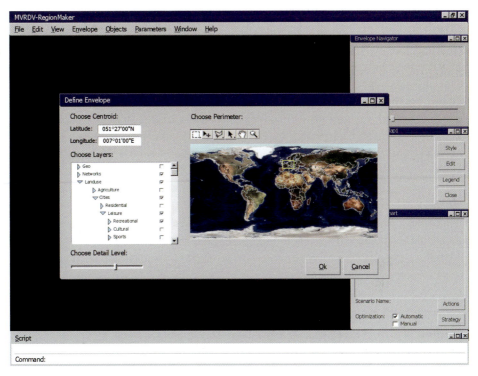

Figure 12.1
**Regionmaker
Software:
MVRDV (2003),
© MVRDV**

The main question highlighted by the Dutch research project was the problem of how to connect and perceive all the information in order to add value and meaning to it. The second issue addressed was how to visually represent the data so that they can make a working tool and make it more accessible and easier for non-specialists in the sector and the public at large (Costanzo, 2006).

The body of information that may be available in relation to a given region is extremely large and constantly changing; integration between hard and soft features is very complex, and it is very difficult to represent the networks of interdependence for a whole region (Thackara and Maas, 2003, pp.89–91).

To handle the huge amounts of data and offer possible scenario to the Rhine-Ruhr region, MVRDV has produced a series of tools called 'The Regionmaker', which combine the functions of a search engine, a graphical interface and a browser. These tools are able to collect demographic data and values provided by the GIS, and allow consultation of maps, access to databases, export of video images from satellites, the internet connection and CAD design.

The software allows the spatial configuration of the region to be analysed and optimized: through the information which is imported, the user is supported in the choice of possible decisions. By displaying the objects divided into categories in a three-dimensional space, once the parameters are defined and all the necessary information is collected, the most suitable configuration of the region can be sought and scenarios created (Gausa *et al.*, 2003).

The same approach to the study of a region was used for the HiperCatalunya project. In this project the Catalonia region was analysed from the population flows perspective. The study also focused on identifying its role in the global context, based on an interaction between data and models. The software developed scenarios for Catalonia in 2050, providing a range of possible ways to transform the region and its role within a local, European and global context.

Research has determined the links which hold together the population dynamics and area configurations, providing 72 possible outcomes, with the aim of ensuring that the Catalan population and its authorities have the information required to decide which scenario to aim for (Gausa *et al.*, 2003).

In adopting the multi-scale approach, the regional scale plays a key role; the tools for surveying and displaying information are modified in order to support the identification of a regional identity and determine configurations of different scenarios. Beyond adding models to represent the flows of people, goods and information, the system is evolving towards assuming a more active and decisive support function to planning policies.

Chapter 13

The configurational approach

The configurational approach concerns the study of a complex of inter-relations. As shown by Bill Hillier and his Space Syntax Laboratory, the method controls the variables of physical complexity, treating built environments as systems of space and analysing them configurationally (Hillier and Stutz, 2004).

The aim of research conducted by Bill Hillier is to discover the models and structure of these variables (Hillier, 1996; Hillier et al., 1986; Hillier and Hanson, 1984). Space Syntax is a method applied to cities to understand how social and economic processes model space through time: it is a way of viewing and conceiving of cities as self-organizing systems.

The most important aspect of the research consists in the set of methods for analysing patterns of space in the built environment in order to find spatial structures and relate them to the way people move, stop and interact.

Space Syntax analyses patterns of real space using simple mathematical tools that typically relate all elements to all others, as far as this is possible.

Hillier uses this method to observe the network of streets and walkways in cities, as well as visibility graph analysis to study patterns of visual fields in public spaces. The result is represented by an axial map of an urban area and its context.

The starting point is the idea that cities are built for subsequent acts. The different character of cities results from the different way in which the spatial network is structured according to culture and era. With this method Hillier's laboratory seeks to demonstrate that cities evolve according to a two-fold principle. The urban structure is shaped by a network of connected centres, created by the influence of micro-economic activity, which maximises movement and groups similar activities within the same space. This construction mode is the basis of the global spatial structures of cities which therefore tend to take a similar form. The local culture, with its differences, makes changes to the modulation and control of movement and flows created by the economic system. These changes may vary not only from city to city, but even within the same city, depending on the types of cultural affiliations and lifestyles.

The urban space is observed at the micro and macro scale in order to understand the interactions and interconnections.

Figure 13.1
**Trafalgar Square, Space Syntax analysis
(Source: http://www.spacesyntax.com)**

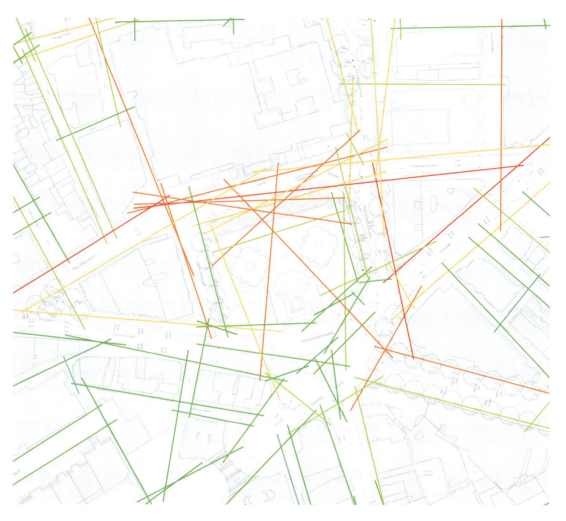

This approach is also used to understand the effects of long- and medium-term project planning, allowing planners and designers to work taking into account the socio-economic process which can be triggered with the projects.

Furthermore, in order to support space syntax analysis, the laboratory has developed a set of software. The instrument most commonly used is Axman, carrying out axial analysis on individual buildings or for whole cities.

Another software package is EVAS which generates virtual environments based on architectural drawings populated by virtual 'agents' or pedestrians. The agents move in the space using the rules 'of perception-action' and may be attracted by objects entering their field of vision. EVAS allows us to calculate the patterns of movement resulting from changes in action of these objects in the environment.

The configurational approach was used by Space Syntax in various projects. In the case of the project for Trafalgar Square, pedestrian flows were studied. Trafalgar Square and Parliament Square are the core of London for many of its users. Despite this, the public space between the two squares was perceived as unpleasant, dangerous and dominated by traffic. Space Syntax analysis identified the activities of pedestrians, particularly noting that the middle of Trafalgar Square was avoided by Londoners, while the space between Trafalgar Square and Parliament Square was not used by tourists.

The pedestrian flow model developed on this occasion led to a series of measures to revitalize the area and make it more attractive for residents and tourists. The project carried out on the basis of that model was able to achieve a 13-fold increase in pedestrian flow in the square (Space Syntax, 2005).

In the case of Margate, the initial consideration was that the historical part of the town of Margate was an area of interest, but underused and situated outside the more extensive town centre. The need was to find ways to attract new investment to that part of town. The analysis was based on the study of the historical development of the centre and its business models, and of its pedestrian flow. The result of this study showed that the historical part of the town had a simple internal organization, but was hard to permeate from the outside and therefore difficult to access. The project was thus based on identifying a highly visible new route through this part of Margate. This potential path was verified by building a pedestrian flow model, which revealed the improvement of this path. Regeneration of the area and the renewed flow once again induced investors to use their resources in that area.

Using the configurational approach, other aspects of the town were also studied: in addition to traffic flows, these included land use patterns, socio-economic changes and crime, in order to investigate the different forms of relationships which can be established between structure and urban functions. Spatial configuration is not always the element which causes all that occurs on a given movement or flow, and effects can vary from place to place. In cases where the effect of the configuration is less strong than in others, Space Syntax collects additional information, such as that relating to transport hubs, land use, the major attractors or the factors which determine aesthetic characteristics (Penn et al., 1998; Turner and Penn, 2002).

Chapter 14

The complex-sensitive approach

The complex-sensitive approach (Sepe, 2009b) studies urban places in all their complexity. It is sensitive because it is open to all the stimuli provided by the places and seeks to identify and represent elements linked to features which are both perceptual and objective, permanent and transitory.

The main method of analysis and design that follows this kind of approach is PlaceMaker (Sepe, 2007b). Unlike other analytical approaches which study only one aspect of the site (perceptive, urban, etc.) or multidisciplinary approaches which collect large amounts of data but find difficulty collating it, PlaceMaker considers the places from all points of view and with different but compatible tools of relief. This method assembles, elaborates and reconstructs data from surveys based on physical reconnaissance, sensory perceptions, graphical elaboration, photographic and video records, and sets these data against those provided by an overview of expectations, an analysis based on traditional cartography and two question-naires administered to local inhabitants. The main products are two final complex maps, one of analysis and one of design, which represent place identity and project interventions in order both to establish a dialogue with local people and support planners and administrators in sustainable urban construction and transformation.

Suitable software supports the different phases of the method for more rapid operations of managing and updating the data collected. PlaceMaker software allows the creation of dynamic and interactive maps. The main characteristics of the software are: flexibility, facility and rapidity of use, strong graphical impact, and indexing of the results. Furthermore, indices such as those of liveability, sustainable place identity and so on can be created by using appropriate calculations able to transform the elements of the complex maps into numerical values.

The main users targeted by the method and software are urban design-ers, planners and administrators, while a simplified form of the complex maps is available for citizens, place users and visitors. As regards administrators and city planners, PlaceMaker enables them to understand, in the framework of the planning process, the potentials and problems relating to any given place, how the place itself is perceived by its users and residents, and what are the possible actions in order to improve its quality. The maps enable the collection of ana-lytical data on the place and data for project interventions. These may be used for specific purposes, including: to redefine the identity and image of a place in regeneration operations (e.g. historical identity, commercial identity, etc.), to assess the compatibility of new activities and urban projects with its identity, to gauge whether the recovery of previous businesses or activities in case of post-disaster reconstructions are still in line with current demands, and to enhance the identity resources in order to sustainably render a place more attractive for locals and visitors.

As to the citizens, PlaceMaker enable them to garner a deeper under-standing of their city's identity, feel stronger ties to it, so that they will protect and safeguard it or play a proactive role by proposing improvements to adminis-trators and participating in planning choices. Lastly, tourists and place users will find that the maps provide an insight into the city that goes beyond mere identifi-cation of major landmarks and captures the complexity of place identity, including its tangible and intangible elements, both permanent and temporary.

Experiments were carried out in Europe, the United States and Japan in areas of historical interest that were emblematic for the city in question.

The next section (Part II) shows the method, software and an emblem-atic index in detail, while Part III presents a selection of the case studies that were carried out.

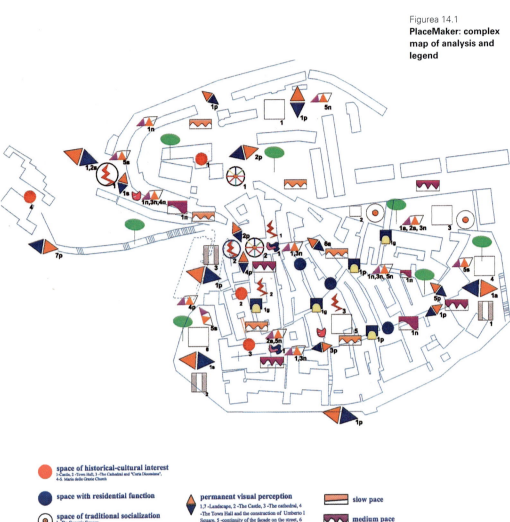

Figurea 14.1
**PlaceMaker: complex
map of analysis and
legend**

space of historical-cultural interest
1-Castle, 2 -Town Hall, 3 -The Cathedral and "Curia Dioomima",
4-S. Maria delle Grazie Church

space with residential function

space of traditional socialization
1- De Sanctis Square

space of random socialization
1- Fischetti Square with the Cathedral

place with multiple values
1 -The area with the Castle- De Andrea Square-
Berardi Street, 2 -Umberto I Square

place of memory
Ruins of: 1 - Solferino Street, 2 - di Savoia Street,
3 -Minghetti Square

symbolic place
1- Monument to the victims on Mancini Street, 2
-Cemented remains standing near the statue of the
Madonna in Piazza Umberto I

empty space
1-Argentino Street, 2,3-De Sanctis Square, 4-
Perspective on Corso V. Emanuele, 5 -area on
Minghetti Street, 6 -seightseeing on the end of
Caracciolo Street

space of limit
1-Area at the end of Emanuele Street, 2 -area at
the end of Caracciolo Street, 3 -Umberto I Square

permanent visual perception
1,7 -Landscape, 2 -The Castle, 3 -The cathedral, 4
-The Town Hall and the construction of Umberto I
Square, 5 -continuity of the facade on the street, 6
-irregularity of the facade on the street

permanent touch perception
1-cobbled paving

transient smell perception
1-smells coming from kitchen

transient sound perception
1-vehicles, 2-recovery works, 3-voices of people,
4-sound of birds, 5- wind

n no-influential perception

p pleasant perception

d annoying perception

s surprising perception

slow pace

medium pace

trees and urban green areas

cats

small size of symbol = presence of
given element in slight percentage

medium size of symbol = presence of
given element in medium percentage

large size of symbol = presence of
given element in considerable percentage

Part II

Making places for people

Section II

The PlaceMaker method

Chapter 15

The method

Phase 0: Construction of the analysis grid

PlaceMaker comprises eight phases in addition to a preliminary one, which consists of the construction of the grid for the set of operations to be carried out.

In phase 0, various types of databases must be created to contain the different types of data collected, namely data from the preliminary analysis (sketches, poems, collages, etc.), denominative survey (words), graphical survey (signs and symbols), perceptive survey, photographic survey (fixed images) and video survey (moving images). Then there are the elements obtained from the study of traditional maps (graphic signs, symbols, etc.) and the questionnaires administered to the users of the places in question (sketches, words, etc.).

The categories of items to be analysed and measurement criteria are also established. Within the reference period chosen to study the urban changes, the most significant days and time slots for carrying out inspections and relative surveys are decided. Furthermore, in order for the calculation of the complex indexes to be provided, characteristics and relative measurement criteria are assigned to the elements to be collected.[1]

The basic categories that can be used for the survey include: built elements (presence of monuments, buildings, etc.), natural elements (presence of landscaped areas, trees, animals, etc.), transportation modes (presence or transit of cars, buses, etc.) and people (presence of tourists, residents, etc.). The categories of elements to be analysed are chosen according to the nature of the place in question. These categories can be modified according to the specific characteristics of the place analysed.

The criteria for measuring the elements to be analysed concern aspects of quantity and quality. The parameter used for measuring the quantity summarizes the data found into small, medium or large percentages, and the parameter measuring quality summarizes the degree of sensation detected as non-influential, pleasant or annoying; as regards pace, this is perceived as either slow, regular or hectic.

As for the choice of the most significant time slices, mornings and afternoons are generally preferred. One working day is used, as well as Saturday and Sunday, while in relation to the period of the year, times of increased seasonal change are preferred. During the survey, any annotations on more suitable categories of elements, measurement parameters or periods than those predicted may make it necessary to replace those previously established with others considered more satisfactory for analysis.

Table 15.1 **PlaceMaker: the method schema**

Phase	Objectives	Actions	Products
0	Construction of the analysis grid	Choice of categories Choice of parameters Choice of significant days Choice of time slices	Database grid
1	Anticipatory analysis	Preliminary observations made prior to the first inspection of the place	Map of the preliminary ideas of the place
2	Denominative and perceptual description of the elements	Denominative survey Perceptual survey Graphical survey Photographic survey Video survey	Map visualizing the results obtained from the surveys
3	Identification with traditional cartography of the elements required for area description	Analysis of traditional planimetry at urban scale Analysis of traditional planimetry at territorial scale	Map with the components of the site deduced from analysis of traditional maps
4	Identification of place elements perceived by users of places	Questionnaire for visitors to the place	Map visualizing the results of the questionnaire
5	Processing the collected information	Overlay of the maps with the different elements observed from the anticipatory and effective analysis Check of the different elements observed through different analysis tools	Graphic system of symbols Complex map of analysis
6	Identification of identity resources	Identification of the identity potential Identification of identity problems Identification of identity qualities	Map of identity resources
7	Identification of identity resources by users of places	Questionnaire for visitors to the place	Map visualizing the results of the questionnaire
8	Identification of the project proposal	Overlay and elaboration of data collected Definition and localization of design interventions	Graphic system of symbols Complex map of identity project

Phase 1: Anticipatory analysis

Phase 1 involves analysis of expectations. This analysis phase, to be implemented before the first site visit, aims to make a preliminary survey of the place; having first chosen the city and the part or parts of it to analyse, the idea one has of that area is sketched using the preferred tool or means of expression, using available information prior to the first visit. This information can be drawn from the memories or associations one has of that place, or from bibliographical research. Information may for this reason be varied, and the product of this phase is a map-mosaic of different ideas of a place emerging. It is a phase where it is important not to go to the site but to define one's own ideas in the form considered appropriate, subsequently being translated into a map containing the items believed to belong to that place. Many tools can be used: from simple use of written text to the use of integrated materials and tools of a type intended to identify the physical location and its characteristics. The first analysis phase is one of the phases most subject to the sensitivity of the individual surveyor and hence conditioned by a high degree of subjectivity. In a multidisciplinary working group expectations analysis is performed by people of different disciplines in order to be able to overlay the data and obtain non-specialist information.

Phase 2: Denominative and perceptual description

The second phase consists of five surveys. The first survey, the denominative one, is to collect data concerning the categories chosen in preparing the grid and related in particular to constructed elements, natural elements, transportation modes and to people. This survey is called denominative because it deals with naming the things that one sees.

The operation of naming urban features[2] is useful both to identify buildings and monuments which are in some way already codified, and to name those elements and places which, though not precisely defined, contribute to constructing the urban landscape and to forming place identity. In this way, it is possible to detect elements whose names are already recognized and, at the same time, name urban components whose effects are known, but whose dynamics or the places in which they occur are less obvious.

Table 15.2 **Template for a denominative survey**

City	Place	Date	Time	Type	Constructed elements	Natural elements	Transportation mode	People
				Low, medium, high percentage				

The categories of elements to be analysed are chosen according to the nature of the place in question. These categories can be modified – replacing or detailing them – according to specific characteristics of the analysed place. Rather than listing all the elements present, the idea is to record the types of elements which go to characterize that particular place: a historical building, a fountain, a form of paving, the presence of cars or bicycles, tourists, hawkers, the type of vegetation, etc.

The location of all these elements, their kind and quantity, expressed as a low, medium or high percentage, are indicated. Each denominative data sheet will be supplemented by a cognitive sheet, a flexible tool for adding elements which were not selected beforehand, but obtained from site visits.

The second survey is the perceptual one.[3] It covers sensory perceptions such as smell, sound, taste, tactile and visual sensations, and overall perception, focusing on location, type, quantity (low, medium, high) and quality (classifying perceptions as: non-influential, pleasant or annoying).

The three alternatives indicated above as to the quantity and quality features of the data collected are provided as synthetic definitions, while during data collection the data may be elaborated in more detail. As for the denominative survey, it is not necessary to register all the perceptions present but only those which are characteristic or salient: the noise of wind or traffic, the smell of flowers or food, the feel of materials used for paving, a striking view, and, in addition, the global perception given by the sum of the sensations.

Perceptions that can be collected can be both permanent and transient. A permanent perception consists for example of the sight of a building or a mountain (visual perception), a historical stone paving (tactile sense), the sound of a waterfall that flows unabated (sound perception). A transient perception may be detected by the sight of a billboard that covers the work of restoration of the facade of a building (visual perception), the noise due to the passage of a machine (sound perception) or the smell from food sold by street vendors (sense of smell).

This survey is a delicate operation because it needs to isolate each sense to identify the sense actually used and the perception which it is capable of causing. This part of the analysis is rather subjective, especially for the survey of perceived feeling. The collective elements observed during the denominative, graphic, perceptual, photographic and video surveys return collected information with a reasonable degree of objectivity.

Table 15.3 **Template for a perceptual survey**

City	Place	Date	Time	Type	Smell P.	Taste P.	Sound P.	Touch P.	Visual P.
				Low, medium, high percentage					
				Non-influential, pleasant, annoying perceived feeling					

A road slope will cause an uncomfortable feeling, detectable for example by photographs or videos depicting greater flows of people who choose less strenuous alternative routes, or from bodily expressions with complaints of fatigue. Likewise, the smell coming from delicious pastries will also be evidenced by a visible concentration of people in that store.

Next comes the graphical survey which consists in sketching the places concerned; the sketches will represent the area in question from a visual-perceptual standpoint and will be supported by written notes as required. This operation is a preliminary study for the construction of the graphic symbols for the first final complex map.

Written notes related to the sketch expand or specify the scope of observation. Sketches show the perception of place expressed in terms of signs. As an example, in this type of survey, the impression of sudden widening of a street, the feeling of empty space caused by a square, or an unexpected limit posed by an unusual barrier are observed. The information, which is collected and transformed into graphic signs, shows on paper not only what is seen but, in particular, the perception of what is seen. Notes written for the sketch expand and/or specify the scope of observation.

Photographic and video surveys of the whole study area are then carried out, focusing more on the recording of facts than on providing an interpretation of the places. The pictures taken during the photographic survey serve to identify elements, facts and relationships. While in previous surveys, particularly in the denominative and perceptual, there is greater attention to identifying single elements, in the photographic survey there is more attention to relationships.

With the video survey, the study of relationships between elements is enriched by measuring their duration and in particular by the pace, cadence and dynamics of places.

Each of the five surveys, taken singly, is not able to give a complete idea of the place. Only when all the data collected during the five surveys are combined is it possible to have comprehensive information on the elements of the place in nominal and perceptual terms, of a sort that does not emerge from traditional analysis. The output of the five surveys is a map collating the results obtained from each.

Phase 3: Analysis of traditional mapping

The third phase consists of an analysis of the traditional mapping of the urban areas selected (ortho-photogrammetry, typological surveys, etc.). The types of maps used in this phase depend on the nature of the area in question; the study is carried out on an urban scale in order to identify the mutual relationships between the elements in the area, and on a territorial scale, so as to identify the relationships between the site and the whole city.

The analysis with the traditional planimetry is based on the survey of the 'materials' and composition of the urban fabric, its matrix and forms, and its connections and fragmentations, relevant to the method of analysis being used.

By way of example, at the urban scale one can observe: squares, the type of urban fabric, places of historic and cultural interest, empty spaces, thoroughfares, visual perceptions of points of interest and urban greenery.

Territorial scale analysis identifies: its position in the town, orography, the type of road layout, squares, buildings of historic and cultural interest, parks, green areas and natural elements in visual perception, including those outside the study area. At the territorial scale the elements which are in relation at both the urban, cultural and visual level with the area in object, have to be identified, in order to comprehend – in the phase of project – the parts of the city to which the design ideas should be interrelated.

The importance of this phase lies in gaining an understanding of all those elements, such as site morphology, the presence of particular types of urban buildings, historical stratification, the main axes, the form of the public squares and concourses, and the relationship of the area with the rest of the city, which can be assimilated by looking at a traditional map but can only be guessed at by a denominative and perceptual analysis. The product of this phase consists of a single map, the third partial map, showing elements which have external and internal relationships with the site.

Phase 4: Questionnaire for analysis

The fourth phase is that of a questionnaire administered to users of the area in order to obtain an idea of the place as perceived by those who are not involved in the study and are not urban planning specialists, but perceive the site only from the standpoint of users, at various levels: namely inhabitants, passers by or tourists.

The questionnaire as a rule opens with brief questions on personal details (age, nationality, occasional or habitual use of the site, etc.), followed by questions related mostly to the overall perception of the site, concerning, for example, the elements of greatest concern (persons, things, etc.), those causing a particular feeling, the elements that disturb, those which could change, the element that symbolises the city, and more specific questions related to objectives proposed by that particular experimentation. Questions addressed to common users of the site are administered during a site visit and may be accompanied by historical and current images of the area in question. Interviewees will not be informed beforehand of the specific purpose of the questionnaire; they will only be told it is part of a scientific study on the cultural characteristics of the place, to avoid influencing their answers.

Where the analysis has a specific objective related to specific groups of people (e.g. the most suitable places for activities undertaken or planned by certain professionals or genders or ages, etc.), one may decide to select people to interview and select the 'privileged witnesses'.

Once again the outcome is a partial map, compiled from the information produced by the questionnaire. This information may well be very heterogeneous, but the map is a record of how the place is experienced, imagined, used and remembered by its users.

Phase 5: Complex map of analysis

The fifth phase is devoted to processing the information collected in previous stages to be carried out through a review of different types of data collected, and the overlay of maps for a selection of useful elements for the final stage of the analysis. The data identified in the four phases are the basis for the construction of a graphics system of symbols to represent elements identifying the urban landscape and develop the final complex map. For the creation of symbols elementary lines and shapes should be used: circles, squares, curves and straight lines, broken lines and their derivatives. In this way the overall map may be easier to read and anyone using the method is enabled to add other symbols in continuity with the shapes of the graphics system already created.

The shape of the symbols is created bearing in mind two components in particular: signs from the graphic survey and similarity of the sign with its meaning. Another criterion adopted is the size of the symbol. Three sizes are used: small, medium and large, indicating the different percentages with which the specific data are quantified – low, medium or high.

We furthermore decided to flank the symbol with a number to indicate the element referred to in the legend. Finally, we decided to summarize sensations referring to the elements of perception as 'non-influential', 'pleasant' or 'annoying', placing the initial letter of these words next to the number to identify them. The colours used are bright and contrasting, aimed at attracting and activating visual and overall perceptions. Each area examined is characterized by peculiar elements and elements common to most areas. The system of symbols for the final map is therefore made up by some basic symbols and further symbols that specify the characteristics of the subject of analysis.

To represent the concept of place, closed circles with either solid or part-solid colour shown in several variants were chosen, conveying the idea of a circumscribed area. Belonging to this category of symbols is the place of historic and artistic interest, places for commercial use, residential use, mixed residential and commercial use, and so forth.

For places of traditional socialization an uncoloured circle was chosen, with a small circle of solid colour inside, to indicate the idea of a space traditionally devoted to aggregation. To represent a place of new socialization, a solid coloured circle was chosen with arrows pointing to a circle with no colour, indicating an area that has become a place of aggregation while not being created only for this function. For places of casual socialization an imprecise curved shape was chosen, referring to the idea of aggregation. A blank square was chosen to indicate an empty space.

Figure 15.1
PlaceMaker method: the basic system of symbols

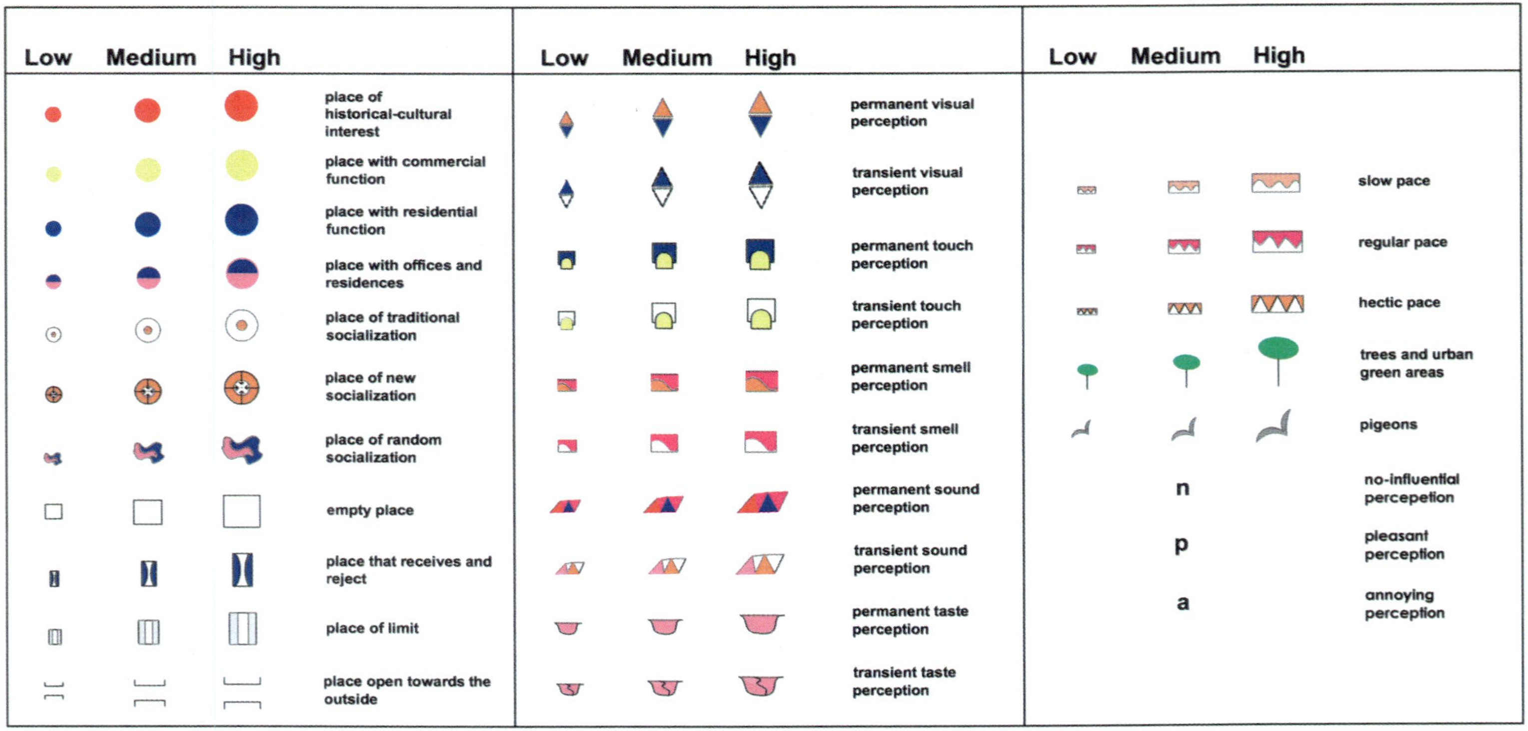

Low	Medium	High		Low	Medium	High		Low	Medium	High	
			place of historical-cultural interest				permanent visual perception				slow pace
			place with commercial function				transient visual perception				regular pace
			place with residential function				permanent touch perception				hectic pace
			place with offices and residences				transient touch perception				trees and urban green areas
			place of traditional socialization				permanent smell perception				pigeons
			place of new socialization				transient smell perception			n		no-influential percepetion
			place of random socialization				permanent sound perception			p		pleasant perception
			empty place				transient sound perception			a		annoying perception
			place that receives and reject				permanent taste perception				
			place of limit				transient taste perception				
			place open towards the outside								

The concave–convex symbol was used to refer to the concept of a place that welcomes and rejects at the same time. The vertically colour-striped square with an uncoloured band in the centre was used to indicate a limit and/or a boundary. Two horizontal square brackets facing outwards were used to indicate a place whose life is carried on beyond its boundaries.

As to symbols linked to perception, we constructed two fundamental types: one for permanent perceptions and the other for transient ones, creating symbols with unbroken lines and solid colours for the former, and dotted lines and semi-solid colours for the latter. The ten perceptual symbols referred to the parts of the body linked respectively to the actions of sight, touch, smell, hearing and taste. For the symbols of pace we used signs recalling the speed to which they refer and the perceptions deriving from them. For the symbols of natural elements we used stylized images of real reference.

Once we had created the symbols, we placed them on the map, whose graphic base consisted of the area outline, placing them at the points where they were noted.

The cartographic base map consisting of the study is defined by its limits and the sign of the urban circuit in simplified form. A proper map is required, showing the correspondence between the symbol and the data found.

The purpose of the map was to represent the identifying elements of the urban landscape and it was accompanied by a legend enabling its interpretation. When reading the map, note the size of the symbols (indicating the elements' quantitative presence), their meaning as given in the legend, and the meaning that may derive from the proximity of two or more symbols. For example, a large symbol indicating a place of traditional socialization (such as a square) shows that the square itself is large. But if this symbol – by way of example – is close to that indicating an empty place, this means that, although the place should serve for socialization, in reality it is not functioning as such (Sepe, 2006b).

Phase 6: Identification of identity resources

The sixth phase is devoted to surveying identity resources in the study area. During this phase, the complex map of analysis drawn up with the PlaceMaker method is used as a basis to detect the resources available for the project. The sixth phase is realized through three measures. The first is identification of the identity potential, namely the elements of the complex map that characterize the area in question in order to recognize those which may assume a focal role in the project. In this respect, both the comprehensive presence of a specific type of element (e.g. how many points of visual perceptions are present) and the quantity measured for each of them (e.g. such an element is assigned a certain size of symbol depending on its visual importance: namely medium size = presence of a given element in a medium percentage) have to be noted.

Then there is the second action where the identity problems are highlighted. The activities are devoted to observing places in the complex map with the presence of *unsustainable* elements and annoying points of perception. With the aim of identifying these places the relationships among the different elements in the map need to be observed. An element may be sustainable in itself, such as a shop which sells typical products; but the presence of several of them may create a site with a concentration of businesses which is unsustainable with respect to place identity. The goal is to understand the impact of people, things and activities, and relative issues.

The third action is the survey of identity quality. The actions to be performed here involve noting places within the complex map of analysis with the presence of sustainable elements and points of pleasant perception.

The elements which contribute to defining that sustainable place or perception will need to be analysed. In this case the aim is again to detect the impact of people, things and activities and relative relationships which are sustainable for the identity of places. The product is a synthesis derived from interpreting the complex map of analysis where the identity resources available for the project are represented: a sort of map of intents, the first step for the construction of the complex map for the identity project in question.

Phase 7: Questionnaire for planning

The seventh phase is identity resource identification from the user of places. The 'project' questionnaire starts with a short request for personal data (age, origin and use of the site, etc.). This request is followed by a series of questions relating to information resulting from the previous phase. We then ask specific questions to ascertain whether the data collected in the sixth stage are congruent with the aspirations, wishes and thoughts of the area's users and to collect further suggestions and proposals. The type of users to be administered the questions are consumers of the area in question. Attention should be paid to survey as many interviewees as possible in order to have a broad vision of the ways the place is perceived, hence not only residents but also locals, tourists, professionals and passers by, irrespective of age, origin, profession or other.

The questionnaire type will usually entail open answers, because as in the analysis questionnaire what is interesting is not only the response, but comments on it as well. In Phase 6 a detailed idea of the characteristics of the place in question concerning quality, critical points and potential is actually gained. With regard to the latter, an idea of possible design interventions to be implemented is beginning to be formulated. This questionnaire will therefore serve to collect suggestions and further proposals on the project ideas, a sort of first test of intents for the area.

Some in situ checks may be made in the initial elaboration of responses. Some answers may be given by respondents too rapidly or inconsistently, or may be due to hurried observation of the place where the questionnaire is administered. It is therefore important to note where the questionnaire was administered, the relationship between that place and the responses, and which parts of the area in question were preferred by respondents for their answers. Not all places are in fact favoured by the respondents. Places close to subway lines or bus stops and routes with little or no presence of shops are less preferred to squares, pedestrian walkways and gardens.

The product of this phase is a partial map which will represent the identity resources from the perspective of users of places and/or privileged actors.

Phase 8: Complex map of project and design interventions

The eighth and final phase consists in the overlay of information gathered in Phases 6 and 7 and identification of project proposals. It represents the final step of the design process where the information contained in the complex map of analysis, after being filtered and transformed into resources, gives proposals for the construction of identity and enhancement of sustainable places. In this phase the sites on which to focus the design hypothesis and the types of interventions to be made are identified, in order to enhance the identity resources. The potential, resources and critical points must therefore be considered, overlaying them with the questionnaire responses.

Interventions should be designed based on the construction of places according to their tangible and intangible characteristics. This is the moment where all the factors noted during the different phases should be put into play in order to ensure that the complexity of the place is not reduced: spaces, architecture, people, transient perceptions, permanent perceptions, urban events, relationships and rhythms. Each element will contribute to a possible solution. This is to draw up guidelines that take into account the identity of the place, its quality liveability. To obtain this result we need to correlate the elements of Phase 6 and understand which represent the place identity, which are the product of globalization, which cause a sense of belonging and which a feeling of insecurity. And, again, what should be preserved and what improved or reconstructed. The more thorough the work of analysis, data collection and subsequent processing, the more consistent will be the design of interventions.

The result of this phase is two fold: on the one hand the construction of suitable symbols which represent the proposed actions, on the other, the development of the overall map for project identity.

As regards the symbols, they are created using simple geometric shapes to allow easy reproduction and use to different surveyors. Symbols are flanked by numbers that show, in the legend, the places where they are positioned. The symbols are developed for any experimentation according with the different place specificities. As regards the map, it is constructed using the base map for analysis and placing the symbols at the points where interventions should be performed.

In this respect, a delicate moment of this final phase is the decision on the level of detail to be given to the interventions identified. Indeed, the complex map of design, in order to allow its realistic use, must provide tangible results that do not result in further interpretation that could stray from the study objectives.

Use of an urban scale is considered a useful reference for choosing the right level of detail. For example, the map will propose maintenance on buildings within a road, not on the individual building. And, likewise, it will not concern details regarding the use of types of paints or technology recovery. In case of urban design furniture intervention, the project will propose a unified design of this, not the draft of the specific bench or flower bed. More detailed project drawings will be delegated to other types of representation which can be added for specific requirements. Finally, an adequate legend supports the reading of the map.

Chapter 16

The software

The product of the PlaceMaker method, as outlined in Chapter 15, consists of two complex maps: one of analysis and one of design. The information collected and systematized in the course of several surveys, questionnaires and analysis is summarized in the maps in the form of symbols, which, although they are effective for illustrating the final results of the method, do not allow all the data collected to be easily viewed, intersected and updated.

The experiments motivated the creation of specific software (Sepe, 2006b, 2010a) to connect and communicate the information contained in the complex map and drive the use of the method. With the PlaceMaker software it is possible to represent and interpret the places in an area by creating interactive, dynamic and multimedia maps (Ayeni et al., 2004; Marinelli, 1999). Places are represented by inserting symbols and elements into maps connected to multimedia schedules that can be continuously updated. Adobe Flex/Air – for their characteristics of flexibility – are the platforms which are used to implement the PlaceMaker software. The programming language is ActionScript 3.

The main characteristics of the software are flexibility, facility and rapidity of use, strong graphical impact, and indexing of the results. Its flexibility makes it possible to store, manage, modify and update in a particular format the multimedia data required to create the multimedia schedule, connected to the symbols placed on the maps. With respect to the facility and rapidity of use, with simple rapid operations the maps are created on the basis of official traditional cartography or other kinds of maps. The maps therefore consist of a cartographic base on which are inserted a series of symbols to which the multimedia database is associated. The multimedia database connected to the symbols contains the data collected in the different phases of the PlaceMaker method, especially written texts, schedules, images, planimetries, maps and audiovisuals. Once the symbols are inserted on the maps, they can be modified, moved or eliminated. Indeed, the software possesses a database that allows the creation and modification of the categories of the PlaceMaker symbols, used for the different maps. Once the database of categories has been constructed, the symbols can be positioned on the base map, making it possible to connect the information that refers to the places with the related multimedia schedule. The symbols may also be linked to other symbols, maps or internet addresses.

In order to facilitate the construction of the final complex maps and consultation of the information when many data are present on one map, it is possible to decide the categories of symbols that must appear on each map and overlay the various maps. The partial maps and the symbols created for the final complex maps can be overlain and connected, the final products being characterized by a strong graphical impact.

With respect to the indexing of the results, the symbols created to construct the complex maps can be translated by PlaceMaker into numerical indices, in order to allow the calculation of data, such as liveability, well-being, chaoticity, etc., useful for the study of the sustainability of the places in question. Furthermore, the map can be adapted to local changes by updating the multimedia database and symbols.

PlaceMaker software supports the method in all its phases. As evidenced by the software scheme, during the preparatory phase in which the construction of the grid for the set of operations is carried out, the software enables the creation of different kinds of databases for the different types of data collected: data from the anticipatory analysis (sketches, poems, collages, etc.); denominative and perceptive (through words), graphical (signs and symbols), photographic (fixed images), video (moving images); elements deduced from the study of traditional planimetries and complex maps (graphic signs, symbols etc.); questionnaires administered to visitors to the places in question (sketches, words, etc.).

Once the categories of elements to analyse and the corresponding measurement parameters, 'within one year' taken as the reference period for urban changes, have been decided, the days which are the most significant and the time slices for the relief need to be connected to the symbols. PlaceMaker allows the construction of the map following the different categories and measurement parameters selected.

Every phase produces a map with multimedia symbols and the related schedule. Each of the first four phases of analysis and the sixth and seventh phases produce a partial map with symbols and the related schedule; the fifth and eighth phases produce the two final complex maps with symbols and related schedule of syntheses.

In the first phase, devoted to anticipatory analysis, it is possible to directly insert the text in word format or insert a sketch or an image in electronic format.

Once the analysis of the expectations has been carried out with a synthesis operation it is necessary to assimilate a text, an image or something else to a symbol; if the database does not contain the suitable symbol, an appropriate one can be created. Such data are necessary in order to construct the multimedia schedule to link to the symbols.

In the second phase, once the five surveys have been carried out, in addition to the denominative and perceptive database, the sketches in digital format, the images and the video are also inserted in the PlaceMaker software. A second partial map with symbols and related multimedia schedule is constructed from the information obtained. The software makes it possible to scroll the images chosen and to edit the video in order to show a specific scene.

Figure 16.1
**PlaceMaker software:
schema**

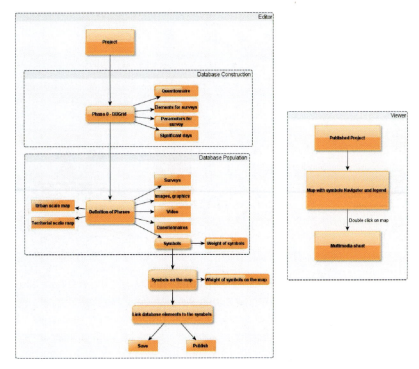

With the third phase, the different types of maps which are used for the traditional analysis are imported by the software. Furthermore, it is possible to either import a map in digital format or download it from the internet. The product of this phase is a map identifying the components required for the site description that can be found only through traditional planimetric interpretation. The symbols in this map will be associated with a multimedia schedule with the two traditional maps, and eventually by historical images and descriptions.

In the fourth phase, the information obtained from the questionnaire is transferred onto the fourth partial map and the schedule for the symbols will mainly comprise images and written text. The schedule shows the specific answer or answers which has/have led to the creation of the symbol in question. At the same time it is possible to visualize all the questions administered, the relative answers and data concerning the respondents. The software will also highlight the relationship between the answers given, nationality/age of the respondent and where the interview was administered.

In the fifth phase, involving assembly of the collected information, the recorded data represents the basis for the construction of the graphical system of symbols and the related multimedia schedule. By a function which makes it possible to overlay the maps obtained from the previous phases, the software can produce the final complex map with symbols and related schedule of syntheses (Sepe, 2010c; Sepe, 2012a and b). The multimedia schedule in this case shows all the data that have led to the creation of that specific symbol.

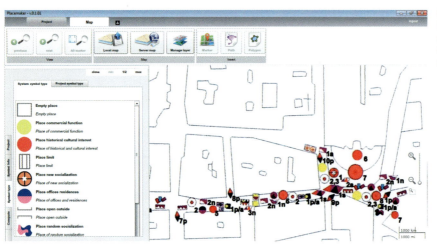

Figure 16.2
PlaceMaker software: window with the complex map of analysis

In the sixth phase, that of detecting the identity resources, the software allows the analysis map to be drawn by selecting the elements that identify the potential, the critical issues and the quality with respect to the identity resources. This operation leads to the identification of possible sites for project interventions. The software makes it possible to draw lines and areas in order to highlight on the map the relevant potentials, critical issues and qualities. The connection to the multimedia schedule will be activated for one or more aggregated symbols related to such intervention areas.

In the project questionnaire phase, Phase 7, the software functions are the same as for the questionnaire in the analysis phase. In this phase, the information will be imported by the software for constructing the map and the multimedia schedule which lists the respondents' questions and answers.

In the final phase of the method, Phase 8, the software allows us to process the results obtained in the analysis and design phases for the construction of the complex map of the project. The schedules related to the symbols will address both the data of the project and analysis phases. The schedules also make it possible to show more detailed design projects related to that specific action.

For both the complex maps, using the software, we can calculate complex indices and update the results by entering new data.

Chapter 17

The sustainable place identity index

As mentioned in Chapter 15 (The method), by associating predetermined characteristics and relative weights to each symbol, the software allows the calculation
of indices in order to give a numerical value used to calculate sustainability. In
particular, the sustainable place identity index is illustrated below (Sepe, 2006d).

The index is characterized above all by referring to the context and its phenomena, and by its flexibility, ease of updating and compatibility with planning tools.
It is defined by the value of a set of elements expressed as symbols shown on the
complex map of analysis drawn up using PlaceMaker. Each symbol is associated with
an element of place, to which is attributed a value of integral weight ranging from 1 to
5. This weight is determined by the typology of the indicator to be calculated. The low-
est value of integral weight, $w_i = 1$, has little impact in calculating the index, while the
highest value, $w_i = 5$, counts for a lot. The overall number of elements is taken to be
n, so that i $\{1,...,n\}$. Each element of the complex map is defined by a set of features
(varying in typology and number from one element to another), each having its own
integral value, c_{ij} ranging from 1 to 5. Thus c_{ij} denotes the feature j of the element
i and j $\{1,...,m_i\}$, where m_i represents the total number of features of the element i.
All the elements denote the quantitative presence of that element in the place. The
value, v_i of an element is given by the median value of its features, calculated thus:

$$v_i = \frac{1}{m_i} \sum_{j=1}^{m_i} c_{ij}$$

It is possible to define an absolute index, I_a and a median index, I_m. The absolute
index is calculated thus:

$$I_a = \sum_{i=1}^{n} w_i v_i$$

and corresponds to the weighted sum of the value of all the elements of a place.
This value in this index depends on both the quantity and the quality of the elements present. The median index, I_m is calculated thus:

$$I_m = \frac{1_a}{n_i}$$

and depends only on the quality of the elements present.

The sustainable place identity index has been calculated for different contexts, with quite satisfactory results. The absolute index is meant to quantify the absolute value of sustainability of the identity of a given place and can be used to compare two different places of the same scale, because it depends both on the number of elements of interest for the sustainability of the identity and on their quality. On the other hand, the median index is normalized with respect of the number of elements, and thus is useful to characterize the sustainability of the place identity of a given place independently of the scale.

As can easily be imagined, each place is characterized by particular features that distinguish it from other places. In order to be able to compare two different places, these features have to be assimilated in categories. This is a delicate operation requiring great care and attention if the specific quality of a place is not to be sacrificed.

Another delicate issue concerns the weighting to be given to each feature. We found that this could in fact change according to the area under analysis: a certain perception, for example, cannot always carry the same weight for every place. In attributing the same weight to the same type of symbol regardless of place, one is in fact introducing an approximation. Finally, we also found that the weighting can change according to the index being calculated, and hence it would probably be more correct to speak of relative weight.

Part III
Case studies

Section I
Preserving place identity

The case studies presented in this section share the question of preserving place identity. The Trevi–Pantheon route in Rome concerns mainly the problems related to anthropic risk, while the South Broadway area in Los Angeles features the loss of traditional functions – this was an historical theatre district – and the consequent abandonment in favour of a not well specified re-use.

With respect to the anthropic risk, this may arise from many factors that are hard to identify due to the dynamic and often uncontrollable nature of phenomena linked to the presence of humans (Boissevain, 1996; Frers and Meier, 2007; Gunn, 2002; Haldrup et al., 2004; Urry, 1995). These include: demographic dynamics, how and when the monument is used and its context, user consumption patterns and management arrangements. In this regard, some useful elements of the urban context to analyse human load include: large concentrations of people; the presence and often the increase in inappropriate commercial activity which can lead to olfactory, visual and noise pollution; urban degradation due to neglect or vandalism (poor maintenance of the built environment, graffiti, etc.); and susceptibility to theft. These elements are able to influence the environmental and cultural quality of place and hence its identity, considering that the construction of relationships between objects and urban factors with the observer plays a fundamental role, as well as the practical or affective meaning they induce in the observer (Lynch, 1960).

Present-day studies in the field of anthropic risk have rarely focused on questions linked to place identity, probably due to the difficulty in obtaining objective results. In the specific case of the Trevi–Pantheon route in Rome, in 1991 this site was subject to pedestrianization, allowing visitors to reach two of its most important monuments – the Trevi Fountain and the Pantheon – without annoying perceptions caused by traffic. Moreover, this route has been equipped with special flooring and directions for the blind. The effects of this operation – which has had the positive effect of eliminating cars from a historic part of town – was a huge increase in the number of tourists in these places, with a clear danger to the preservation of place identity.

In order to mitigate the risk in question, areas close to these sites can be identified so as to extend the visitor's range of action and offer alternative activities integrated with the main site and in continuity with its identity. The purpose of the Trevi–Pantheon case study – carried out in the framework of the European Project Culture 2007–2013 *Preserving places. Managing mass tourism, urban conservation and quality of life in historic centres* (Coordinator: ICVBC CNR Rome Division) – was to distribute the main site over a wider range, with activities closely connected to the site so as to decongest it. The cultural places and appropriate activities were identified by tracing the current identity of the places, their characteristics and potential, in order to provide a sustainable and integrated enhancement and fruition (Appleyard, 1981; Carter *et al.*, 1993; Castells, 1997; Christensen, 1999; Dickens, 1990; Gospodini, 2004; Hague and Jenkins, 2005; Massey and Jess, 1995; Nasar, 1998; Nijkamp and Perrels, 1994; Urry, 1995).

The second case study presented in this section concerns a different question, which, even though related to the topic of preserving identity, involves the renewal of theatres. The topic of recuperating sizeable disused theatres is common to many cities (Zukin, 2010). The advent of multi-screen cinemas, and multi-containers which often include multiplex cinemas, has led to the closure and disuse of many traditional single-screen theatres. The recuperation of theatres covers a wide range of functions including commercial, residential and leisure. Residents and locals are typically linked to these places because in many cases they represent part of their life and contribute to the sense of belonging to that part of the city. Thus the choice of the new function should pay particular attention not to upset the previous identity of the place.

The problem becomes more difficult if the theatres are of historic interest, whether history of the cinema or the architecture of the building itself. And especially if it is a matter of an entire thoroughfare containing a large number of historical theatres such as Broadway in Los Angeles (www.BringingBackBroadway.com; Donofrio, 2010; Fuller-Seeley, 2008; www.LA Conservancy.org; Zukin, 2010; Scott and Soja, 1996).

Broadway is one of the oldest streets in the city – and one of few pedestrian streets – which during the first half of the twentieth century was one of the prime theatre districts. More than twelve theatres and many buildings in the classical style were built. After the Second World War, with the rise of multiscreen cinemas and the consequent closure of most theatres, a slow decline in the thoroughfare set in. In these years, the Hispanic population 'settled' in this place using many of the historic buildings and theatres as stores, quinceanera boutiques and different kinds of businesses (Reynoso, 2012).[1] Over recent years the state of decline of Broadway – even though the street is heavily populated – is increasing, and it has been gradually losing its place identity. This case study aims to identify the identity resources in place nowadays and propose design interventions able to make the historical tradition of this place re-emerge, reinterpreted according to the new needs.

Chapter 18

Rome
The Trevi–Pantheon route

Phase 1: Anticipatory analysis

The Trevi–Pantheon area contains fine monuments of outstanding historical and architectural interest. The anticipatory analysis concerning the monuments, and in particular the Trevi Fountain and the Pantheon, was carried out using the memory of these sites; whereas the analysis of expectations related to the route linking the two monuments was carried out using a logical and deductive approach.

The selected area is a preferred tourist destination, located at the heart of Rome's historical centre. The buildings are historical and in a good state of conservation. The streets are narrow, for pedestrians only, and receive natural light for only a few hours a day. The area is heavily used by tourists and residents. There are many shops, particularly selling souvenirs, as well as cafés, bars and restaurants. The Piazza at the Pantheon is highly evocative, an almost magical place where history, art and sacredness are united. The Piazza at the Trevi Fountain constitutes a sort of counterpart to the Piazza at the Pantheon, the place of the 'profane', its imagery linked to Rome in films, where people go to toss a coin into the water and express a wish. History and art somehow seem to recede into the background, giving pride of place to the emotions. The study-itinerary is thus a sort of link between the sacred and the profane. The Piazza at the Hadrianeum is spacious, enhancing the magnificence of the monument. Rome is an international city and this characteristic is clearly perceived in these places; with tourists from all over the world, public notices are put up in at least two languages. The most common perceptions concern: visually, the major monuments, in particular the Pantheon and Trevi Fountain; for touch, the paving in flint cubes or large stone slabs; for taste and smell, the presence of cafés, bars and restaurants selling local specialities but also fast food; for hearing, voices and footsteps, and repair work in progress. The global perception is very agreeable, even if there is occasionally some chaos and confusion.

Phase 2: Denominative and perceptual description

The route starts in Piazza della Rotonda, accessible only to pedestrians, from Via dei Pastini. The denominative and perceptual identification of the elements that make up the identity of place using five types of surveys are summarized below.

Arriving here the visitor is immediately struck by the beauty of the piazza and its monuments. Piazza della Rotonda is a typical location for traditional socialization; its conformation, the extraordinary beauty of its monuments, the presence of restaurants and outdoor tables and the pleasant atmosphere ensure a constant throughput of people.

The first element that draws the eye is the Pantheon, an ancient religious edifice, circular in shape, which dominates the scene and somehow embraces it. With its colonnade and monumental elegance, the temple draws a constant throughput of tourists and visitors who troop endlessly into the building, where a round opening in the centre of the dome creates a particular lighting effect which together with religious chants accompanied by classical organ music make for a very evocative atmosphere. The voices of visitors and the noise of the constant tramping of feet constitute an additional acoustic perception.

Not only those who come to visit the monument but also passers by often pause for a while outside the monument, sitting at the foot of the columns or on the perimeter walls, chatting or having a snack, creating a scenario which at times gets rather chaotic. A large nondescript throughput of people ebbs and flows in front of the Pantheon, that invariably includes hawkers, perhaps selling concert tickets dressed in historic costume or souvenirs or miscellaneous goods.

There are often school groups. It is also possible to hire bicycles or go for a ride in a horse-drawn carriage.

In front of the Pantheon a fountain with an obelisk and dolphins forms a focal point which not only characterizes the piazza and adds to the overall scenario but becomes a place of socialization for many visitors and tourists. The steps around the fountain encourage many visitors to pause or stop for lunch, photographing the fountain and the Pantheon or reading a guidebook or feeding the pigeons. The noise of their voices often drowns out the noise of the water flowing in the fountain. The Piazza is surrounded by unbroken facades of historical buildings, largely devoid of decoration and differing in width, mostly with pitched roofs, the plasterwork in colours ranging from brick red to pale blue.

A large *votive aedicule* featuring the Madonna occupies one of the facades, while a large panel conceals the refurbishment work in progress on another.

Figure 18.1
Graphic survey: Piazza della Rotonda with the fountain and the Pantheon

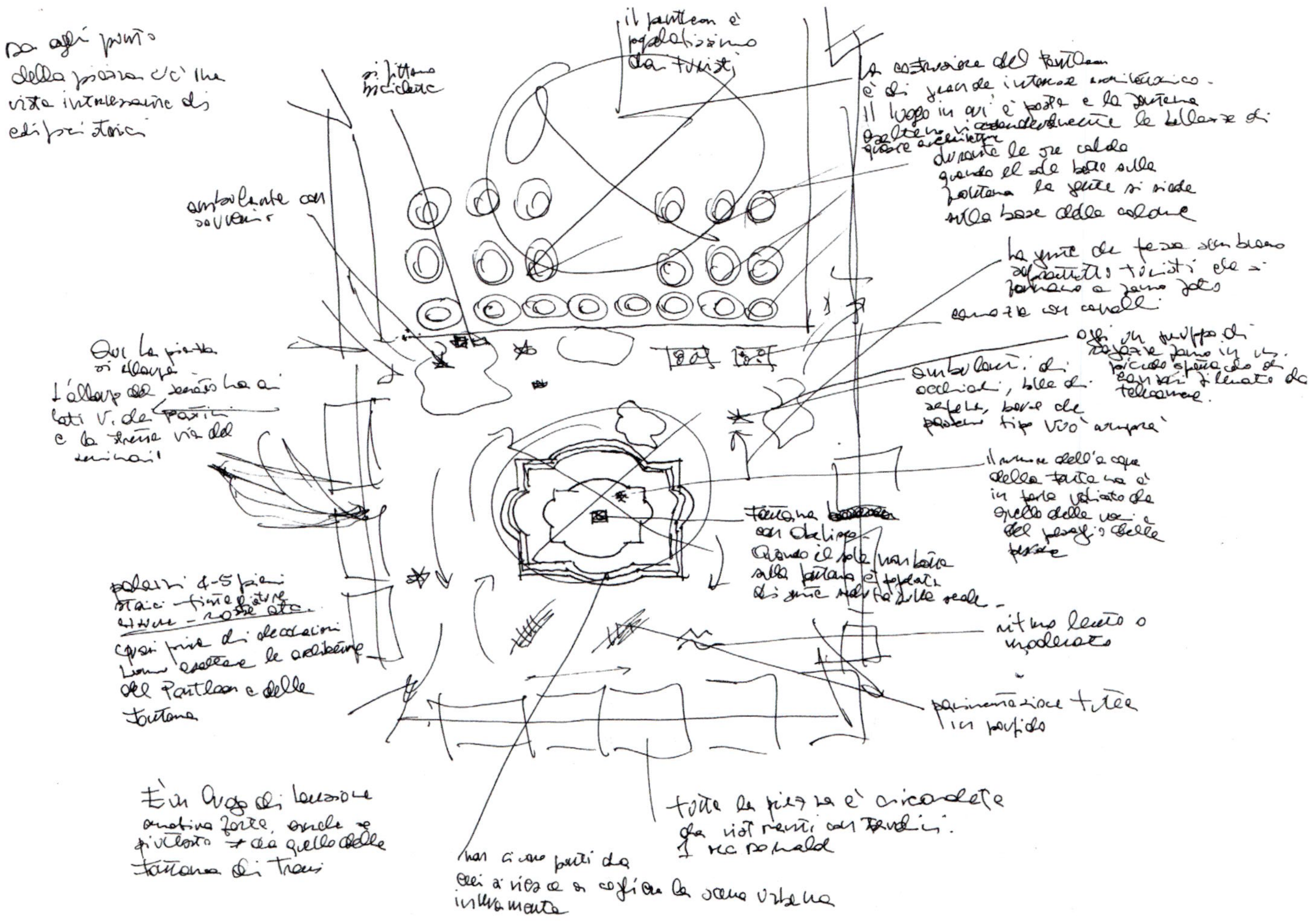

Figure 18.2
**Photographic
survey: Piazza
della Rotonda
with the
fountain and the
Pantheon**

Figure 18.3
**Photographic
survey: people
visiting the Piazza
della Rotonda**

Figure 18.4
**Photographic survey:
Via dei Pastini**

The ground floor of the buildings is occupied by bars and restaurants with outdoor tables that are always thronged with people. One of the restaurants emanates the unmistakable smell of fast food, while smells of food and coffee colour the atmosphere. A grocer selling local products on one side of the piazza attracts many tourists. In spite of the large throughput, the overall pace here is moderate and tranquil. The urban decor comprises old-style street lighting, litter bins and round metal bollards marking off the concourse; the paving, in small flint cubes, slopes at different angles and makes for a pleasant tactile perception.

Continuing along the study-itinerary one comes to Via dei Pastini, a narrow winding street for pedestrians leading only from Piazza della Rotonda to Piazza di Pietra. Along the sides the paving is in flint cubes, and down the centre special paving has been laid for the blind. There are also some modern stelae made of burnished metal which recount the history of this 'route of Hadrian' in Italian, English and Braille, with a plan of the itinerary. Walking along the street, one has the impression of going through a long funnel that opens out into the piazza, with unbroken facades of historical buildings, some with refurbishment work in progress, restaurants with outdoor tables thronged with people, a *votive aedicule*, hawkers and the occasional beggar. Many of the buildings have shops at street level. One is surrounded by a continuous stream of people of different cultures, white collar workers and local residents.

Many stop to purchase souvenirs or takeaway food and continue into Piazza della Rotonda. The atmosphere is lively, verging on chaotic. There are shops selling eccentric souvenirs, including foodstuffs, Venetian masks and one with wooden craft products with a bench in front occupied by a life-size Pinocchio, making a photo opportunity for passers by. The pace is mostly moderate. Apart from streetlamps in wrought iron projecting from the facades there are no other items of urban decor.

The perceptions involved are: above all tactile, on account of changes in the street paving; taste and smell, for the restaurants and cafés offering typical products; and acoustic, for people's voices. The street receives little natural light on account of its narrow width and the height of the buildings.

As one arrives from Piazza della Rotonda, the first striking feature is the Hadrianeum, the temple of Hadrian with its towering columns lining one side of Piazza di Pietra. The remains of the temple house the Chamber of Commerce; two trenches dug in front of the colonnade reveal some archaeological remains. Although it is massive the building maintains a 'silent' presence in the piazza, as though sure of itself, not needing to attract attention. The monument is flanked by boxes of painters. The piazza is surrounded by soberly decorated historical buildings from different periods; it is in practice a thoroughfare which in spite of its impressive monument favours a casual socialization with people stopping to drink and admire the temple or the archaeological remains before going on their way. It gives the impression of being empty rather than full. The paving is in flint cubes; the tactile route for the blind continues from Via dei Pastini, passing in front of the Hadrianeum. The pace is tranquil. The olfactory perception from the products of the café is ephemeral and agreeable; the acoustic perception due to the passage of the occasional resident's car and far-off building works is practically nil.

Piazza di Pietra leads into Via di Pietra, which shares many of the characteristics of Via dei Pastini: it is narrow, with paving along the sides in flint cubes and down the centre special paving for the blind; there are metal stelae illustrating the route; and there are unbroken facades of historical buildings, restaurants with outdoor tables, souvenir shops and hawkers.

Figure 18.5
Photographic survey: Piazza di Pietra with the Hadrianeum

The type of road user is similar, although here the throughput seems slightly less animated. There is the occasional beggar. One begins to hear the noises of cars, buses and motorcycles from Via del Corso. At the end of Via di Pietra, or the beginning if approaching from Via del Corso, there is a sign indicating 'special itinerary for the blind'. The perceptions involved are: above all tactile, on account of changes in the street paving; taste and smell, for the restaurants and cafés offering typical products; and acoustic, for people's voices and vehicles from the nearby traffic in Via del Corso.

On arriving in Via del Corso, before continuing along the route in Via delle Muratte, one is struck by the sight of Palazzo Venezia in one direction and the Obelisk in Piazza del Popolo in the other. The pace here becomes busier. There is a distinct contrast with what has gone before. The street is very wide and busy with both pedestrians and vehicles. Crossing Via del Corso leads to Via delle Muratte, another pedestrian-only street. As before the paving is in flint cubes with special paving for the blind, and there are the metal stelae found throughout the study area. In this street there is a certain disparity in building periods and styles, and the presence of sidestreets that interrupt the unbroken facades. The urban decor comprises bracket-mounted street lamps and litter bins. The street can be divided up into three sections, each with its own features and constituting a sort of gradual lead-up to the Trevi Fountain.

The first section is broad and lined with historical buildings four storeys high, which cater for offices.

Down the middle of the street, space is set aside for hawkers selling primarily calendars, postcards and posters that predominantly feature Rome; further on are other hawkers and painters displaying and selling their creations. A beggar. The pace is moderate. With the second section the street begins to narrow. On the right is the Palazzo delle Telecomunicazioni with decorations and other historical buildings from different periods rising to about four storeys. In both sections the throughput comprises above all tourists and white collar workers.

The third section gets narrower still; the historical buildings form an unbroken facade as far as Piazza di Trevi. The street here is full of souvenir shops offering both typical and eccentric wares, ice cream parlours, takeaway outlets, restaurants and cafés with outdoor tables.

Table 18.1 **Detail of the denominative survey**

Place	Date	Time	Type	Constructed elements	Natural elements	Transport mode	People
Trevi	June	14.00		Scenic fountain in white marble	–	Horse-drawn carriage (Touristy)	Tourists Gladiators
			Low, medium, high percentage	High		Low	High Medium

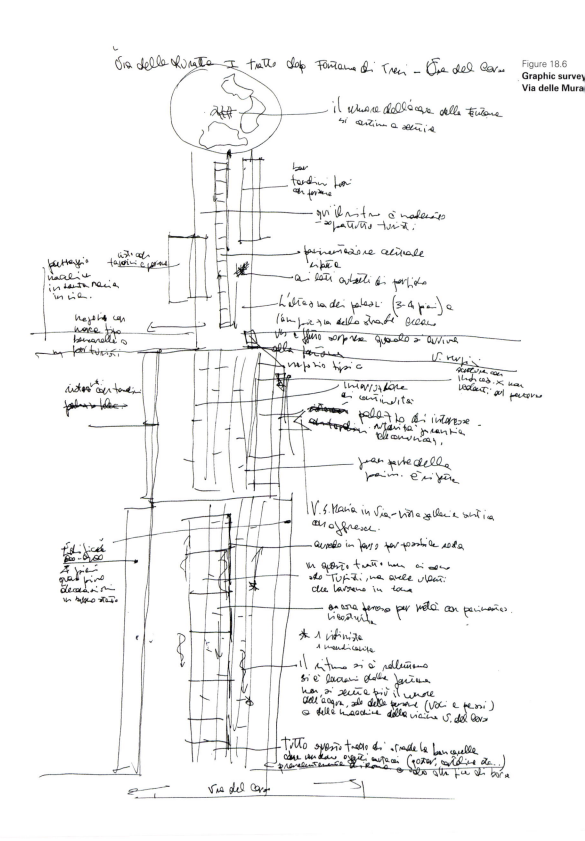

Figure 18.6
Graphic survey
Via delle Mura

Table 18.2 **Detail of the perceptive survey**

Place	Date	Time	Type	Smell p.	Taste p.	Sound p.	Touch p.	Visual p.
Trevi	June	14.00				Noise of the water	Porphyry paving	
			Low, medium, high percentage			Medium	High	
			Non-influential, pleasant, annoying, surprising perceived feeling			Surprising	Pleasant/ annoying	

Here, too, there is a continuous stream of people, above all, tourists drawn from all over the world.

The visual perception is monopolized by the Trevi Fountain at the end of the street; taste and smell, by the food on offer in the various shops; and acoustically, the noise of the fountain becomes louder and louder on approaching Piazza di Trevi. The loud noise of the water flowing in the fountain seems to herald a special event. Even before reaching Piazza di Trevi one catches sight of the scenic Trevi Fountain in white marble with ramps and the statue of 'Ocean' as its centrepiece. Walking into the piazza feels like taking part in a scene or an event rather than merely arriving somewhere. The scene is made up of the spectacular fountain but also the enormous quantity of people who throng the piazza observing, admiring, listening, taking photographs, throwing coins into the water, eating ice cream or a sandwich, sketching, relaxing or buying souvenirs. There are hawkers selling souvenirs and other goods, a roast chestnut seller, men dressed up as gladiators who tourists can be photographed next to, living statues, disabled people begging.

The fountain is built against one side of a building. There are flights of ramps which gradually lead from the street level to the fountain and stairs fitted in the scenic scene created by the fountain, giving different perspectives and encouraging people to linger.

At street level there are bars, cafés and souvenir shops. It features the Baroque church of San Vincenzo e Anastasio. The paving is in flint cubes, the urban decor streetlamps and litter bins in decorated metal, with angular iron benches around the fountain. The tactile perceptions include: porphyry paving, for its material and unevenness, probably due to the constant tramping; the materials and sculptures of the fountain; and the water in the fountain, which people often use to cool down.

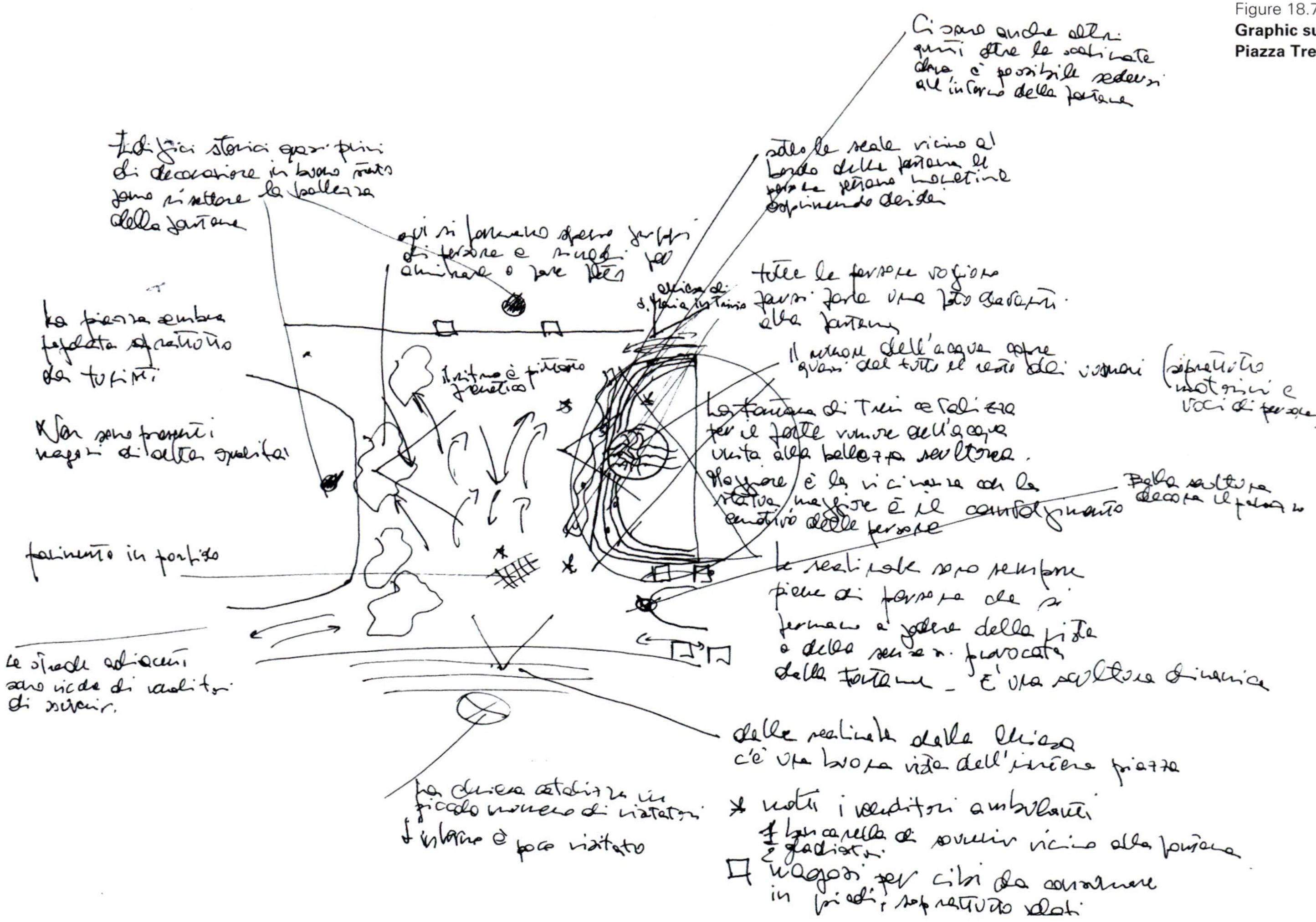

Figure 18.7
Graphic survey: Piazza Trevi

Figure 18.8
Photographic survey: special stela marking the route for the blind

The visual perceptions are the churches of San Vincenzo e Anastasio and Santa Maria in Trivio, and the sacred aedicule at one corner of a building. The acoustic perceptions are the predominant noise of running water, and the voices of the people who throng the piazza. The perceptions of taste and smell concern the products of the cafés, ice cream parlour and fast-food outlet; the smells hang in the air without being oppressive. The pace is slow.

After the denominative and perception survey came the graphic survey, which involved elaborating graphic-perceptive sketches of some of the places we considered significant for our analysis. They could then be correlated with notes taken during the inspections, providing the first indications of symbols for use in drawing up the final complex map of analysis. In the specific case of the sketch provided for Via delle Muratte the graphical signs were used in order to create both the symbols for the special paving for the blind and the continuous flows of people of different cultures.

For the photographic survey, 300 photos were taken during the inspections. Most of these show the continuous flux of people and the high presence of visitors around the Trevi Fountain. Others show some relationships among urban details that would escape the other kinds of survey. For the video survey the episodes filmed served a dual purpose: registering data concerning variations of pace on the Trevi–Pantheon route, often rapid, and recording the sound data. Sound levels are high in the two main squares of the itinerary due to great presence of people visiting the Pantheon and the sounds of the Trevi Fountain and voices of people in the Trevi square.

Figure 18.9
**Photographic survey:
Via delle Muratte**

Figure 18.10
Photographic survey: the huge amount of people sitting by the Trevi Fountain

Figure 18.11
Photographic survey: the high concentration of people visiting Piazza Trevi

Phase 3: Analysis of traditional mapping

The third phase aims to identify the elements that characterize the place, using traditional maps on the urban and territorial scale. Here we sum up the findings.

On the urban scale, the section from Piazza della Rotonda to Piazza di Pietra reveals a predominantly irregular layout, typical of the Medieval period. The urban grid for the route appears to comprise successive stratifications of the blocks with various prospects and orientations. The major axis of Via del Corso divides the study itinerary into two parts. The subsequent section, Via delle Muratte, is characterized by a more regular layout featuring rectangular blocks in the first stretch. Continuing along Via delle Muratte the route becomes narrower but maintains its prevalently straight orientation. The maps show blocks of different shapes, most with internal courtyards.

There are two religious buildings. The first is the Pantheon, built in 126 AD, with its round central chapel, a predominant feature in the layout of the piazza. This concourse is irregular in shape, being at the confluence of streets coming from different directions. It functions as a catalyst and focus for the various tensions that characterize the adjoining streets.

The second religious building is the Baroque church of San Vincenzo e Anastasio, built around 1650, in Piazza di Trevi: the maps indicate its importance in the construction of the piazza. Here the route marks a pause, and its continuity is interrupted. This is due to the Piazza di Pietra with the monument known as the Hadrianeum, built in 145 AD. This concourse has a regular, rectangular shape but is 'empty', since the Hadrianeum and adjacent buildings seem to have been designed to ensure the regular site conformation.

There is in fact a clear distinction between Piazza di Pietra and Piazza della Rotonda, whose form is the result of the juxtaposition of various strata. The interruption in continuity is due to Via del Corso, an imposition which is out of scale with respect to the study itinerary. This interruption is clear not only in the breadth of the street and the typology of the buildings but also for the diversity of the first section of Via delle Muratte, where the blocks are very regular.

In Piazza Trevi the focus of attention seems to lie in the fountain; the lozenge-shaped concourse, made up of the facades of the buildings and the church together with the conformation of the Trevi Fountain, completed in 1762, seems to be off-centre, in the confluence of the four adjacent side streets. There are no areas of vegetation.

Analysis on the territorial scale suggests that the route gets lost in the dense urban layout that characterizes this area. It borders on the so-called 'trident' departing from Piazza del Popolo and comprising Via di Ripetta, Via del Corso and Via del Babuino. Via del Corso is particularly evident as a 'major thoroughfare'.

Figure 18.12
Traditional analysis: detail of the planimetry of Rome
(Source: Rome City Hall, 1960)

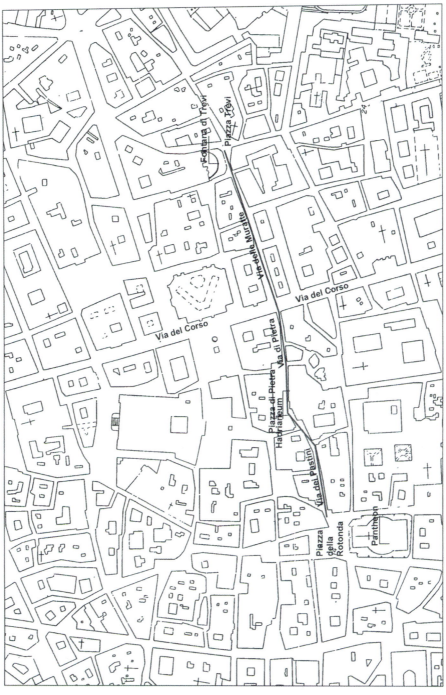

The study itinerary does not stand out on the map, partly because of both its regular slope and the lack of any vegetation. It features three piazzas: Piazza di Trevi, Piazza di Pietra and Piazza della Rotonda, while, outside its precincts, lie the nearest, Piazza dei Crociferi and Piazza Sant'Ignazio, and Piazza Venezia, Piazza di Spagna, Piazza del Popolo and Piazza Navona. There are various places and monuments of historical interest bordering on the study area. The major monuments observed by the analysis inside the study area are: the Trevi Fountain, the Pantheon, the fountain in Piazza della Rotonda and the Hadrianeum. The significant monuments situated outside the study area are the nearest churches of Sant'Ignazio and Santa Maria in Trivio. While, outside its precincts, the monuments include the 'Vittoriano' (or 'Altare della Patria'), the Obelisk in Piazza del Popolo, the church and steps of Trinità dei Monti and the church of Sant'Agnese and the fountains in Piazza Navona. With respect to the visual perspective of interest obtained from traditional cartography, a fine prospect stretching from Via del Corso to Piazza Venezia and Piazza del Popolo is observed. At a certain distance from the area there is also the River Tiber.

Phase 4: Questionnaire for analysis

The questionnaire is designed to take between 10 and 30 minutes to complete and consists of the questions listed below. The analysis gives a reasoned summary of the answers obtained.

0)   Nationality, age
Passing through the study area:
1)   What elements strike you most (persons, things, etc.)?
2)   Is there one or more elements which produce a particular sensation?
3)   Is there any one element which brings to mind a moment important to you for any reason?
4)   Are there any things which bother you?
5)   Is there any one element which produces a strong sensation?
6)   If you could change anything, what would you do?
7)   Is this area comparable to another area of Rome or elsewhere?
8)   If so, why?
9)   What is the symbol of this city?

Questions were posed to people who used the site during the analysis without making any kind of distinction with respect to age, nationality or otherwise. Most of the respondents were tourists, who represent the majority of the throughput, and come from the USA and Europe (Italy, France, Britain, Austria, Sweden, Holland). English was the language used above all for foreigners, and Italian for the Italians. About 30 people were interviewed, with an age range from 20 to 60.

The questionnaire was proposed above all in the three piazzas in the study area, and all the people approached took a genuine interest. There was a notable uniformity in the answers in spite of the difference in age and provenance.

The first question asked what were the most striking elements, and the replies were evenly distributed: the monument that was in front of them at the time, meaning the Pantheon, Trevi Fountain or Hadrianeum; the atmosphere; the presence of crowds; the history of the site; the urban scenario and the architecture.

The second question asked which elements evoked a particular sensation, and the replies were above all: the Pantheon, for the aperture in the dome, its grandeur and the size of the columns; the Trevi Fountain and the architecture of Piazza di Trevi; the Hadrianeum, for the contrasting styles of architecture and the state of conservation of the buildings.

The third question asked whether there was one element that brought to mind an important event for whatever reason, and the replies were mainly generic, referring to holidays with parents or a book that talked about these places; a smaller percentage replied that there was no element bringing to mind an event; and one or two indicated the water in the fountain.

The fourth question asked whether there was anything that constituted a nuisance, and half the respondents answered in the negative; the other half gave replies that were evenly distributed between the crowds, the litter, the fact that people sit on the columns and damage them, and the lack of vegetation.

The fifth question asked whether there was one element that caused a strong sensation, and the replies mainly referred to the sheer size of the Pantheon and its columns, seen by some as a power symbol; and the Hadrianeum. Some chose not to answer.

The sixth question asked what people would change if they had the chance, and half the respondents answered nothing, while the other half indicated the presence of too many tourists and the fact that the areas around the monuments were not kept clean.

The seventh question asked whether respondents could compare this site to somewhere else in Rome or another city, and this produced a great variety of answers. Most people, irrespective of age and provenance, indicated the Colosseum. Some from the USA named Washington D.C., other respondents named Piazza Navona, or gave a list of monuments in Rome and Europe in general including St Peter's in Rome, the Parthenon, the temples of Agrigento, Les Invalides in Paris and the Duomo in Milan. Nobody was able to say why these monuments were comparable to the study area; some gave the generic answer that it was on account of the crowds (eighth question).

For the last question almost all respondents indicated the Colosseum as symbolising Rome, followed by the Pope and St Peter's and religious power. One person chose the Trevi Fountain.

Phase 5: Complex map of analysis

The fifth phase involved elaborating the data collected to construct the system of symbols and draw up the complex map of analysis.

The Trevi–Pantheon route is in the historical centre of Rome and its historical urban elements are well known and recognized as such. Thus, in the construction of the complex map we tried to bring out not only the historical monuments but also the elements that point to both the intangible and tangible heritage and are undermining the place identity perception. To achieve this many symbols were added to the basic PlaceMaker system of symbols.

To indicate hawkers selling souvenirs a symbol with three coloured rectangles was chosen, the fan-shape suggesting the seller displaying his various wares.

To indicate a horse-drawn carriage a symbol with two large wheels was chosen placed in a rectangle evoking the carriage.

To indicate the special paving for the blind a symbol was chosen representing paving placed in a rectangle with an arrow indicating the route and the symbol of tactile perception.

To indicate graffiti a stylized image of a wall marked by graffiti was used.

To indicate the stelae marking the route in Italian and English, and in Braille with a map for the blind, the stylized form of the stela was chosen (Sepe, 2010e).

Furthermore, the symbol relating to a marked concentration of people was initially assimilated to the traditional symbol for a place of socialization. But it was then realized that a sizeable concentration of people does not necessarily imply such a place.

To indicate traders selling local souvenirs the symbol of a place of commerce was chosen placed in a square showing that the goods take on a symbolic value. Subsequently, we decided to create a specific symbol for a trade location selling souvenirs because this does indeed characterize this route, in particular concerning souvenirs which have nothing to do with Rome, representing a singular anomaly.

Phase 6: Identification of identity resources

Identity resources were identified through observation of identity potential, problems and quality.

Looking at the complex map of analysis, with respect to the potential, various interesting features of the whole route are not immediately apparent. The streets linking the three monuments are regarded merely as thoroughfares in spite of the presence of historic buildings. Some monuments, such as the church of Sant'Attanasio in Piazza Trevi and the nearby churches of Santa Maria in Trevi and Sant'Ignazio, and the Galleria in Santa Maria in Via do not seem to be given enough attention. Then again, nobody seems to notice the remarkable religious icons scattered along the route. The lack of vegetation, remarked by some of the respondents, is another element to be evaluated. In spite of the creation of a route for the blind, it does not seem to be used.

Figure 18.13
Complex map of analysis of Trevi–Pantheon route

LEGEND

⬤ **place of historical and artistic interest**
1- Pantheon, 2- Fountain with obelisk , 3- Palazzo Cini, 4- Hadrianeum, 5- Telecommunication building, 6- Fontana di Trevi, 7- Church

⬤ **space with commercial function**

⬤ **space with residential function**

⬤ **places with offices and residences**

▨ **places of commerce selling local souvenirs**

▨ **places of commerce selling local e non-local souvenirs**

◉ **place of traditional socialization**
1- Rotonda Piazza and Fountain, 2- bars and restaurants with outdoor tables, 3- Piazza Trevi

⬤ **place with high concentration of people**
1- Pantheon, 2- Pantheon colonnade, 3 -Piazza Rotonda Fountain, 4- bars and restaurants with outdoor tables, 5- Via dei Pastini, 6- Via delle Muratte, 7- Fontana di Trevi, 8- Piazza Trevi

✳ **place of new socialization**
1- fast-food

🦋 **place of random socialization**

▢ **empty place**
1- Piazza di Pietra

▥ **place of limit**
1- bollards marking off the concourse

▢ **place open toward the outside**

▼ **permanent visual perception**
1- votive aedicule , 2, Piazza Rotonda with Pantheon, fountain, buildings, 3- floral decoration, 4- Hadrianeum, 5- Piazza del Popolo, 6- Piazza Venezia, 7-Galleria, 8- buildings perspective, 9-Fontana di Trevi, 10- Church

▼ **transient visual perception**
1-panel conceals the refurbishment work in progress

◩ **permanent taste perception**
1- paving in porphyry

◥ **transient smell perception**
1- horses, 2- smells from cafeteria and restaurants

▽ **permanent taste perception**
1- grocer's local products , 2- typical coffes

▽ **transient taste perception**
1- tastes from cafeteria and restaurants

◣ **permanent sound perception**
1- water from fountain

◢◣ **transient sound perception**
1- acqua fontana, 2- voci di persone, 3- mezzi di trasporto

n no-influential perception

p pleasant perception

a annoying perception

s surprising perception

▨ **stele marking the route for the blind**

▨ **hawkers selling souvenirs**

◉ **live statue**

▨ **horse-drawn carriage**

▨ **graffiti**

▨ **special paving for the blind**

▨ **continual flow of people of different culture**

◣◣ **quiet pace**

◣◣ **regular pace**

◣◣ **hectic pace**

🕊 **pigeons**

○ **small size of symbol = presence of given element in slight percentage**

○ **medium size of symbol = presence of given element in medium percentage**

○ **large size of symbol = presence of given element in considerable percentage**

Figure 18.14
**Complex map of
analysis of Trevi–
Pantheon route:
detail of Via delle
Muratte-Piazza
Trevi**

The main problems are due to the increasing use of this area by mass tourism rather than residents and locals. This has led to the concentration of various kinds of trading activities – sometimes of low quality – that is slowly diminishing the perception of the identity of place and the cultural enjoyment of the area. Indeed, this trend is triggering a series of events where, paradoxically, the culture is becoming a cause of impoverishment of the quality of places rather than the engine of sustainable development: from the increase in fast-food outlets, street vendors and non-local souvenir shops, to the wearing out of the historical pavement and monuments; from an inappropriate use of colour in facades to frame ground floor shops, to the spread of the open-air tables of cafés and restaurants.

With respect to the identity qualities, due to the great historical, architectural and urban interest of this place, such qualities are various and clearly deducible from the complex map of analysis: namely not only the squares and historical monuments, buildings and urban fabric, but also the pleasing and sometimes surprising visual, acoustic and tactile perceptions and the slow pace which pervades this route.

Phase 7: Questionnaire for planning

The identity resources identified in the sixth phase were developed in the form of questions listed below to be administered in the questionnaire to users of the places as the first test of project interventions to be proposed.

0) Nationality and age.

Passing through the study area:

1) What do you think about inserting breaks in the path?
2) Would you be interested in alternative paths with the aid of multimedia guides?
3) What do you think about the quality of this place?
4) Do you think that the presence of too many people, street sellers, open-air cafés and restaurants, etc. diminishes the benefits of this place and its perception?
5) Did you know that there is a path for the blind (the visually impaired) which doesn't work? Do you think it would be better to restore it?
6) Did you feel threatened at any point?
7) Do you think that there are any points where there is a perception of dirtiness?
8) Did you notice any graffiti?
9) Did you notice the state of the road paving?
10) Do you think that the presence of shops selling souvenirs not only of Rome creates problems for the preservation of place-identity?
11) What site have you come from and where are you going now?
12) Do you think it could be useful to insert gardens in this area?

The questionnaire was administered to tourists, both foreign and Italian, and local residents. Most foreign respondents were from Europe (Italy, France, UK, Belgium, Czech Republic, Netherlands and Luxembourg) and the United States, with a few from Australia. In this respect the language used was mainly English for foreigners and Italian for Italians. About 35 people were interviewed with an age range of between 25 and 65. The 'project' questionnaire, like the 'analysis' questionnaire, was proposed in the three squares, due to the difficulty in asking questions and especially receiving sufficient attention to the responses in the rest of the route where there are no points for a break. Most of those interviewed showed interest in the questionnaire.

With respect to the first question concerning the possible inclusion of breaks along the route path, approximately 60 per cent of respondents, regardless of age and nationality found them useful. 20 per cent of respondents, particularly those of Italian nationality, interpreted breaks in the sense of pausing to sit down and identified the Piazza di Trevi and Piazza della Rotonda as the places where the breaks could be placed. Those who responded negatively to this question, mostly Belgians and British, argued that the presence of benches could lead to people taking longer to eat takeaway food or even sleeping on them at night.

As regards the second question concerning the possibility of creating alternative routes including the use of media guides, almost all interviewees responded positively. They were particularly interested in the possibility of personalized itineraries. A small minority of different ages and nationalities stated they were not interested because, with little time at their disposal, they had already planned a tour of the most famous historical monuments of Rome.

With respect to the third question related to the quality of the place, almost all respondents replied in an articulate fashion, describing the emotions offered by this route. Approximately 80 per cent of them, whatever their age or nationality, observed two things: the particularities of that place and its very pleasing atmosphere and, at the same time, the presence of too many people. They paid little attention to the upkeep of the individual buildings along the route, looking at the place as a whole and linking quality only to the emotion that the place itself is capable of transmitting. A smaller proportion of respondents, about 20 per cent, including some local residents, noted that the route in its entirety should be better maintained, but referred to no particular element.

The fourth question was designed to specify the previous question, asking in particular whether some elements detracted from the enjoyment of the route in question and its perception. About 50 per cent of interviewees, almost all Italian and locals, said that the presence of open-air tables outside restaurants and cafés cover the sight of buildings, especially in Piazza della Rotonda, and generally cause difficulty in the fruition of the place, becoming a sort of barrier. Another 30 per cent, chiefly foreigners of any age, said that open-air cafés added a pleasant atmosphere and livability. The remaining respondents belonging to different ages and nationalities had a generally depressing perception of the presence of street vendors, fast food outlets and too many open-air tables. Taken together, they led to a decline in the quality of the place.

The question about restoring the itinerary for the blind received the same response almost universally: respondents agreed on the desirability of renewing it. Nevertheless, no one had noticed the presence of stelae that indicated the route in Braille and no one knew of the existence of the route for the blind. A small percentage, comprising Italians and local residents, pointed out that a blind person would find it difficult to move along such a crowded route and at the same time fully appreciate its beauty, primarily consisting of monuments which act on visual perception.

On the question concerning the feeling of safety, most people never experienced a feeling of insecurity. A lower percentage, of locals in particular, claimed they felt a sense of insecurity on the streets along the route rather than in the squares, and another small percentage, once again locals, after 10 p.m.

With respect to the question about the cleanliness of the place, the answer, regardless of age and nationality, for 50 per cent of the respondents was negative and for the other 50 per cent was that there was little cleanliness especially around places with takeaway food and close to open-air tables. In relation to the question about the presence of graffiti, only one interviewee – a young Belgian – detected its presence. On the question regarding the state of pavement maintenance, respondents at the time of the question had not noticed the state of the pavement. After subsequent inspection of the pavement most replied that it was uneven and partly worn and needed maintenance. Approximately 20 per cent of foreigners replied that it was historic paving, which is often worn.

As regards the question about the presence of non-local souvenir shops, almost all respondents replied that there are in general too many low-quality souvenir shops and that they contribute to the loss of identity of the place. Only a small percentage – most of Italian nationality – answered that the presence of shops selling non-local souvenirs may generate confusion among foreigners.

With respect to the question about the itinerary, most of the respondents regardless of age and nationality, had come from the Piazza di Spagna, Piazza di Trevi and Piazza della Rotonda, and would respectively continue to Piazza Navona, Piazza della Rotonda and Piazza di Trevi. They would later reach the Colosseum and Piazza San Pietro.

Finally, the last question concerning the possible inclusion of gardens, people answered positively to the inclusion of urban green spaces along the itinerary. A small percentage (10 per cent) of local residents responded that greenery has no part to play in the historic centre.

Phase 8: Complex map of project and design interventions

And finally, we highlighted the project interventions to be made to allow for sustainable enhancement and fruition of this place, and mitigate anthropic risk (eighth phase). Differentiating and restoring, slowing down, introducing vegetation, denoting and giving identity to what is transitory, and virtualizing are some of the interventions which, if duly integrated, should prove beneficial.

One might well start from the differentiation of routes. This might involve: creating different linking routes between the monuments of the Pantheon and the Trevi Fountain – a short route (Hadrianeum) and a longer one featuring the stratification of the urban fabric as well as the monuments; creating alternative routes focusing on the elements of perception – this solution may well prove both educational and sustainable – it would show visitors how pleasing perceptions can be easily blotted out by unpleasant ones; restoring the route for the blind – perhaps adding other perceptions; and creating integrated historical-cultural-perception routes meeting specific requisites – by introducing routes featuring the sound of water playing in the fountains, the ancient materials found along the route, admiring religious icons, buildings, churches and architectural features which pass unobserved in a hasty visit, sampling local produce, and breathing in the scent of Rome.

The second intervention is differentiating and restoring traditional activities. This intervention might include restoring handicrafts producing local products, including high-quality goods, so as to reduce the commercial confusion in these streets and rescue vanishing skills. Furthermore, we suggest the design of a coordinated project for shop signs and windows, above all as regards the streets which connect the squares, eliminating graffiti on the facades and respecting their traditional colour. In this way, redesigning the critical points would ensure greater balance in the set-up of spaces and organization of the various activities, it would act as a dissuader to additional fast food outlets and would pressurise those already in place to conform.

A third intervention designed to reduce the excessive physical and emotional load is the creation of breaks, to be introduced in: Piazza di Pietra, the only true moment of relaxation, where one might build, for example, a little conceptual garden, also serving as an educational function, where people can pause and indulge their perceptions and then proceed to the central space of the Hadrianeum; the Galleria in Santa Maria in Via, currently underused, not strictly on the route but close by, could serve as a break with the inclusion of exhibitions, featuring the route of Hadrian for example, and other functions.

A fourth intervention involves the introduction of vegetation, currently lacking in the area: in a small garden in Piazza di Pietra; in small well-defined spaces, for example at the start of Via delle Muratte, and also close by the study area such as at the end of Via del Seminario (parallel to Via di Pietra) in Piazza Sant'Ignazio.

A fifth intervention consists in giving identity to what is transitory by creating lightweight multifunctional structures to be introduced at the focal points of monuments and street commerce, variable in extension and dimension, opening and closing, where artists, hawkers, living statues and others can create their own fluid spaces within a dynamic, light grid which nonetheless constitutes a framework. This form of urban decor can be equipped for various functions including multimedia.

A sixth intervention involves virtualizing the graffiti and the path. In the first case at some points, where there is more graffiti and the historical pavement has been replaced by a recent one, a special pavement could be inserted that allows the creation of virtual graphic signs which may visualize the steps of visitors. In the second case it involves going online with the creation of multimedia guides. The various routes can be presented and made more user friendly by means of multimedia guides via satellites accessible for example from mobile phones. In this way visitors can be oriented towards alternative personalised routes which they can follow with the help of multimedia texts and maps (Sepe, 2010a).

Conclusion

The Trevi–Pantheon route we have analysed links two major monuments located in two piazzas, Piazza della Rotonda and Piazza Trevi, and we have characterized it as a (musical) piece of the city which leads from the sacred (point) to the profane (counterpoint). The most significant break along the route comes in Piazza di Pietra which in historical terms is no less important, but which has to some extent escaped the magnetism of a tourist, cultural and commercial attraction. In spite of its impressive appearance, the study has identified that the Hadrianeum is less of a tourist pull, probably on account of its current function as Chamber of Commerce, so that passers-by may pause here briefly but then go on to visit other monuments. By contrast, the break represented by Via del Corso appears merely an interruption rather than a change in pace on the route.

Figure 18.15
Complex map of design of Trevi–Pantheon

L E G E N D

differentiating and restoring routes
1 - creating different linking routes between the monuments of the Pantheon and the Trevi fountain to learn about the stratification of the urban fabric as well as the monuments
2 - creating integrated historical, cultural and perception routes meeting specific requisites, with information about the history and identity of the places
3 - restoring the route for the blind, also adding other perceptions

differentiating and restoring activities
1 - differentiating activitie s
2 - restoring handicrafts producing local products, including high-quality goods
3 - coordinating shop signs and windows

slowing down
slowing down the excessive physical and emotional impactof the route through the creation of *breaks*, to be introduced at some points such as Piazza di Pietra and the *Galleria* in Santa Maria in Via

giving identity to what is transitory
creating lightweight multifunctional structures to be introduced at the focal points of monuments and street commerce, where artists, hawkers, living statues and others can create their own fluid and dynamic spaces

making more natural
introduction of vegetation in a small garden in Piazza di Pietra; in small well-defined spaces, for example at the start of Via delle Muratte, and also close by the study area such as at the end of Via del Seminario and in Piazza Sant'Ignazio

virtualizing graffiti
developing an equipped pavement which allows the creation of virtual graphic signs which may visualize visitor footprints

virtualizing the path
creating multimedia guides with multimedia texts and maps to orient visitors towards alternative and personalised routes

137

The streets linking the piazzas constitute a sort of recurrent motif with similar characteristics. Via di Pietra, Via dei Pastini, Via delle Muratte are primarily thoroughfares with several possibilities for eating and souvenir shopping.

The objective of this case study of anthropic risk due to ever increasing mass tourism was to provide a decongestion of the itinerary identifying interventions that are suited to the area's ancient culture and tradition. In order to meet this goal a long period of monitoring – lasting three years – was carried out with the PlaceMaker method in order to capture the slow but evident changes that are diminishing the quality of this place.

Differentiating and restoring, slowing down, introducing vegetation, denoting and giving identity to what is transitory, and virtualizing are the interventions that were identified in order to provide for cultural sites and appropriate activities for a sustainable and integrated fruition and preservation of the site.

Some questions were noted during the traditional phase of analysis and the two questionnaires were particular useful for the investigation. With respect to the traditional analysis, in an historical centre like Rome there are any number of monuments and places of interest and, in the study of the cartography, it was difficult to decide whether to take note of all of them or only those which seem to be more closely related to place identity.

With regard to the questionnaire of analysis, there were places where people were more willing to spend time answering a questionnaire, such as the Piazzas and others where people are primarily intent on walking and thus have little wish to respond. Furthermore, it was interesting that the question 'Can you compare this area to another area in Rome or in another city?' elicited answers including the Colosseum and all sorts of places throughout Europe and America, denoting a certain confusion among some tourists.

Finally, with respect to the questionnaire of project (seventh phase), this was composed of a greater number of questions (12) than that of the analysis (9), requiring more time for answers, and was preceded by a brief explanation of its purpose. One may notice a certain difference between the answers given by respondents of Italian nationality and those of other nationalities. While the former have mostly observed the effects of mass tourism, the latter only detected the presence of too many people.

Chapter 19

Los Angeles
South Broadway

Phase 1: Anticipatory analysis

Los Angeles is a city whose international fame is due to Hollywood and the film industry. The expectations are that the city areas are therefore often known because movies and television series have been filmed there. Just look at the image of the hill with the Hollywood sign that takes the imagination of many people back to places such as Beverly Hills, Sunset Boulevard, Rodeo Drive and Venice, as well as famous actors.

Another particular aspect of Los Angeles is that it is a County which consists of a set of rather different cities and that the overall urban fabric is crossed by an extensive surface area of highways. This leads to two preliminary considerations. The first is that most likely there is no real centre – given the existence of different areas placed a highway apart – and that there is no peculiar architectural or urban character. And the second is that the use of the car is an indispensable element for getting around in different parts of Los Angeles and, consequently, the perception of places is likely to be filtered by the fact that – except in a few areas – the road is not used as a 'public space' to walk, stop, etc.

These considerations make the uniqueness of South Broadway in downtown Los Angeles stand out even further. South Broadway is one of the few pedestrian streets in the County: it is therefore necessarily a road on a human scale, although at present little frequented by locals.

It is also, in the section between Third Street and Olympic Boulevard, the street with the greatest concentration of historic theatres in the United States. At present, few theatres are open, but an atmosphere full of history is still possible to breathe, and the buildings, albeit in disuse, are mindful of their old function. Broadway will be of interest as a location for filming and for tourists.

There is a certain degradation probably due to it still being an area waiting to rebuild its identity, returning to its historic use or reconstructing a new one. The contrast could be made even greater by the proximity of the new downtown area, with its skyscrapers and head offices.

The entire study will focus on the part between Third Street and Olympic Boulevard deemed of particular interest from the standpoint of preservation of place identity.

Phase 2: Denominative and perceptual description

The area involved is the section of South Broadway between Third Street and Olympic Boulevard, which is about 2.5 km long. First the right-hand side and then the left-hand side are described, from Third Street to Olympic Boulevard, showing the denominative, perceptive, graphics, photographic and video surveys.

The road pavement of the thoroughfare is fairly uniform within the section in question and has a central part for vehicles with four lanes – two in each direction – and sidewalks. South Broadway differs notably from the rest of the downtown area. Some characteristics common to all sections may be observed.

The curtain of the buildings is generally continuous, though differing in height, style, state of maintenance and use. Furthermore, the large colourful window frames or signs of many shops tend to hide the beauty of many historic buildings and theatres, which often go unnoticed to the passer-by. The visual chaos is enhanced by the presence of several stores with no shop windows that display their goods outside.

The current use of the street is predominantly commercial with rather diverse goods being sold, especially formal and *quinceanera* clothing. In several sections, shops on the ground floor are shuttered up. There are typical kiosks, all identical, selling newspapers along the whole section. The street furniture is discontinuous and diverse, and consists of some iron benches, ornate or stylized streetlights, flowerpots and waste bins.

People who use these spaces are predominantly Hispanic, as can also be observed by the sign 'English is spoken' in an opticians. There also theatre-goers, police outside most jewellery stores, professionals and some beggars.

A few trees have been planted somewhat haphazardly on sidewalks in a seemingly random and discontinuous manner. Various transportation modes are in evidence: in the road, there are cars, buses and coaches; on the sidewalks, bicycles and skateboards.

We begin on the right-hand side, describing the section between Third and Fourth Street.

Third Street to Fourth Street right-hand side

This first section has a continuous curtain of buildings varying from one to eleven storeys in height and in different architectural styles. The most characteristic buildings in this part are the Stability Building with a Spanish Baroque facade and the Million Dollar Theatre inside, and the Homer Laughlin Building occupied at street level by the Grand Central Market with a facade of mixed styles. Both buildings are in good condition.
The Million Dollar Theatre has bright signs that advertise the shows and, outside on the sidewalk, a special billboard illustrating the history of the theatre.

The Grand Central Market has a pleasing display of products within, and various places to eat and drink food from different parts of the world. After these buildings come low newly-built constructions for commercial purposes, selling products of various kinds. A formal and quinceanera clothing shop stands out from the others. Another feature is the colour of the storefronts which are sometimes quite vivid.

Table 19.1a **Detail of the denominative survey**

Place	Date	Time	Type	Constructed elements	Natural elements	Transport mode	People
Sixth Street	September	10:00		Los Angeles Theatre	Trees	Bus and cars	Latinos
			Low, medium, high percentage	High	Low	High	High

Table 19.1b **Detail of the perceptual survey**

Place	Date	Time	Type	Smell P.	Taste P.	Sound P.	Touch P.	Visual P.
Sixth Street	September	10:00				Latino music by shops		Theatre facade with shop lights and goods exposed outside
			Low, medium, high percentage			Medium		High
			Non-influential, pleasant, annoying, surprising perceived feeling			Non-influential		Annoying

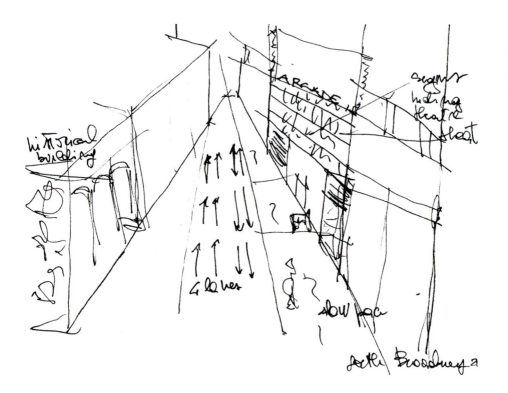

Figure 19.1
**Graphic survey:
the Arcade
Theatre lights
hidden by shop
signs**

Figure 19.2
**Photographic
survey: South
Broadway with th[e]
mural representin[g]
Anthony Quinn, o[n]
Third Street**

Figure 19.3
Photographic survey: South Broadway with a view of the Calle de la Eternidad mural and, behind, skyscrapers

Figure 19.4
Photographic survey: view of the Los Angeles Theatre

The most evident and pleasing visual perceptions concern two murals that can be seen from both the right- and left-hand side. These are the murals that represent Anthony Quinn, on Third Street, and the Calle de la Eternidad mural, drawn at the end of this section of South Broadway. Visual perception is also captured by goods displayed outside shops, often creating a feeling of chaos. Perceptions of smell and taste are triggered by the presence of different food from the Grand Central Market. Sounds include music from a store. The pace is moderate.

Fourth Street to Fifth Street right-hand side

This section has a continuous curtain of buildings – from one to eleven storeys tall – of different styles. The first building – the Broadway Department Store in the Romanesque Revival style and in a good state of maintenance – has ground floor premises closed for business. The buildings that follow are for commercial uses and mostly of recent construction. This section concludes with the Metropolitan Building which is also in Romanesque Revival style, with shops on the ground floor. A formal and quinceanera dress shop is observed. The prevailing visual perceptions are those relating to the iron KRKD radio tower which is pleasing and eye-catching, and the products displayed outside the shops. In terms of sound, this consists in particular of music from stores. Along the final part of the section some trees have been planted. The pace is moderate.

Fifth Street to Sixth Street right-hand side

This section has a continuous curtain of buildings of variable height between one and ten storeys. The predominant use is commercial: the ground floor premises of one building appear closed. The section is dominated by shops with goods on display outside. It is also apparent that there are shops selling formal and quinceanera clothing. There is a tree with a large canopy and some plants. Attention is likely captured by the KRKD Radio Tower and white advertising signs that are projected onto the sky. Visual perception is also triggered by shop signs arranged very differently in different stores, creating a sense of visual chaos. The flooring in front of a jewellery store has a diamond-shaped design. The pace is moderate.

Sixth Street to Seventh Street right-hand side

This section is dominated by the Los Angeles Theatre which, with its light-coloured French Baroque facade and red neon signs, forces itself onto the urban landscape. The height and style of buildings are different. There is a commercial use of street-level premises and several of them sell formal clothes for quinceanera.

The end of the section has a large commercial space for the sale of jewellery. On the sidewalks are some plants in large pots. Visual attention is captured by the facade of the Los Angeles Theatre and the paving which in some sections varies to draw attention to a shop or features artistic designs, as is the case in front of the Los Angeles Theatre. The sense of touch is triggered by short stretches of irregular paving. The pace is moderate.

Seventh Street to Eighth Street right-hand side

This section has a continuous curtain of buildings, which vary from one to twelve storeys, in different styles. The building that mainly dominates the scene is Loew's State Theatre currently used as a church. The use of the buildings at street level is mostly commercial, with some selling formal clothing. Along this stretch several shops have closed down. As for natural elements, some trees with spreading canopies have been planted.

Figure 19.5
Photographic survey: perspective of the street with quinceanera clothing shops

Figure 19.6
Photographic survey: view of the Loew's State Theatre currently used as a church

Figure 19.7
Photographic survey: perspective with the United Artists Theatre Eastern Building

In terms of visual perception, the eye is especially attracted towards the end of this section by the Tower Theatre facade on the opposite side of the street and later, on the original side, by the Eastern Columbia Building, both pleasing. As in the previous sections some shops display goods outside, creating visual chaos. Other perceptions are not placed under particular stress. The pace is moderate.

Eighth Street to Ninth Street right-hand side

This section is completely dominated by the historic Asher Hamburger Department Store where on the ground floor there is the Broadway Trade Center, with shops of different types, and by the Eastern Columbia Building facade with its 14 levels – in Art Deco style with terracotta walls and bright blue and gold trim – now used as a film location. In particular, the Eastern Columbia Building, with its height and its particular style and colour strongly attracts the observer's eye. Between the two buildings there is a low building of recent construction with some premises that are not used.

Outside the Broadway Trade Center and the Eastern Columbia Building, there are some trees. The steps of the Broadway Trade Center, also due to the presence of a bus stop, often become a place where people socialize at random.

Visual perception is captured by the facade of the Eastern Columbia Building and the characteristic floor in front, and by the KRKD radio tower and white advertising signs that are projected onto the sky. The pace is quiet.

Ninth Street to Tenth Street right-hand side

This section has a discontinuous frontage due to the presence of buildings – between six and 12 storeys – and car parks. In the first part there is a building from the early twentieth century with shops on the ground floor, followed by a parking lot with a small Mexican food kiosk. Next, there is the Texaco Building, with a 12-storey facade in Spanish Gothic style that houses the United Artists Theatre. After that, there is an early twentieth century building with shops on the ground floor, some of which are closed, and another car park.

Like the previous section, this has different characteristics from the other sections. The buildings are mostly well maintained, there are no shops with goods displayed outside and it is not very frequented by people. The pace is quiet. In terms of visual perception, the eye is captured by the paving, the signs of the United Artists Theatre and large signs pointing to parking lots. The sense of smell is stimulated by the Mexican food wafting from the kiosk near the parking lot. At the end of the street a sort of interruption of continuity with the first section is perceived.

Now the left-hand side of the road is analysed.

Third Street to Fourth Street left-hand side

This section has a curtain of continuous buildings (one to five storeys) interrupted by a public space. The building of greatest interest is the Bradbury Building, built in Romanesque Revival, mainly used as a film location and then a historical cutlery store. The other buildings are mainly used by businesses selling various kinds of products, with a quinceanera clothing shop standing out. This section has the only designed public space on the whole route: Biddy Mason's Park. This space, with stylized furniture, sculptures, trees and panels with the history of Biddy Mason is widely used at times of rest by professionals from the street parallel to Broadway.

In visual terms, this section is the most striking: what captures the eye are the billboard with the history of the Bradbury Building, the mural of Anthony Quinn in Third Street, the Calle de la Eternidad mural and the skyscrapers of downtown buildings that can be seen from the low height constructions on the opposite side of the street. The pace is moderate.

Fourth Street to Fifth Street left-hand side

This section has a curtain of buildings, which vary in height from one to twelve storeys, of different styles. The buildings have ground floor shops, some of which have goods displayed outside. The buildings which attract most attention are the Broadway mall and the historic Chester Williams Building, which has some shuttered-up stores on the ground floor. There are some plants in pots on the sidewalks.

Visual perceptions concern the goods displayed outside the shops and the scaffolding of the Chester Williams Building. The sense of smell is stimulated by the smell of food from a fast food outlet. The pace in this section is moderate.

Fifth Street to Sixth Street left-hand side

This section has a continuous curtain of buildings which, albeit of different height (from three to thirteen storeys) and architectural styles, present a fairly homogeneous visual scene. In this section, there are three theatres: the Roxi, Cameo and Arcade. The Roxi, thanks to its impressive Art Deco facade and the tower with a sign with the name of the theatre, is that which most captures the attention.

The Cameo has a facade in Renaissance Revival style, whose sign is partly obscured by the many bright signs of the shops below. As with the Arcade, despite its Beaux Arts style facade it would not be easily recognized if it were not for the particular paving in front. At street level there are commercial premises which have closed down.

Another characteristic building in this part of Broadway is the Broadway Arcade Building in Spanish Renaissance Revival style, a large commercial block stretching parallel to Spring Street. On this building rises the KRKD radio Tower, in iron with a bright sign.

Figure 19.8
**Photographic survey:
South Broadway,
perspective of the
Rialto theatre**

Figure 19.9
**Photographic survey:
view of the Arcade
Theatre**

Figure 19.10
Photographic survey: perspective of the Tower Theatre

Figure 19.11
Photographic survey: detail of the Orpheum Theatre

Figure 19.12
Photographic survey: perspective with the Clifton's Cafeteria

Figure 19.13
Photographic survey: car park

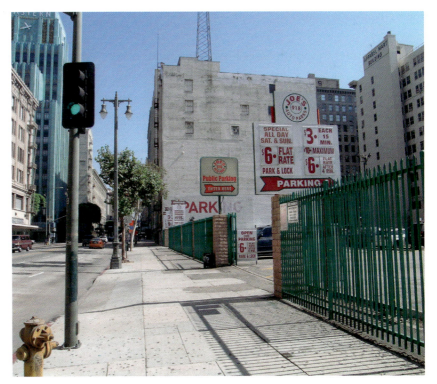

The ground floors of buildings have different kinds of shops, including a clothing store and a bakery, both for ceremonies, and other premises for selling jewellery. There are some trees.

The visual attention is captured by the signs of shops and theatres as well as the particular paving of the Arcade and by goods displayed outside shops. The sense of taste is heightened by the bakery, and the sense of touch by the pavement which in some places is uneven. The pace is moderate.

Sixth Street to Seventh Street left-hand side

This stretch has a continuous curtain of buildings between one and 12 storeys tall, most of historical interest.

The first building is the Walter P. Story Building with its ornate white marble facade, followed by the Palace Theatre with its facade in Florentine Renaissance style. In this section there is also a historic café – Clifton's Cafeteria.

At street level there are shops that sell different types of products, especially jewellery. Furthermore, some shops have closed down. There are some trees and some plants in large pots.

In terms of visual perception, what stands out is the facade of the Los Angeles Theatre on the opposite side and the floor of Clifton's Cafeteria. There are also products displayed outside shops.

The senses of taste and smell are activated especially by the products of the historic café. The sense of touch is stimulated by stretches of rough pavement. The pace is moderate.

Seventh Street to Eighth Street left-hand side

This section has a curtain of buildings with a height between seven and 12 storeys in different styles. However, despite the presence of large parking lots, it maintains a sort of continuity in the townscape. The first car park has several fast food restaurants at street level. It is followed by two historic buildings: the Garland Building with its Neoclassical facade and the Chapman Building with a Renaissance Revival style facade. The Garland contains the Globe Theatre, whose red sign really stands out.

On the ground floor of the buildings there are shops selling various types of goods whose window frames and colour signs liven up the scene – although it becomes chaotic at times. Several shops have closed down.

In terms of visual perception, there are goods displayed outside shops, shuttered-up shops and the Eastern Columbia tower. The smell is that of fast food. The pace is moderate.

Eighth Street to Ninth Street left-hand side

This section has buildings from one to fourteen storeys in height in different styles. The continuity of the curtain is interrupted by a space for parking.

The urban scene is dominated by the Tower Theatre, and its tower, located at the beginning of this section. The theatre, with an angular facade in the French Renaissance style with Spanish, Romanesque and Moorish influences, has the word 'Tower' written vertically on it. There follows the Rialto Theatre, with a facade of minor architectural interest, and the Orpheum Theatre with its imposing French Gothic style facade and eye-catching signs that indicate the name of the theatre and shows.

A historic building in art deco style, the Ninth and Broadway Building, concludes the section. On the ground floor there are many shops that have closed down, some with goods of various kinds and a so-called co-working shop in the final stretch.

In terms of visual perception, what causes most disturbance are the sight of businesses closed and goods displayed outside shops, the bright signs of theatres and large signs pointing to car parks. The sense of touch is also somewhat stressed by the uneven surface of the pavement. The pace is moderate.

Ninth Street to Tenth Street left-hand side

This section has a discontinuous curtain of buildings due to the presence of a spacious car park. The height of the few buildings ranges from one to seven storeys, some of which have no particular architectural style. The building that attracts the most attention is the Burns Building, located at the beginning of this section, with its Gothic Revival facade.

Continuing in the central part of the section is a car park. There are few ground floor shops, but some trees. In terms of visual perception, what catches the eye is the presence of closed-down shops, the signs pointing to parking lots and the sight of the Eastern Columbia on the opposite side. The sense of touch is stimulated by the rough pavement. The pace is slow.

At the end of this section, we perceive an interruption of continuity with the next stretch of road and a sense of disorientation.

With regard to the graphical survey, the sketches mainly served to transform the visual scene into symbols, rather than the pace or flow of people, and provide input in order to create specific symbols for Broadway such as that of the coloured facades. The most striking feature is the presence of different kinds of goods on display outside the shops and the large variety of shop signs that tend to obscure the prospect of the theatres and historical buildings, leading to different experiences at street level. With regard to the photographic survey, about 400 images were taken during the inspections due to the route's considerable length. In this case, the pictures were an important tool of analysis because they were able to capture better than eyes the relationships among different heights of buildings, the theatres and their signs, shops and people. Finally, the video survey showed a mainly moderate pace in the various parts and strong auditory perceptions.

Phase 3: Analysis of traditional mapping

Phase 3 is devoted to traditional analysis carried out on maps of both urban and territorial scale.

The part of Broadway between Third Street and Olympia Boulevard under analysis consists of a large continuous thoroughfare for vehicles and pedestrians. The roadway consists of four lanes, flanked by sidewalks. This road is part of an urban fabric with a checkerboard pattern, which is regular for the stretch in question.

Broadway is one of the major thoroughfares of downtown Los Angeles and runs from Mission Road (North Broadway) and merges into Main Street, before the San Diego Freeway (South Broadway). One of the oldest streets in the city, Broadway was laid out by Edward Ord under the plan of 1849 and its original name was Fort Street, stretching from south of Fort Moore Hill to Sand Street. In 1890, the name of the street between First Street and Ten Street was changed to Broadway – today South Broadway – while the section from First Street to California Street became North Broadway.

During the first half of the twentieth century, Broadway was deemed the main commercial street in Los Angeles and one of the first districts of theatres, where people went to see movies or shop in department stores. Between 1920 and 1930 many large buildings were erected, which are now listed in the National Register of Historic Places.

The original use of many buildings was as department stores or residences, or, as in the case of the Bradbury Building, for film locations. After the Second World War, with the rise of multiscreen cinemas and shopping malls, as well as the financial district moving south-east of downtown LA, a slow decline in the thoroughfare set in. Contributory factors were the closure of nearly all the theatres and department stores.

Analysis at the urban scale shows the presence of many historic buildings, constructed, as stated above, in the first half of the twentieth century, with diverse styles ranging from various forms of Art Nouveau and Revival style, which include: the Stability Building, Bradbury Building, OT Johnson Building, the Metropolitan Building, Chester Williams Building, Walter P. Story Building, J.D. Hooker Building, Garland Building, Charles C. Chapman Building, Wurlitzer Building, Eastern Columbia Building, Texaco Building and the LL Burns Building. There is also the historic Grand Central Market.

There are no plazas or squares, although there is a small park between Third and Fourth Street on the Bradbury Building side. The park, named after Biddy Mason, is the only green space of the section of South Broadway under analysis. Few trees are present. Due to the constant height of the axis no visual perceptions of interest emerge on the planimetry, outside that of the buildings of the road itself.

Figure 19.14
Traditional analysis: downtown map of historic Los Angeles (Source: DLANC, the Downtown Los Angeles Neighborhood Council)

At the regional scale, the analysis shows the central position of the whole Broadway axis with respect to the downtown area. The regularity of the checkerboard pattern of the urban fabric beyond Spring Street – to the East side – is loosened in order to show larger and less rigid meshes.

Broadway is part of the Historic District and Theatre District in downtown LA which includes two other important thoroughfares, Spring Street and Main Street, and a short section of Hill Street. The historic part of downtown LA borders with other districts, such as the Jewelry District, Fashion District, Toy District and the Civic Center, each with their own particular characteristics. Other districts are present downtown, including: Bunker Hill, El Pueblo – which is the oldest – Little Tokyo, Downtown Center, South Park, Warehouse District and Figueroa Corridor.

The main north–south thoroughfares crossing downtown LA are Broadway, Spring Street, Hill Street and Main Street. Three freeways cross Broadway, namely the 101, 110 and 10. Among the secondary roads, those which intersect Broadway include: Cesar Chavez Avenue, Temple Street, First Street, Third Street, Fourth Street, Sixth Street, Eighth and Ninth Street, crossing downtown LA from east to west. A historic cable car, the Angels Flight in the Bunker Hill district, connects Hill Street and California Plaza.

The Los Angeles River runs from north to south parallel to the main axes mentioned above, intercepting North Broadway in its final stretch before flowing into Spring Street. The green areas, while not representing the main feature of this area, are located at Pershing Square, The Plaza and at the northern edge of downtown LA in Elysian Park.

The buildings of cultural interest, considering the entire downtown area with which Broadway is related in different ways, include: the buildings of the parallel Spring Street and Main Street with architectural style in keeping with the Beaux Arts and revival in the style of Broadway, such as the Braly-Continental Building; the Los Angeles City Hall in the Civic Centre; the skyscrapers of Bunker Hill and the Financial District – of which the Library Tower designed by I.M. Pei is the largest. Furthermore, there are several museum buildings which contribute to create well-known landmarks, including: The Walt Disney Concert Hall, designed by Frank Gehry, and the MOCA Museum of Contemporary Art designed by Arata Isozaki, both in Bunker Hill. Among the religious buildings, those of historical and cultural interest include: Our Lady Queen of the Angels Church, in the historic Plaza of El Pueblo District – the original settlement of the nineteenth century in Los Angeles – and Our Lady of the Angels Catholic Church, the monumental Church recently designed by Rafael Moneo, again in Bunker Hill.

Pershing Square, regular in shape, and the Plaza, not regular in shape, are the squares which are observed. Some of the most interesting among the visual prospects are the Los Angeles City Hall, the skyscrapers of Bunker Hill and the Financial District, and the Walt Disney Concert Hall.

Phase 4: Questionnaire for analysis

The questionnaire consists of 10 questions. The expected length varied between ten and thirty minutes and consisted of ten questions listed below. This is followed by a summary of responses.

   0) Nationality, age
   Passing through the study area:
   1) What elements strike you most (people, things, etc.)?
   2) Is there one or more elements which produce a particular sensation?
   3) Is there any one element which brings to mind a moment important to you for any reason?
   4) Are there any things that bother you?
   5) Is there any one element which produces a strong sensation?
   6) If you could change, improve or enhance anything, what would you do?
   7) Is this area comparable to another area of Los Angeles or elsewhere?
   8) If so, why?
   9) What is the symbol of Los Angeles?
   10) What is the symbol of Broadway?

The interviewees (roughly 30 in number) comprised locals, workers and visitors. Their countries of origin were the USA, Mexico and, to a lesser extent, Honduras. The language used was mainly English, except in the case of some Mexicans and Hondurans when Spanish was used. The age of respondents varied between 40 and 70. The points at which we conducted the questionnaire were Biddy Mason's Park on Third Street, where people were having a break, and along sections of Broadway close to historic buildings and theatres where the pace was slower and people stopped to admire their surroundings. The interviewees showed interest in responding to the questionnaire.

As regards the first question, the striking elements, most people – regardless of nationality and age – answered the architecture of buildings. The others gave rather diverse responses, including the variety of people, the homeless, food and stores.

With respect to the second question, the elements which produce a particular sensation, again the answers referred to the architecture. Most respondents mentioned the sculptural details of historical theatres and buildings and, in general, the history of Broadway, while a small percentage mentioned the variety of activities taking place there.

As regards the third question, the elements which bring to mind an important moment, hardly any interviewees had specific memories connected to elements or places in Broadway. A small percentage of Mexicans responded with 'work', while a few Hondurans mentioned the homeless.

In response to the fourth question, concerning the things which cause most annoyance, almost all referred to the traffic, the homeless and unpleasant smells coming from sidewalks. Few people mentioned the change in function of some buildings and theatres.

As regards the fifth question, the elements which produce a strong sensation, most people – regardless of nationality and age – answered 'nothing'. Just a small percentage referred to the variety of people. When asked (question 6) if they would change, improve, or enhance anything, the answers were quite different, though all shared the same idea of improvement of the place.

More than half the people – regardless of nationality and age – wanted cinemas brought back to Broadway by renovating the old theatres, and the historical buildings restored and enhanced. With respect to the rest of the interviewees, almost all – consisting mainly of locals and professionals aged between forty and fifty – wanted cleaner sidewalks, while a small percentage wanted more restaurants to be open. Only some older people from the USA were quite sceptical about the possibility of improving the quality of the street.

With respect to the comparability of Broadway to another area of Los Angeles or elsewhere, almost all answered that there were no other areas like this. A small percentage of people gave very different responses such as the East of Los Angeles or New York in general without giving specific motivations.

As to the symbol of Los Angeles (question 9), this had the largest number of different responses, probably reflecting the many districts which make up the city. The most frequent answer was Hollywood, followed by City Hall given by both younger and older people from the USA. The other responses were the Skyline, the diversity, and the climate, given by Mexicans and Hondurans.

In response to the last question, concerning the symbol of Broadway, almost all – regardless of nationality and age – mentioned the theatres or the historical buildings in general. Few people gave a specific answer, including the Eastern Columbia (people from the USA), and the State Theatre (Mexicans). A very small percentage of people from Mexico mentioned the Central Market.

Phase 5: Complex map of analysis

In this stage, the data collected in order to draw up the complex map of analysis are re-elaborated. The place identity of Broadway is not static, consolidated or prey to globalization, but in continuous evolution. What emerges is a vibrant and contrasting mix given by the colours, sounds, smells of the Latino culture and the historic theatres with their architecture, signs and relative memory. The symbols which were used in order to draw up the complex map were taken, as in each case study, from the basic PlaceMaker system of symbols, adding those specifically created in order to represent the peculiarity of this place.

As for the symbols specifically created for South Broadway Street, most of them are related to theatres and places of different kinds of commerce – which represent the main components of the place identity – and are drawn with shapes and colours strictly related to the full circle used for the concept of place.

Figure 19.15
**South Broadway:
complex map of
analysis and legend**

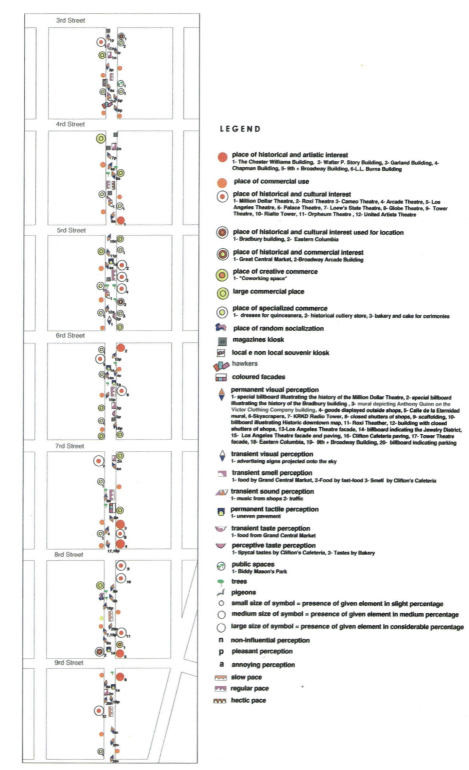

3rd Street

4th Street

5rd Street

6rd Street

7rd Street

8rd Street

9rd Street

LEGEND

● **place of historical and artistic interest**
1- The Chester Williams Building, 2- Walter P. Story Building, 3- Garland Building, 4- Chapman Building, 5- 9th + Broadway Building, 6-L.L. Burns Building

● **place of commercial use**

◉ **place of historical and cultural interest**
1- Million Dollar Theatre, 2- Roxi Theatre 3- Cameo Theatre, 4- Arcade Theatre, 5- Los Angeles Theatre, 6- Palace Theatre, 7- Loew's State Theatre, 8- Globe Theatre, 9- Tower Theatre, 10- Rialto Tower, 11- Orpheum Theatre , 12- United Artists Theatre

◎ **place of historical and cultural interest used for location**
1- Bradbury building, 2- Eastern Columbia

◎ **place of historical and commercial interest**
1- Great Central Market, 2-Broadway Arcade Building

◎ **place of creative commerce**
1- "Coworking space"

◎ **large commercial place**

◎ **place of specialized commerce**
1- dresses for quinceanera, 2- historical cutlery store, 3- bakery and cake for cerimonies

🕮 **place of random socialization**

▦ **magazines kiosk**

▦ **local e non local souvenir kiosk**

▦ **hawkers**

▦ **coloured facades**

⬇ **permanent visual perception**
1- special billboard illustrating the history of the Million Dollar Theatre, 2- special billboard illustrating the history of the Bradbury building , 3- mural depicting Anthony Quinn on the Victor Clothing Company building, 4- goods displayed outside shops, 5- Calle de la Eternidad mural, 6-Skyscrapers, 7- KRKD Radio Tower, 8- closed shutters of shops, 9- scaffolding, 10- billboard illustrating Historic downtown map, 11- Roxi Theather, 12- building with closed shutters of shops, 13-Los Angeles Theatre facade, 14- billboard indicating the Jewelry District, 15- Los Angeles Theatre facade and paving, 16- Clifton Cafeteria paving, 17- Tower Theatre facade, 18- Eastern Columbia, 19- 9th + Broadway Building, 20- billboard indicating parking

⬇ **transient visual perception**
1- advertising signs projected onto the sky

▭ **transient smell perception**
1- food by Grand Central Market, 2-Food by fast-food 3- Smell by Clifton's Cafeteria

▱ **transient sound perception**
1- music from shops 2- traffic

▣ **permanent tactile perception**
1- uneven pavement

▽ **transient taste perception**
1- food from Grand Central Market

▽ **perceptive taste perception**
1- tipycal tastes by Clifton's Cafeteria, 2- Tastes by Bakery

◉ **public spaces**
1- Biddy Mason's Park

🌳 **trees**

🕊 **pigeons**

○ small size of symbol = presence of given element in slight percentage

○ medium size of symbol = presence of given element in medium percentage

○ large size of symbol = presence of given element in considerable percentage

n non-influential perception

p pleasant perception

a annoying perception

〰 slow pace

〰 regular pace

〰 hectic pace

As regards places of historical and cultural interest, for the historical theatres we used the symbol of historical and artistic interest with an empty circle, in order to indicate an historical place connected to the culture of this specific street. For places of historical and cultural interest used as locations for filming, we used the symbol for a site of historical and cultural interest, with a full orange circle inside the red circle, linked to the creative function of film-making.

With respect to sites of historical and commercial interest, the symbol for sites of historical and cultural interest was used, with a full yellow circle inside the red circle. The meaning which is attached to that symbol is of historical value, related to the commercial function.

As regards sites of creative commerce, the symbol for a commercial site was used, with a full orange circle inside – linked to the specific creative function of the shop.

For a site of specialized commerce, we used the symbol for a commercial site within an empty circle in order to indicate shops which sell specific goods that can be found mostly in this street, becoming part of its place identity. For the coloured facades, we choose a rectangular shape within coloured rectangles in order to indicate the colorful frames of shops found along many parts of the street. For newspaper and magazine kiosks, in keeping with other symbols of stalls used for other case studies, we chose a square symbol in grey, referring to the shape of the stalls themselves and what is on sale.

To indicate hawkers selling different kinds of goods, a symbol with three coloured rectangles was chosen, the fan-shape suggesting the seller displaying his/her various wares.

Phase 6: Identification of identity resources

From the observation of the complex map of analysis, several critical issues emerged which do not allow the perception of place identity in South Broadway or of its theatre culture. The retail trade, which constitutes a major element in the part of South Broadway under analysis, is in its current form at risk of lowering the quality of this place. The frames and signs of shops differ from one another and often cover not only the facades of theatres, but also those of historical buildings, almost hiding them from view.

Furthermore, many shops do not have windows and the goods are displayed outside, creating a chaotic perception of the road. Many retail outlets are vacant, creating a feeling of abandonment of the place sometimes combined with the poor state of maintenance of some buildings. This feeling is heightened by the striking contrast with parallel streets downtown where, from some points of Broadway, modern skyscrapers and well-maintained roads and buildings can be seen. The state of abandonment is probably also perceived by some homeless who walk on the sidewalks. The retail trade is the dominant activity. Cultural activities, despite the historical spirit of place, are left to the only theatres still in use. The almost total dominance of retail businesses means the road is rarely occupied after the closing of stores, increasing the perception of insecurity in the evening.

With regard to the road, the sidewalks are wide, but almost totally devoid of benches. The greenery consists of a few trees and some neglected plants which appear haphazardly inserted into the surroundings. The street furniture is discontinuous, as well as the maintenance of different road sections. The four-lane carriageway is very busy, and the lack of a green filter from trees contributes to the noise of vehicles spreading to the sidewalks.

As regards the identity potentials, the section of South Broadway in question has considerable potential, first as regards the early-twentieth-century architecture of its buildings which range from Art Nouveau to the various forms of Revival style. The architectural and sculptural details of different buildings often go unnoticed due to the above issues in relation to identity problems. Similarly, the theatres, some of which have facades that seem designed to dominate the cityscape, almost all with interiors of architectural and artistic interest, in several cases do not appear well-maintained, or perform business functions which hide the architecture. Even the signs which are an integral part of the theatres – hence of the cityscape – are often confused or replaced by shop signs.

While trade is very much present, partly with the sale of low-cost products, there are few global chain stores in Broadway except for some fast food outlets, mostly situated in a large parking lot. This represents huge potential for this place because it continues to maintain its own character when it comes to history. In addition, the Hispanic population who have 'settled' in this place, albeit in ways that often create visual chaos, have enriched the street with colours that suit the architectural context, maintaining an atmosphere of liveliness on Broadway. There is also the scenic mural in the section between the Third and Fourth Street entitled 'Calle de la Eternidad' which is of artistic interest but underexploited as a cultural landmark.

As regards the thoroughfare itself, the presence of wide sidewalks, though often poorly maintained, is an invitation to experience the street on foot. The presence of historic sections of paving, such as those in front of the Eastern Columbia, the Los Angeles Theatre and Clifton's Cafeteria, could also be better highlighted.

Finally, with respect to identity qualities, one of the first qualities is the distinctiveness of Broadway, which entirely differs from other roads downtown and has maintained its historical character. The curtain of the buildings along Broadway has no ultra-modern skyscrapers. Despite the varied height and architectural style of its buildings, it has maintained the overall continuity in the cityscape. The presence of two theatres in use, and the use for film locations of two of the buildings with the most historical and artistic value in Broadway – the Bradbury Building and the Eastern Columbia – constitute elements of importance for site quality. There is also the historic Grand Central Market, with food for all tastes, which attracts, with its architecture and its variety of products from all over the world, a large number of people. Other historical stores with quality products are the Clifton Cafeteria and the Cutlery store.

On the stretch of Broadway between Third and Fourth Street on the left-hand side there is a small urban park recently built to honour Biddy Mason, which, besides having commemorative value, is a place for many to enjoy breaks and free time. Also from this first section, the mural entitled 'The Pope of Broadway' representing Anthony Quinn when he received an Oscar for his portrayal of Zorba the Greek can be seen painted on the Victor Clothing Company building on Third Street. The paving painted in the mural is the floor of the Bradbury Building, thus recalling a historic building. In addition to the visual impact of this mural and, whilst walking along Broadway, the visual image of the well-maintained Eastern Columbia Building, several other senses are activated by the taste and smell of the products in the Central Market and Clifton's Cafeteria. Finally, the pace is generally moderate, allowing pedestrians to walk calmly, without the hectic pace found in business-oriented areas.

Phase 7: Questionnaire for planning

We administered a ten-point questionnaire concerning possible interventions. The interviewees (approximately 30 in number) were passers-by in Broadway and aged between 40 and 70. Their countries of origin were the USA and Mexico. The language used for the interviews was mainly English, except in the case of some Mexicans when Spanish was used.

    0) Nationality, age
  Passing through the study area:
    1) Why do you come to this street?
    2) What do you think about the quality of this place?
    3) Have you noticed the historic buildings?
    4) What do you think about making this street or part of it just for pedestrians and introducing a cycle lane?
    5) Did you feel threatened at any point?
    6) What do you think about restoring buildings to create a museum or perform other cultural functions?
    7) What do you think about restoring the theatres as cinemas or to perform another cultural function?
    8) What do you think about redesigning the street section, restoring the sidewalks, introducing more trees and enhancing the historic stretches of pavement?
    9) What do you think about the new urban furniture, including the shop windows?
    10) What about creating new urban spaces?

The places where the questionnaire was administered were almost the same as the questionnaire of analysis, namely Biddy Mason's Park on Third Street, and on stretches of Broadway close to historic buildings and theatres where people often stop to look at buildings. All the interviewees showed interest in responding, albeit briefly, to the questions.

With respect to the first question, concerning the reason for their using Broadway, regardless of the nation of origin and age, almost all answered 'for work'. A small percentage of interviewees answered 'for visiting' or 'just looking at the historical buildings'. As regards the second question, about the quality of Broadway as it now appears, 70 per cent considered the quality to be poor, because of the use and poor state of preservation of the street and its buildings. The rest answered in a range between not very good to medium. The third question, as to whether the interviewees noticed the historic buildings, all replied in the affirmative, denoting awareness of the history and tradition of the place.

Conversely, on the question of the possible pedestrianization of Broadway, interviewees did not give expected answers. Although almost all felt discomfort from the traffic noise, only a few interviewees, the younger ones, responded positively to banning cars and other motorised vehicles. Most agreed with the use of the car, whilst reducing vehicle speed. All agreed with the idea of introducing a lane for bicycles.

As regard the perception of security, people answered in different ways. Half the interviewees regardless of age and place of origin feel insecure while walking down the street. Almost all of the other half feel unsafe while walking down Broadway during the evening, and a small percentage – the older people – feel safe at all hours.

The two questions concerning the restoring of historic buildings and theatres, both as regards architecture and function, had positive answers. With respect to the new functions of buildings almost all the interviewees added their preference for museums and cultural functions in general, while as regards the theatres, they opted for functions not all necessarily connected to the cinema.

Also, with respect to questions 8 and 9 concerning the redesign and enhancing of the street section in different ways, introducing trees and new urban furniture and redesigning the shop windows, almost all people responded positively. Very few people had doubts about inserting trees anywhere along the street. Finally, in response to the last question about creating new urban spaces, such as Biddy Mason's Park, people were generally positive. Some of them specify that they would use these public spaces close to the historical buildings and theatres, in order to better admire them.

Phase 8: Complex map of project and design interventions

As regards the seventh phase, the construction of the complex map of the identity project, the interventions which emerged in the design phases of PlaceMaker concern: improving the street quality; recovering the historical and cultural heritage; enhancing elements of historical, cultural and identity value; differentiating activities; introducing entertainment; improving urban green spaces; virtualizing the path. Each intervention envisages different actions.

The main objective is to preserving the place identity of Broadway, recovering its historic culture while introducing some new elements of the Hispanic culture. With its traditions this culture is protecting Broadway from possible globalized markets which could diminish the peculiarities and specific attraction of this thoroughfare.

The first intervention is to improve street quality. This intervention primarily translates into creating small public spaces within the path. Even though all five actions are devoted to creating a street with place identity, the first aim is to create small spaces containing sculptures, designed green spaces, benches, specifically recalling the history of the theatre and all historical cultural activities on Broadway. These spaces can be built using the street itself, small parts of open parking lots, unused spaces between buildings and so on.

The second action is to widen the section used by pedestrians and use some of the four-lane roadway to create a cycle lane. The whole street section is quite wide and would allow the sidewalks to be widened. This operation would improve the possibility of inserting good quality urban furniture and result in higher pedestrian flows to the street.

The third action, strictly related to the previous one, is to create a single project for lighting and seating. These aspects include different results: light is an important tool both to highlight points of interest (such as theatres and historic buildings) and illuminate the street during the dark, improving attractiveness and security. Seating is necessary both to allow a break during the itinerary, admire buildings, people-watch and in general appreciate the street scene. This should be combined with good quality paving, which suitably matches existing historic or artistic paving and allows easy walking (fourth action).

The last 'improving' action concerns shop windows, many of which have to be created *ex novo*. Indeed, the lack of shop windows in many retail outlets means that goods cannot be suitably displayed: they are often relegated to improvised stands which result in both chaotic visual perception and difficult walkability. The shop windows and a single design for signs and frames that do not cover the buildings would improve street quality and the sale of goods.

The second intervention is to recover the historic and cultural heritage. In this regard, the first action is recovering the historical theatres in disuse. As observed in the various phases of analysis and design of PlaceMaker, the Broadway Theatres have still a strong historical, cultural and identity value.

Different reasons caused their decline, but collective memory of this place has persisted, both with respect to the theatres which are still used for performances and those in disuse or used for retail.

In strict connection with this action, there is that related to the recovery of historic buildings. There are various buildings in Broadway of architectural and identity value. The recovery of less famous historic buildings also needs to be carried out. With their Art Nouveau or various forms of Revival style, these strongly contribute to the particular urban character of this street.

The third action is to recover the murals. Beyond the more famous murals representing Anthony Quinn on the Victor Clothing Company building on Third Street and the scenic mural on the stretch between Third and Fourth Street entitled 'Calle de la Eternidad' – both of artistic interest – there are also others, on the side of building facades, representing advertising products or other kinds of signs. Albeit less impressive, such murals testify to the history of the place and could be profitably restored.

The fourth action is to restore the old theatre building and shop signs. The latter form part of the history of Broadway to the same extent as theatres and buildings. Suitable recovery of the old signs would contribute to the roots of identity in this place.

The third intervention is to enhance elements of historical, cultural and identity value. In continuity with the second intervention – recovering the historical and cultural heritage – the first action is to enhance the historic theatres in disuse as well as those in use. Programmed maintenance has to be carried out so that the theatres are not slowly forgotten.

At the same time, again in continuity with recovering the historical and cultural heritage, enhancement of Broadway will necessarily include programmed maintenance of historic buildings, both of the most famous such as the Eastern Columbia or the Bradbury Building – already in a good state of maintenance – and the others, most of them hidden by chaotic shop signs or in a state of abandonment (second action) (Sepe, 2012d).

The third action is to exploit – through suitable urban furniture – the visual perception of murals of historic or artistic interest. The main murals are those representing Anthony Quinn on the Victor Clothing Company building on Third Street and the more recent mural on the stretch between Third and Fourth Street entitled 'Calle de la Eternidad'.

The fourth action is to enhance the historic pavements, such as those in front of the Eastern Columbia, the Los Angeles Theatre and Clifton's Cafeteria, which are of artistic interest. The new design of the street cannot fail to take account of these historically paved areas. They should be included in the design which will improve the overall image of Broadway.

The fifth action is to enhance colours. This means enhancing the bright colours of the Hispanic culture, which has become part of the identity of Broadway and may be observed in many street details, including shop windows and signs. The bright colours are part of the present place identity and have to be enhanced, using them to design the street more innovatively and more harmoniously. The sixth action is to enhance the creative activities of the place. Beyond enhancing the historic theatres and buildings, it is important to foster suitable activities that will be hosted inside them. These should include creative activitities – meant in its broader meaning – which are the most related to this place, namely the use of theatres for entertainment and the use of buildings for museums.

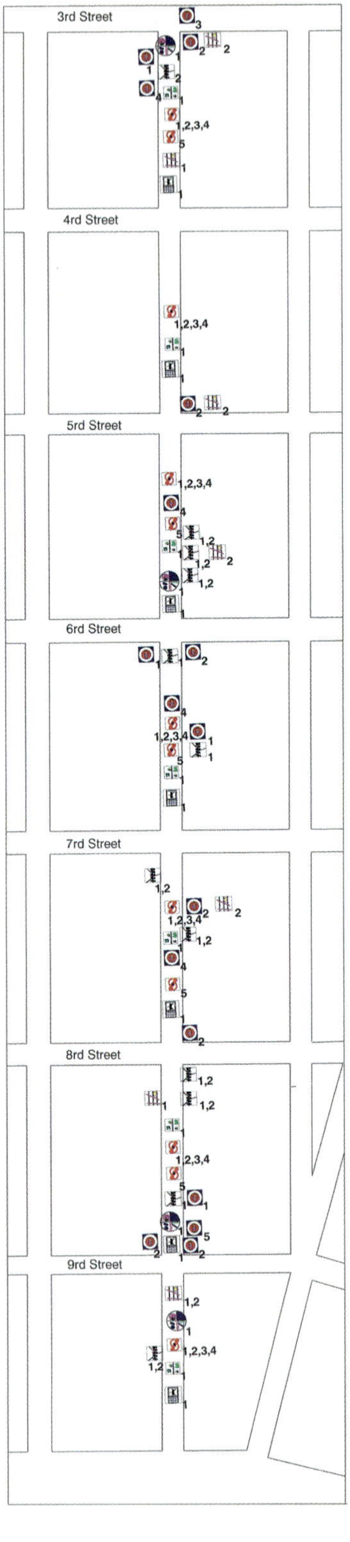

Figure 19.16a
**South Broadway:
complex map of
design**

3rd Street

4rd Street

5rd Street

6rd Street

7rd Street

8rd Street

9rd Street

Figure 19.16b
South Broadway: complex map of design legend

L E G E N D

Improving the street quality
1- creating small public spaces within the path
2- widening the section used by pedestrians
3- creating a single project for lighting and seating
4- realizing good quality paving
5- realizing shop windows

Recovering the historical and cultural heritage
1 - recovering the historical Theatres in disuse

2 - recovering the historical buildings

3 - recovering murales

4 - restoring old Theatre, building and shop signs

Enhancing elements of historical, cultural and identity
1 - providing for the maintenance and enhancement of the historical Theatres in use

2 - enhancing Historical Buildings

3 - enhancing historical murals

4 - enhancing histotrical pavements

5 - enhancing the coulor

6 - enhancing creativity

Differentiating activities
1 - inserting shops with quality local products

2 - including cultural activities

Introducing entertainments
1 - introducing entertainments and street artists devoted to the history of cinema

Improving green
1 - inserting trees or plants

Virtualizing the path
1 - creating multimedia guides with multimedia texts and maps for personalized paths

The fourth intervention is to differentiate activities. The present use of Broadway in many stretches is characterized by the sale of generic goods with no local interest, some of them of low quality. The only shops that sell quality products, such as the historic caféteria and cutlery store, are practically hidden by the majority of generic retail outlets. In accordance with the peculiarity of Broadway, new shops would be inserted, also using currently closed structures, including film set materials, books about actors and directors, and so on (first action). Furthermore, new cultural activities, beyond those of theatrical performances, have to be inserted. These could include the history of the cinema and theatre exhibitions, and experimental forms of performances (second action).

The fifth intervention is to introduce entertainment. Entertainment is an element which, if suitably inserted, could contribute to the enhancement of theatres and the (re)activation of cultural activities. Accordingly, entertainment and performances by street artists should be in strict connection with street re-design and the re-use of theatres and historic buildings in order to create a more lively place with sustainable place identity.

The sixth intervention is to improve urban greenery. The new design envisaged for Broadway should include the insertion of trees and plants, improving those which already exist. Such improvements would have various positive effects, including the liveability of the place and the creation of a sort of green filter from transport smog and noise. Attention is required as regards choosing the tree species in order to both not to hide the theatres and buildings, and to ensure green treetops for most of the year.

The seventh intervention is to virtualize the path. Broadway is a thoroughfare with an evolving place identity. Even though this is related to its history and culture mainly connected to its theatres and historic buildings, new cultural uses would be added in order for its overall image to be improved. The possibility of virtualizing the path by creating multimedia guides in order to foster a wider range of users and visitors who could create their own paths would contribute to the recovery and re-use of this place.

Conclusion

The case study was carried out on a major thoroughfare, South Broadway, in a representative downtown area of Los Angeles. The street is known for its historical theatres, most of which are at present in disuse as is also the case in many European cities. It is one of the few streets in the city that caters to both cars and pedestrians. The purpose of the study was not only to ascertain whether the present identity of this place is still related to the history of the theatres involved, but also to determine how to halt its decline and think in terms of urban re-design, enhancing identity, improving the quality of its image, walkability and urban safety.

With respect to the experiment itself, the second phase presented some problems understanding which buildings were the former theatres. While the architecture and signs of some of them were very evident, others were hidden by new shop signs which obscured the original theatre signs. Likewise, the historical buildings were often hidden from view due to the presence of shops at street level with wares often displayed outside, or in other cases due to the closure of many retail outlets. Furthermore, the historical paving passed unobserved.

Indeed, the interest in this place lies precisely in its history – related to its theatres and use for film locations – and, from some angles, in the colours and music introduced by the Hispanics who work there. Almost all the interviewees wanted cinemas brought back to Broadway by renovating the old theatres, and the historical buildings restored and enhanced. Further, in response to the question concerning the symbol of Broadway, almost all mentioned the theatres or historical buildings in general: most of the interviewees wanted museums or, in general, cultural functions in the historical buildings, with the theatres staging cultural events not necessarily connected to the cinema.

Several urban and architectural details, such as the historical signs, murals and pavements, if appropriately included in a new design, could enhance the overall beauty of this street, encouraging roots to be established among both locals and tourists. The central position within downtown Los Angeles and hence the proximity to various LA landmarks represents an important factor that would ensure – should Broadway be regenerated – greater use of the street by Angelinos and visitors alike. Furthermore, the quiet pace found along this stretch of Broadway is another element to enhance. The street's considerable width would allow suitable re-design to reduce the width of the roadway and widen the walkways, inserting a cycle lane for good measure.

Accordingly, a series of interventions are proposed, namely improving street quality, recovering the historical and cultural heritage, enhancing elements of historical, cultural and identity value, differentiating activities, introducing entertainment, improving green spaces and virtualizing the itinerary. Each of these interventions envisages different actions to preserve the historical memory of the street and enhance the positive aspects of its present use. New public spaces need to be designed, and buildings and shops re-used, following the leitmotif of the history of the cinema.

Part III
Case studies

Section II
Reconstructing place identity

The devastation wreaked by earthquakes, floods and other natural catastrophes occurs on a time scale which is inversely proportional to that involved in reconstructing and readapting the places, their values and sense of identity (Bauman, 2004; Carter *et al.*, 1993; Castells, 1997; Oncu and Weyland, 1997). At the same time, the latter activities bring about a rapid transformation in the movements of people and objects, and in ways of thinking.

In post-seismic reconstruction, interventions carried out with little or no consideration for reconstructing the identity of a place have led in many cases to far greater damage than that caused by the earthquake itself: towns which have been duplicated, whole quarters eliminated, historical centres and buildings destroyed or made unrecognizable, sites intended for emergency use which have become permanent. As Pantelic affirms:

> Urban ambiance, historical heritage and traditional architectural values are frequently victims of earthquake destruction, but very often reconstruction programs sacrifice these values, thus intentionally or unintentionally disrupting the social fabric of the community. Refusing to accept development simply as economic growth, Weitz (1986) states that a 'major reason for the recurrent failures of past development efforts is the neglect to involve values systems in development planning and implementation. The analysis of recovery programs after earthquakes and other disasters too link the many reconstruction programs to the lack of respect for the social and cultural values of the affected community. Two most significant objectives of reconstruction in this domain can be defined as strengthening the local community through active employment of its resources and incorporating the cultural values of the community into the reconstruction process'.

There are three main factors in safeguarding the cultural and identity resources of a place subject to natural disasters: to establish a culture of risk in the population in relation to the historical identity of places; to provide for a conservation plan before a disaster; and to adopt a multidisciplinary approach to damage and assessment.

In this respect the Guiding Principles for Cultural Heritage Conservation issued by the Jha *et al.* (2010) identified some key issues:

> Cultural heritage conservation helps a community not only protect eco-nomically valuable physical assets, but also preserve its practices, history, and environment, and a sense of continuity and identity; Cultural property may be more at risk from the secondary effects of a disaster than from the disaster itself, therefore quick action will be needed; Built vernacu-lar heritage offers a record of a society's continuous adaptation to social and environmental challenges, including extreme events, such as past disasters. This record can often be drawn on to design mitigation strate-gies for new construction or retrofitting; Communities should prioritize which cultural assets to preserve, considering both cultural meaning and livelihood implications, although reaching a consensus may be difficult; Cultural heritage conservation plans are best designed before a disaster, but, in their absence, heritage authorities can and should collaborate to develop effective post-disaster heritage conservation strategies.[1]

What is necessary in order to achieve a reconstruction attentive to all factors is an integrated norm which includes questions related to technical, economic and planning – and hence also cultural – aspects. Furthermore, clearly an earthquake will never reverse a trend in course; it can merely accentuate current tendencies, whether of development or crisis. Economic growth will be furthered, while an economic crisis will deepen. The damage linked to the loss of identity is more evi-dent where the catastrophes and the problems existing prior to the event were greater. Thus recognising the value of place identity serves as a reference point in the reconstruction process both in terms of the wishes of the collectivity and in safeguarding the urban image (Cullen, 1961).

In this section, two emblematic case studies of post-seismic recon-structions are presented: Kitano-cho in Kobe, Japan, an historic district affected by an earthquake in 1995, and Market Street in San Francisco, California, struck by two earthquakes in 1906 and 1989 – the latter specifically occurred in the South of Market Area (SOMA).

The reconstruction operations in the two cities were different, because, in general, each reconstruction follows local rules, trends and particular situations at the moment of the disaster.

In the case of Kobe, most of the large-scale project reconstruction was completed by 2005. On the other hand, as Edgington (2010) asserts, this achieve-ment did not always lead to new development opportunities.

> The Japanese planning system has the advantage of certainty, as in most cases it guarantees funding for infrastructure repair and replace-ment. Major disadvantages are its lack of flexibility and its lack of autonomy for local governments. Local urban planners eager to improve Kobe after the quake found themselves in collision with a rigid approach

to post-disaster redevelopment at the national level that contributed to the frustrations experienced by residents and small business owners, who felt especially vulnerable and disempowered.

Kitano-cho is an historical district of Kobe, where foreign businessmen settled in the late-nineteenth century, building houses that later became museums. Analysis of this case, carried out in the context of the Progetto Dimostratore Irpinia promoted by the Regional Centre for Environmental Risk Analysis and Monitoring (AMRA),[2] involved recognition of the identity of the place following reconstruction, an assessment of the extent to which the earthquake still affects current reality, and the review of possible interventions for harmonising sustainable rebuilding with place identity.

As regards San Francisco, which has seen many earthquakes including those of 1906[3] and 1989, the post-seismic reconstruction was carried out in different stages.

The Community Safety Element[4] identified specific objectives and relative policies. With respect to the topics of the Market Street case study, Objective 2 states:

> reduce structural and non-structural hazards to life safety, minimize property damage and resulting social, cultural and economic dislocations resulting from future disasters. Most earthquake-related deaths and injuries will result from the failure of buildings and other structures as a result of shaking or ground failure. Damage to structures results in substantial economic losses and severe social, cultural and economic dislocations. In addition to the characteristics of the earthquake and of the site, a structure's performance will depend on structural type, materials, design, age and quality of construction and maintenance.

The Policy 2.8 reads:

> Preserve, consistent with life safety considerations, the architectural character of buildings and structures important to the unique visual image of San Francisco, and increase the likelihood that architecturally and historically valuable structures will survive future earthquakes.

Market Street was subject to reconstruction which has mainly privileged the part including the financial district, leaving the other parts in a slow decline, apart from the Castro area. Furthermore, even though present buildings of historical interest are well maintained, the stretch between Embarcadero and Powell is mainly used by workers and less lively during weekends.

This is one of the major thoroughfares of San Francisco, which for its position is related to many parts of the city and is recognised by residents as an emblematic axis. Thus, the objective of this case study was to identify the place identity with respect to the current cultural resources and provide for interventions able to restore the identity of Market Street as a whole.[5]

Chapter 20

Kobe

Kitano-cho

Phase 1: Anticipatory analysis

When one thinks of Japan the first thing that comes to mind is the strong contradiction between technology and tradition that exists in this country. In places
where technology prevails, one notices large infrastructures, skyscrapers,
highways everywhere, bright lights from advertisement posters, the typical background noises of large cities, the smells of fast-food restaurants, and precisely
timed subways, trains and buses. In places where tradition prevails, one notices
instead many minimalist buildings, the use of wood, few noises, a calm pace,
many cult buildings, and theatres for wrestling shows. We also expect that in
many places the streets do not have numbers, making it hard for foreign people
to figure out what point of the street they are at.

As for Kobe, this city was struck by a violent earthquake in 1995, which
caused immense damage, especially to infrastructure, and subsequently further
building collapse and damage due to the fires that broke out in much of the city.
This earthquake claimed thousands of victims. It can be presumed that the reconstruction of the city is still not complete in 2012.

The study area, the historic neighbourhood of Kitano-cho, extends on
to a hill. We can expect it to be much frequented by tourists. Considering its
location, it will presumably offer several interesting views. We expect Kitano-cho
to be an especially distinctive area, completely different from other places in
the city. It was home to businessmen from Europe who built houses here that
were somehow remindful of the architecture of their places of origin. The fact
that Kobe is an international port makes it rather open to other cultures, and this
aspect is also to the fore in Kitano-cho. Finally, we can expect to find signs of the
earthquake or post-earthquake reconstruction.

Phase 2: Denominative and perceptual description

The Kitano-cho area extends on to a hill. It begins where Kitanozaka Avenue
intersects Kitano Street, the main axis of the area, from which all the streets and
paths leading up to Mount Rokko branch out. The mountain marks the limit of
our study area. Few of the streets here have names, and street numbers, while
existing, are almost never indicated on building fronts.

The five surveys concerning the second phase show that at the entrance point to the area there is an information point where one can learn about the most interesting museum houses and buy an inclusive ticket to visit them. Here there are also some souvenir shops and cafés, and many typical Japanese soda vending machines. The many museum houses in Kitano-cho originally belonged to European businessmen who lived here in the late nineteenth century. They were all recently rebuilt. The neighbourhood also houses several apartment buildings of different types and sizes, but all built in reinforced concrete, with an average height of five or six storeys and displaying a rational style devoid of decorations. There are also temples and sanctuaries of different religions. In the museum houses, built by businessmen from various countries (Germany, France, Italy, etc.), visitors can admire furniture and objects from these countries, and purchase souvenirs. Visitors are received by attendants who are often from the country in question and are dressed in its traditional costume. An especially remarkable feature of this area is that the apartment buildings and museum houses are built alongside temples and sanctuaries of a variety of religions.

Table 20.1 **Detail of the denominative survey**

Place	Date	Time	Type	Constructed elements	Natural elements	Transport mode	People
Kitano-cho Plaza	July	12:00		Sculpture of musician Fountain	Trees		Japanese tourists
			Low, medium, high percentage	High High	Medium		Low

Table 20.2 **Detail of the perceptual survey**

Place	Date	Time	Type	Smell p.	Taste p.	Sound p.	Touch p.	Visual p.
Kitano-cho Plaza	July	12:00				Fountain water Jazz music Voices		Rheine House
			Low, medium, high percentage			Medium Medium Low		High
			Non-influential, pleasant, annoying, surprising perceived feeling			All pleasant		Pleasant

The area is densely populated. In the residential zones one sees parked cars, laundry hanging out to dry on balconies, etc.

There is a youth hostel. The most interesting museum houses are in the east zone. There are also some exquisite contemporary buildings on the itinerary leading to the mountain and on Kitano Street, a broad street with a pleasant touristic atmosphere, along which one finds museum houses, souvenir shops and wedding dress boutiques.

The western zone has less interesting buildings and some empty areas overgrown with weeds. The typical artefacts of the globalized world are scarce here, especially when compared with the rest of the city. The most visible among them are probably the satellite dishes on residential buildings and the typical Japanese soda vending machines. The urban decor is of no particular interest. Its most remarkable feature is the manhole covers decorated with symbols of the city of Kobe – the tower, the port, etc.

Figure 20.1
**Photographic survey:
Kitano-cho visit
starting point**

Figure 20.2
**Photographic survey:
Kitano-cho Plaza
with the sculpture
depicting a jazz
musician and the
Rheinen House**

Figure 20.3
**Photographic survey:
Weathercock House**

Figure 20.4
**Photographic survey:
Denmark House**

Figure 20.5
**Photographic survey:
detail of a place of
worship**

Figure 20.6
**Photographic survey:
a public space**

Figure 20.7
**Photographic survey:
a place for weddings**

Figure 20.8
Photographic survey: sightseeing of Kobe from the top of Kitano-cho

Figure 20.9
Photographic survey: detail of Kitano-cho with electricity pylons

Figure 20.10
Photographic survey: some empty places and buildings in reconstruction

Figure 20.11
Graphical survey: sketch with empty place

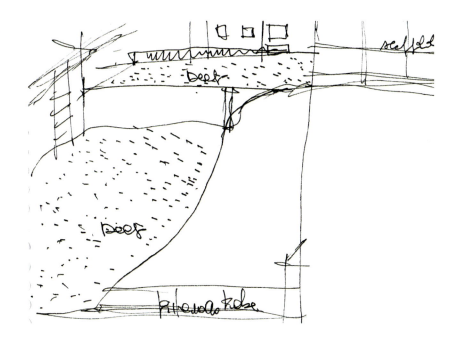

Kitano-cho Plaza is the hub of the whole area as well as one of the most photo-graphed tourist sights. It is circular in plan, with broad ramps where people can sit and linger to take pictures. The sounds heard in the square include the water splashing in the fountain, jazz music broadcast over loudspeakers and people's voices. From this vantage point you can see various sights of Kitano-cho: the Rheinen House, sculptures depicting jazz musicians, and a cluster of skyscrapers on the other side of the city.

Traces of the earthquake can be seen in a wooded area below the Dutch House, where, among the trees, one can see a house that was completely dev-astated by the quake. The route through the neighbourhood is on a slope, with some stretches so steep that they provide strong tactile sensations. Almost all the streets running perpendicular to Kitano-cho Street carry one-way traffic, which blocks out the views. Some streets and paths further up are more level and narrower, with more vegetation and a more harmonious appearance. The paths leading up to the mountain are very pleasant, with panoramic viewpoints and playgrounds. The main sights are the mountain above and the skyscrapers below in the modern part of the city. The most notable acoustic perception is the silence. The only sounds occasionally interrupting this silence are those of pass-ing tourists – almost all of them Japanese and carrying parasols – the fountain, the jazz music from Kitano-cho Plaza, the cries of crows, and passing cars. The most noticeable smells are those of green tea, which is used as an ingredient in ice cream, and of butter, which is widely used in local cuisine. An especially strong smell of butter comes from some kiosks in the first stretch of the itinerary. The pace of life is invariably calm, except for Kitano Street where it is moderate and at times hectic. As mentioned before, few reflections of globalization are observed. Among these, beyond the satellite dishes on houses and the typical Japanese soda vending machines, are the ungainly electricity pylons lining the whole route. In the eastern part are the Shinkansen station, a subway station and a cableway.

This peculiar area is much visited by Japanese tourists and also used for weddings. Indeed, there are several wedding-dress boutiques and some isolated properties hosting weddings and receptions.

The graphic-perceptual sketches were combined with some notes: use-ful elements identified by the graphical survey mainly concern the difference between the two parts. Furthermore, signs of the earthquake were noted. For the photographic survey we took about two hundred photographs of the whole district. The photos reveal unexpected visual perspectives of the Kobe panorama, the relationships between Mount Rokko and many parts of the area, the empty places, and the peculiarity of the businessmen's houses. The selected images show some photographs from our survey of Kitano-cho, sorted by areas and elements. The video survey had the dual purpose of recording both the pace – mainly quite – and the sounds of the area, which were mainly represented by the silence.

Phase 3: Analysis of traditional mapping

The third phase involved traditional analysis of the area at the urban and territorial scale.

The neighbourhood of Kitano-cho is one of the historical centres of Kobe. Foreign businessmen settled here in the late-nineteenth century, when the port of Kobe was opened up to international trade. The businessmen's houses, built in the late Meiji and early Taisho periods (1868–1912 and 1912–1926, respectively), are predominantly in the Victorian or Gothic styles. Today they have become museum houses showcasing the culture of the countries their dwellers came from. There is thus a German House, a French House, an Italian House and so on, fitted with furniture and objects from their respective countries. The foreigners' residences that have not been converted into museums have become shops or restaurants.

The catastrophic earthquake that struck Kobe in 1995 also impacted the Kitano-cho area. Kobe was rebuilt in a short time. Special effort was devoted to the reconstruction of tourist areas.

Our study area is built on a slope and has a somewhat irregular layout. Kitano Street marks its southern limit. From here, several streets branch out in several directions, eventually reaching Mount Rokko, which constitutes the northern limit of the area. Kitano Street, is a strongly characterizing feature of the neighbourhood and its widest street. It revolves around the central Kitano-cho Plaza.

In our urban-scale analysis, we singled out the following elements of interest: Kitano-cho Plaza, a central square, circular in plan and stepped; the paths and axes, the principal of the latter being Kitano Street; and the rotation of the urban fabric.

Places of cultural-historical interest include in particular the museum houses on the eastern stretch of Kitano-cho, namely, the English House, the French House (Yokan Nagaya), Ben's House, the Italian House, the Choueke House, the Yamate Hachibankan, the Uroko House and Uroko Museum, the Parastin House (or Russian House), the Dutch Museum, the Fragrance House, the Panama House, the Rhine House, the Austrian House, the Danish House, the Former Chinese Consulate, the Moegi House, the Weathercock House and the Kitano Foreigners Association. There are also some museums, including the Platon Decorative Arts Museum, the Kitano Museum and the Minato Miharashidai Observatory, an astronomical observatory.

Besides the museum houses, there are various temples and sanctuaries of a variety of different religions, including a mosque, the Kansai synagogue, a Jain temple, and Catholic, Baptist and Russian Orthodox churches.

As regards green areas, Kitano-cho has several green and treed spaces. Also to be remarked is the presence here of the Shinkansen station and a cableway station. Due to its steepness, the area offers interesting views of Mount Rokko and the sea port.

Figure 20.12
**Traditional
analysis: detail
of the Kitano-
cho planimetry**

Kitanozaka Avenue

Kitano Street

Sannomiya Station

At the territorial scale, we highlighted the central position of the study area within the city. We also indicated the area's higher altitude than the rest of the city.

The main axes, besides Kitano Street, are Ijinkan Street, Pearl Street, Yamate Kansen running southeast–southwest, and Flower Road, running north–south.

The area is close to China Town, where there are some interesting buildings, including the Kobe City Museum. It also has a connection with the port, since this is visible from several points in Kitano-cho, although it does not border on it. In the port area is Meriken Park with several interesting buildings and monuments, including the Kobe Port Tower, built of red steel, the Kobe Maritime Museum, and a Memorial to the victims of the Hanshin earthquake.

Among the worship places in Kitano-cho, one that stands out is the Ikuta Shrine, dedicated to Waka-hirumeno-Mikoto, the goddess of ancient Japan. Natural features include Mount Rokko – a very significant presence in Kitano-cho, both as a natural resource and visually – the Nunobiki Herb Park, and the Sorakuen Garden. On the opposite side one looks out to sea.

Finally, one notices the presence of a residential area lying outside the study area.

Phase 4: Questionnaire for analysis

The questionnaire administered in Kitano-cho included six questions, to which we added a summary of answers. The estimated completion time was between ten and thirty minutes.

0) Age and nationality
1) What is your idea of Kitano-cho today?
2) What is the most representative or symbolic place in Kobe?
3) What is the most representative or symbolic monument in Kobe?
4) What place or monument in Kitano-cho arouses a particular emotion in you?
5) What part of Kitano-cho do you prefer?
6) If you could change something in Kitano-cho, what would you change and how?

The interviewees were mostly tourists or museum-house owners, aged 30 to 50. All were Japanese. The language employed was English.

The interviewees showed a certain reluctance to answer, probably because of their imperfect understanding of English, or possibly due to a veiled mistrust or the reserved nature of many Japanese. The few who answered the questions were the owners of the museum houses, who are used to answering visitors' questions. We thus rephrased and simplified the first questions to speed up the questionnaire. Our synthesis of the answers gave the following results.

To the first question the interviewees answered that after the earthquake of 1995 reconstruction mainly focused on the destroyed or damaged museum houses, which were rebuilt as they were, partly because they are the distinctive feature of Kitano-cho.

To the question about the most representative place in Kobe, about 50 per cent answered that it is Kitano-cho, while the rest could not think of a place in particular.

To the third question, about the most representative monument or monuments, most of the interviewees said that it is the Kobe Port Tower in Meriken Park, while for the rest it is the museum houses of Kitano-cho.

To the question about places in Kitano-cho capable of evoking a particular emotion, most of the interviewees could not think of any. A smaller percentage indicated a still not rebuilt part of Kitano-cho where one sees a house covered with weeds showing evident signs of earthquake-induced collapse. This house aroused emotions in them by reminding them of the earthquake. Some added that in the port, part of a collapsed wharf has been made into a memorial of the disaster.

As to the question regarding which part of Kitano-cho they preferred, all the interviewees replied that they preferred the museum houses. Finally, to the question about what they would change in Kitano-cho, the interviewees replied that the part where the museum houses are is fine as it is. Any changes would have to be made where the earthquake damage is still visible.

Phase 5: Complex map of analysis

The place identity that emerges from the elaboration of the surveys comprises elements, which include: the history of the area – foreign businessmen settled here in the late nineteenth century; the natural environment – mainly Mount Rokko; tourism – visitors to business houses which have become museums; wedding sites – reflecting the particularity of the area; worship places – created for different kinds of cults; the dwellings – mainly present in the western part; some signs of earthquake damage; and a calm pace.

The symbols which were used for the complex map of analysis include the PlaceMaker method basic system and others specifically created for Kitano-cho. These concern a variety of symbols related to the different types of place which characterize the district such as: the places of historical and touristic interest, places of scientific and touristic interest, and places for residential and touristic use.

Furthermore, for worship places, we used a square with a circle inscribed in it. The circle is divided into four wedges of four different colours to indicate a meeting place for different cults. For places of memory, we devised a symbol constituted by a group of broken lines filled in dark red, to indicate a break of continuity. The symbol is also meant to evoke the emotional scars left by a tragic event. For wedding celebration places, we chose two rectangles of different colours joined by a circle to indicate union. We used a plain, uncoloured square to designate empty places. For symbols of natural elements such as trees and other vegetation, or crows, we used stylized images of each. We did the same for two other elements characterizing the area, namely, the conspicuous electricity pylons and the typical Japanese soda vending machines (Sepe, 2006c).

Figure 20.13
**Kitano-cho: complex
map of analysis**

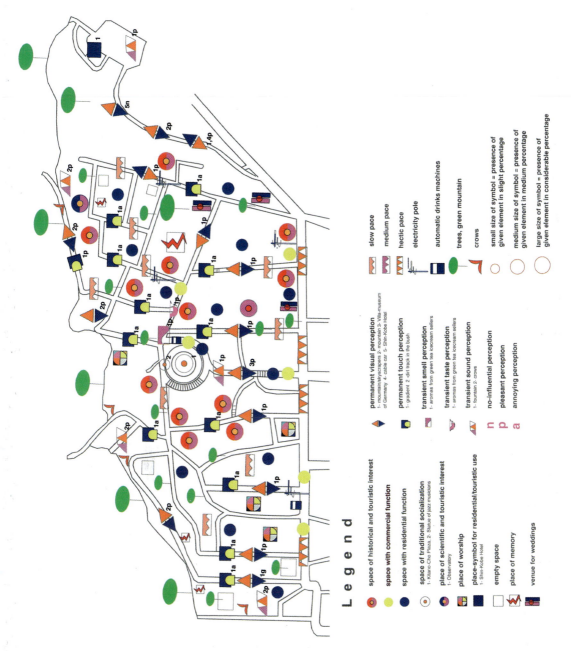

Legend

space of historical and touristic interest

space with commercial function

space with residential function

space of traditional socialization
1- Kitano-Cho Plaza. 2- Statue of jazz musicians

place of scientific and touristic interest
1- Observatory

place of worship

place-symbol for residential/touristic use
1- Shin-Kobe Hotel

empty space

place of memory

venue for weddings

permanent visual perception
1- mountains/skyscrapers 2- mountain 3- Villa-museum
of Germany 4- cable car 5- Shin-Kobe Hotel

permanent touch perception
1- gradient 2 -dirt track in the bush

transient smell perception
1- aromas from green tea icecream sellers

transient taste perception
1- aromas from green tea icecream sellers

transient sound perception
1- fountain 2- crows

no-influential perception

pleasant perception

annoying perception

slow pace

medium pace

hectic pace

electricity pole

automatic drinks machines

trees, green mountain

crows

small size of symbol = presence of
given element in slight percentage

medium size of symbol = presence of
given element in medium percentage

large size of symbol = presence of
given element in considerable percentage

Phase 6: Identification of identity resources

The observation of the complex map of analysis carried out with PlaceMaker has sin-gled out the following problems, potentialities and qualities concerning place identity.

As regard problematic aspects, Kitano-cho, like the whole city of Kobe, was impacted by the violent earthquake that destroyed large parts of the city. The reconstruction of the foreign residences – the ijinkan – in the eastern part of the area damaged or destroyed by the earthquake was carried out rapidly, since the livelihood of the Kitano-cho district is essentially based on tourism. The western part of the area and some places in the eastern part – such as the destroyed house below the park of the Dutch House – still show signs of earth-quake damage.

One thus observes a lack of continuity between the western and the east-ern parts. Indeed, Kitano-cho appears to be divided into two parts. One, although pleasant, is built only for the tourists and comes across as somewhat phoney, as if crystallized in time. The western part of the district, instead, is mainly used for dwellings, but appears extraneous to the rest of the area and almost, as it were, 'on hold', due to the presence of several empty lots overgrown with weeds and buildings under construction. Furthermore, this part lacks public spaces. The dis-continuity of the neighbourhood's urban fabric, due to the gaps in it, is matched by a discontinuity in the architectural style and quality of its buildings.

The same discontinuity can be observed in urban furniture and street paving. The electric pylons found in the whole area – as in the rest of the city – have a strong visual impact on the natural and urban landscape.

Finally, the steepness of the streets, especially in the upper part of the district, and the lack of benches make the visit of the ijinkan strenuous in some stretches.

As regards the area's potential, its atmosphere is agreeable and it is much visited by tourists. The tourists, however, are mainly Japanese. Besides, the district has many cult places, and is hence also visited for reasons connected to people's religion.

The buildings under construction and the gaps in the urban fabric are as much an opportunity as they are a problem, as they could be used to restore the continuity of the two parts of Kitano-cho and, at the same time, create public spaces and interesting buildings for both the locals and foreign tourists.

Kitano-cho also has a cableway station. Its narrow boundary with Mount Rokko is an interesting factor, both from a natural and a perceptual standpoint. Its connection to the routes used to visit the foreigners' residences could be improved.

Kitano-cho's connection with other places of interest, such as China Town and the port – the latter, while not actually near, is visible from many spots in the neighbourhood – is another element to be taken into account in a broad project for the improvement and thematisation of Kitano-cho.

As to quality, the museum houses are one-of-a-kind attractions. They are complemented by several museums. The presence of worship places for many religions makes the area interesting for different kinds of visitors.

Kitano-cho Plaza is a place for socialization for many tourists who come to watch the performances staged there or have their picture taken next to the statue of the jazz musician.

Because of the narrowness of many streets and the small size of houses, the scale of the place is very human.

The peculiar qualities of Kitano-cho are also appreciated by the people who choose to get married here. Thus, the neighbourhood has several wedding dress boutiques and places for the celebration of marriages.

In the district one observes many treed and green spaces, as well as perceiving the strong presence of the adjoining Mount Rokko. There is also a playground.

Several spots in Kitano-cho offer views of the whole city all the way to the sea, including some especially interesting ones.

The pace as a rule is calm. The eastern part, in particular, provides an agreeable atmosphere for a stroll.

Phase 7: Questionnaire for planning

Phase 7 involved the administration of a questionnaire about possible actions to be undertaken to improve the neighbourhood.

1) What do you think of the quality of this place?
2) Why do you come to this place?
3) What do you think about the idea of implementing a plan for Kitano-cho that will also improve its western part?
4) What about creating public spaces for residents as well as tourists, partly exploiting the still not reconstructed areas?
5) What about creating a memorial of the earthquake in Kitano-cho?
6) What about improving the integration of Mount Rokko with Kitano-cho?
7) What about creating cultural spaces providing information about the history of Kitano-cho as a means to draw more visitors from other countries?

We interviewed users of the place and people who work at the museum houses. As in the case of the analysis questionnaire, it was mostly the people who work in the museum houses who answered the questions. The questionnaire includes seven questions based on considerations that had come up in the sixth phase, where we singled out Kitano-cho's identity resources. The interviewees were aged 30 to 50 and all Japanese. The questionnaire was in English.

To the first question, about the quality of Kitano-cho, almost all the interviewees answered positively, mentioning both the museum houses and the presence of restaurants and cafés offering opportunities for a pleasant break. The few who did not answer positively did not express any judgement about the quality of Kitano-cho.

To the question about their reason for coming to Kitano-cho, most of the interviewees answered that they came here to work, being employed at the museum houses. The rest answered that they were tourists.

As to the third question, regarding the implementing of a project also taking account of the western part of Kitano-cho, where the earthquake has left its most evident traces, the interviewees answered positively. Some mentioned that some traces of the earthquake are still to be seen in the eastern part, too.

As to the fourth question, about the creation of public spaces for residents rather than just for tourists, half of the interviewees answered that they thought it would be a good idea, while the rest, had no answer to offer.

To the question about the building of a memorial in Kitano-cho, most of the interviewees answered positively. Many mentioned the already existing monument at the port of Kobe.

As to the sixth question, about the integration of Mount Rokko with Kitano-cho, all the interviewees showed a strong interest in the mountain as a symbolic place in Kobe, and answered positively, since they consider Mount Rokko to be already strongly connected to Kitano-cho, not because it borders on it, but as a natural presence dominating the neighbourhood.

To the last question, about the creation of places that could make Kitano-cho more attractive to non-Japanese visitors, the interviewees who work in the museum houses answered positively. The rest had no answer to offer, but said they would have been interested in a museum about the history of Kitano-cho and Mount Rokko.

Phase 8: Complex map of project and design interventions

The recommendations for the completion of the reconstruction of Kitano-cho take into account the different requirements of users and the specific characteristics of the place.

The first intervention to be undertaken is to realise urban continuity through a general improvement plan for the whole district of Kitano-cho.

One of the first things one notices about the neighbourhood of Kitano-cho is that it is divided into two parts, a mainly residential one to the west and a mainly touristic one to the east, although the latter part does have some residential buildings. The two parts do not seem to interact. There is thus a discontinuity both in the use of the place and in its quality, which is inferior in the residential part. This results in a trend towards the creation of a crystallized place, as in the case of the zone where the museum houses are, which is mainly used by Japanese tourists.

The first action to be taken is to introduce cultural activities in the buildings under reconstruction that will draw tourists or non-resident locals to the western part of the neighbourhood. Some of the most interesting uses for these buildings would be as museums, university buildings and libraries. Furthermore, traditional street entertainments could be organized not only in the Kitano-cho Plaza but also in other less utilized places of the district.

The second action is to introduce a single street paving design for all of Kitano-cho, and provide urban furniture and benches along the routes through the neighbourhood, especially in the western area. This would make the continuity of the place more visible to its users and would allow opportunities for stopping, resting – an important consideration when we think of the steepness of the north–south streets – and admiring the houses and landscape.

The second intervention is to complete reconstruction, especially in the western zone. This intervention should go hand in hand with the first. The reconstruction should be carried out according to a master plan aimed at improving the whole district of Kitano-cho. The post-earthquake reconstruction completed the museum houses and other buildings of cultural and touristic interest. In the study area one can still observe traces of earthquake damage. One of the most emblematic lies below the Dutch House in the eastern part. There are several buildings under reconstruction and empty lots overgrown with weeds, especially in the western part.

The first action is thus to reconstruct the buildings to restore their original functions or create new ones. The second action is to create new spaces or buildings in the empty lots to make the western part of the Kitano-cho district more attractive.

The third intervention is to improve urban attractivity. The square in Kitano-cho that is best known to tourists is Kitano-cho Plaza. There are few public spaces in the neighbourhood. Besides Kitano-cho Plaza, there is a playground near the Dutch House. The first action is to create public spaces for residents, especially in the western part. Residents do not use Kitano-cho much, since the place is mainly designed for tourism. The second action is to create public spaces in the eastern area, especially around the earthquake memorial – to be created as our fourth action – so as to obtain a space that is not only pleasing to the eye but also usable.

The third action is to build new electricity pylons with less visual impact on the landscape than the current ones. In consideration of the fact that this is a historic neighbourhood, a plan for electricity pylons and street lighting harmonising with the prevalent style of the museum houses would improve the appearance of the whole district.

The fourth intervention is to create an Earthquake Memorial in Kitano-cho. There are other memorials elsewhere in Kobe, but a new one here would be something the neighbourhood residents could share with the rest of Kobe, improving their sense of belonging. The museum-house area, and especially its eastern limit, where one sees an empty lot and further on a collapsed house, could be a suitable place for this memorial, which would help to make the eastern area less 'crystallized'.

The fifth intervention is to create places of culture capable of attracting visitors from other countries as well as Japanese ones. As we have repeatedly observed, not only is Kitano-cho only visited by tourists, but these tourists are mainly Japanese, with the exception of visitors to the worship places. To make this special place also attractive to tourists from other nations, the first action is to create a museum illustrating the history of Kitano-cho and its principal attractions, such as the museum houses and Mount Rokko.

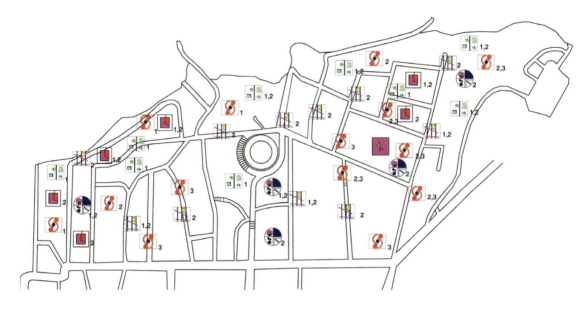

Figure 20.14
Kitano-cho: complex map of design and legend

L E G E N D

Realising urban continuity

1 - to introduce cultural activities and street entertainments
2 - to introduce a single street paving design

Completing the reconstruction

1 - to reconstruct the buildings
2 - to create new spaces or buildings

Improving urban attractivity

1 - to create public spaces for residents and locals especially in the western area
2 - to create public spaces in the eastern area
3 - to build new electricity pylons

Creating an Earthquake Memorial

1 - to create a monument for the earthquacke victims

Creating places of culture

1 - to create a museum illustrating the history of Kitano
2 - to set up spaces for exhibitions

Improving urban green and natural resources

1 - to create or transform the existing green spaces
2 - to integrate Mount Rokko

The second action is to set up spaces for exhibitions, readings, and showing images and films about or by contemporary or past artists from the nations of the museum houses.

The sixth intervention to be undertaken is to improve urban green and natural resources. Although there is no scarcity of urban green in this district, several spots are overgrown with weeds. As we have observed above, these are found especially in the western part of the area. The first action is therefore to create or transform the existing green spaces into play parks, panoramic gardens or gardens for meditation. The second action is to integrate Mount Rokko in the Kitano-cho itineraries. The Japanese see Mount Rokko as a symbolic place but, in spite of Kitano-cho's nearness to the mountain, on which it borders, the neighbourhood is not regarded as being at one with it. An improvement plan for Kitano-cho taking account of its natural assets could establish a connection between the local mountain paths and the streets of Kitano-cho through the setting up of panoramic points, spaces and urban furniture in a perspective of mutual enhancement.

Conclusion

The case-study of Kitano-cho has examined an unusual area, a historic district in Kobe which, like the whole city, was struck by a violent earthquake in 1995 and subsequently reconstructed. The reconstruction focused especially on the more touristic part, that of the ijinkan, which were restored or completely rebuilt.

The first impression of this district was that here the reconstruction has striven to erase all signs of the earthquake. At a closer look, however, it becomes apparent that the reconstruction has consisted of individual reconstructive actions rather than being informed by an overall plan. Thus, in the western part of Kitano-cho there are still several empty lots and buildings under reconstruction.

What we have proposed here is a unitary project for Kitano-cho aimed at promoting its heritage and identity resources, and especially the neighbourhood as a whole.

To realize urban continuity, to complete reconstruction, to improve urban attractivity, to create an Earthquake Memorial in the district, to create further places of culture and to improve urban green and natural resources were the interventions that were identified.

The use of a place for exclusively touristic purposes exposes its cultural heritage to the risk of losing its authenticity and identity value over time.

The lack of public spaces is another element that poses a similar risk. Without places offering residents opportunities for socialization, the difference between the two parts of Kitano-cho may further increase, to the detriment of its liveability.

Chapter 21

San Francisco
Market Street

Phase 1: Anticipatory analysis

The expectations of Market Street are based especially on images preserving the memory of the earthquake that hit San Francisco in 1906, destroying many parts of the city, including this thoroughfare. Images of the damages caused by the earthquake to this important city street are also the point of departure of our preliminary investigation, based on a bibliographical and Internet search. Prominent among our sources are images from films or well-known TV series with scenes set in San Francisco.

To better place Market Street within the general context of the city of San Francisco, we started to imagine the whole city with its distinctive characteristics. A first consideration is that San Francisco's landscape is constituted by its sea and hills. One of the distinctive traits of the image of San Francisco is indeed the high gradient of its hill slopes, resulting in steep streets that, we imagine, will offer especially pleasant views. The Bay must be another place from which to watch San Francisco's skyline with its skyscrapers. It is presumably lined with many quays equipped so as to be also enjoyed in people's leisure time.

The image of San Francisco is also made up of certain landmarks. First of all, the Golden Gate Bridge, whose architecture and red colour places a strong stamp on the urban landscape. It is hard to imagine San Francisco without thinking of its skyline with the Golden Gate Bridge in the background. Another distinctive feature of the city are its historical streetcars transporting citizens and tourists, which presumably create an atmosphere of liveability.

In this context, an axis such as that of Market Street, probably one of the most evident signs in the urban fabric of San Francisco, can be assumed to be of emblematic significance both for the city's inhabitants and for visitors. Its reconstruction must have taken account of its original commercial function, restoring it.

The street will presumably include recent buildings lacking a distinctive architectural style and some reconstructed buildings that survived the earthquake. Finally, considering the remarkable length of the axis and its commercial destination, we can expect it to be very busy with traffic and tourists.

Phase 2: Denominative and perceptual description

Market Street has a total length of five kilometres. It runs from the sea at Embarcadero to the foot of the Twin Peaks hill at Portola Drive. Our study will focus especially on the stretch from Embarcadero to Castro, which is characterized by strong axial continuity.

Considering both the remarkable length of Market Street and the different street grids with which it borders, in order to make the description of our results clearer we have divided it into three stretches (left and right hand): Embarcadero to Powell, left-hand and right-hand side; Powell to Van Ness, right-hand side, and 5th street–11th street, left-hand side; and Van Ness to Castro, right-hand side, and 11th street–Castro left-hand side.

Market Street comprises a carriageway with two to four lanes and two sidewalks lined with trees. Its width remains approximately constant until the intersection with Van Ness. From this point it becomes wider until the intersection with Castro.

Market Street shows strong continuity as regards both its visual impact and functional use, especially in the Embarcadero–Powell stretch. This continuity decreases in the Powell–Castro stretch. Neither of these stretches have a homogeneous urban character. They both show several different characters.

In the first stretch, historical buildings mostly from the early 1900s alternate with skyscrapers housing banks or financial companies. All these buildings are in good condition. In the second stretch, the historical buildings, although erected roughly in the same period – late-nineteenth to early-twentieth century – are in different styles and alternate with recent buildings mostly lacking architectural distinctiveness, and with gaps left by the 1906 earthquake.

Over the whole length of the street, transportation is provided by cars, various kinds of buses, streetcars, the subway, the Bay Area Rapid Transit (BART) and bicycles.

Embarcadero to Powell, left-hand side

This stretch of Market Street begins right after the Embarcadero Plaza, which in the present study is regarded as part of the area under scrutiny, along with the Ferry Building.

The Embarcadero Plaza is a vast square with fountains, sculptures, palms, benches, staircases and cafés with open-air seating. The square is used to hold markets, to sell various kinds of products on stands, for events, and by street performers. The overall impression is that of a partially incoherent and occasionally chaotic place. The Ferry Building, which dominates the urban landscape, is in the Classical Revival style and features a clock tower. Being used as a market place, it is intensely frequented by tourists and locals alike.

Figure 21.1
Photographic survey: Embarcadero Plaza with the Ferry Building

Here perceptions are mainly visual, and include views of the sea, which can be glimpsed from several spots in the square, and the Main Bridge. Looking out with one's back to the Ferry Building, one gets a view of the hill. This spot where one can see the hill – one of the few on Market Street – creates a special contrast with the perception of the sea and the high rises in the background, giving one a clear feeling that the street is an axis. The pace of the square is moderate.

Table 21.1 **Detail of the denominative survey**

Place	Date	Time	Type	Constructed elements	Natural elements	Transport mode	People
Embarcadero Plaza	September	12a.m.		Ferry Building Fountain Stairs	Trees Pigeons		Tourists Street vendors
			Low, medium, high percentage	High Medium Medium	Medium Low		Medium High

Table 21.2 **Detail of the perceptual survey**

Place	Date	Time	Type	Smell p.	Taste p.	Sound p.	Touch p.	Visual p.
Embarcadero Plaza	September	12a.m.				Voices Transport		The sea The bridge The hill
			Low, medium, high percentage			Low Medium		Low Medium
			Non-influential, pleasant, annoying, surprising perceived feeling			Non-influential Annoying		Pleasant

The Embarcadero–Powell stretch is predominantly characterized by skyscrapers housing banks and company headquarters, historical buildings and public spaces. It begins with the eleven-storey Southern Pacific Building, in the Chicago School style, with shops on the ground floor. This is followed, after the intersection with Spear Street, by a tall modern building with a continuous glass facade and a gallery on the ground floor. On the sidewalk is a flower kiosk. Further ahead is a BART exit and then a series of large round marble vases with plants. After the intersection with Main Street, one observes the Matson Building and the Pacific Gas and Electric Building, both eighteen storeys high and in the typical Beaux Arts style. On the sidewalk is another flower kiosk.

Figure 21.2
Graphic survey: sketch of Market Street with historical and new buildings

Following on past Beale Street, one observes a skyscraper with a glass facade for bureaus and a colonnade with stores on the ground floor and, further ahead, a space with flower pots and benches. After the intersection with Fremont Street is another modern skyscraper housing offices, with a glass facade, a colonnade, and bank offices on the ground floor. This is followed by a seven-storey building, also of glass, and also having a colonnade, stores and bank offices on the ground floor. Between the two buildings is a public space with flower pots and wooden benches. This space, like the previous one, appears to be made with quality materials and well kept, but is little used by people.

After First Street one observes another skyscraper, followed by the Market Street Plaza, a public space with benches and green spaces with a curvilinear design, much frequented especially for lunch breaks. It is followed by two more modern skyscrapers with porticoes. The second of these has stores and fast food restaurants on the ground floor. In the space between the two skyscrapers is a small garden and access ramps of transparent material leading up to the buildings. Then comes a low building, presently unutilized, and yet another skyscraper with fast food restaurants and bank offices on the ground floor.

On the sidewalk are a BART exit and some typical cylindrical newspaper kiosks. Such kiosks are found along the whole Embarcadero–Powell stretch, but they are all closed.

Continuing along the stretch of Market Street intersecting Second Street, one observes Neoclassical buildings, seven to 14 storeys high, predominantly with bank offices or fast food restaurants on the ground floor, as well as an historical Boudin Bakery. On the sidewalk is a typical shoeshiner's movable kiosk.

Past the intersection with New Montgomery Street are a Beaux Arts style building housing a hotel and a small public space with greenery, then the ten-storey Monadnock Building in the Beaux Arts style, used for offices, and the angular Hearst Building, 12 storeys high, in the Modernist style. On the ground floors of the Monadnock and Hearst buildings are stores and a café with tables in the open air. One observes a BART stop.

Most of the urban furniture on the sidewalk is homogeneously designed. It includes waste baskets and street lights with decorations, newspaper boxes and billboards.The people who use this stretch of Market Street are mainly professionals and locals, but as one walks on some tourists are to be seen as well. Near the Embarcadero one mostly encounters tourists and locals. Usually some homeless people can also be observed here.

Figure 21.3
Photographic survey: public space on Market Street with no benches

Figure 21.4
Photographic survey: public space on Market Street between two buildings

Figure 21.5
**Photographic survey:
Market Street,
stretch with a
shopping centre and
a kiosk of flowers**

Figure 21.6
**Photographic survey:
Market Street, a
visual perspective
with the Hearst and
Hobart buildings**

Figure 21.7
Photographic survey: Market Street, a visual perspective with the Flatiron building

Figure 21.8
Photographic survey: Market Street, a visual perspective with the Hobart building and skyscrapers

In this first stretch, visual perceptions are agreeable. Notably, there are several views of skyscrapers, such as the Hobart Building on the opposite side and the Transamerican Building, also on the opposite side but on a street running parallel to Market Street. At intersections one can make out the Main Bridge in the distance. One often notices bicycles leaning against trees. Disagreeable acoustic perceptions are caused by vehicle noise. The pace is moderate, occasionally sustained.

Past the intersection with Third Street one observes a row of buildings of different heights, including a 21-storey modern-style skyscraper called the Central Tower and, further on, a skyscraper with a full glass facade. On the ground floors of these buildings are various kinds of stores and fast-food restaurants. Further on one observes a small square, then a café with open-air seating, a Beaux Arts style skyscraper, and an eight-storey building with a large storehouse. This part of Market Street has a more relaxed atmosphere than the previous one. After crossing Fourth Street one observes a continuous row of buildings, five to ten storeys high, in the Beaux Arts style. They are predominantly house stores and department stores, including the higher floors. On the sidewalk is a BART exit and, as in the previous stretch, some bicycles leaning against trees.

Most of the urban furniture on the sidewalk is homogeneously designed. It includes waste baskets and street lights with decorations, newspaper boxes and billboards.

The people who use this part of Market Street are mainly residents and locals. There are also a few beggars, some peddlers and street performers.

Permanent visual perceptions here include the view of the facade of the Hearst Building on Third Street and of the Phelan Building. Transitory visual perceptions include those of the advertisement posters outside some of the stores. Near the intersection with Powell Street, one observes the Ferry Building with its clock tower to the north-east and, on the opposite side, the hill.

Disagreeable acoustic perceptions are caused by vehicle noise. The pace of the square is predominantly moderate.

Embarcadero to Powell, right-hand side

Returning to the beginning of the stretch of Market Street, starting from Embarcadero, on the right we observe a modern reinforced concrete building about 28 storeys high and the Hyatt skyscraper. On California Street we see a cable car stop.

On the ground floor of the modern building are cafés with open-air tables. In this stretch one observes peddlers and beggars, a cylindrical newspaper box (closed), a public toilet cubicle, a bicycle rental space and a shoeshiner's stand with wooden chairs.

Permanent visual perceptions include the view of the hill and skyscrapers; transitory ones include the advertising posters on store fronts. Following on past Drumm Street, one notices two modern skyscrapers for offices, one with a full glass facade and plants and round benches in the space fronting it. On the sidewalk is a subway and BART exit.

Going on past Davis Street, one observes a 26-storey building of triangular shape with food stores, both international and American chains, on the ground floor. Past the intersection with Front Street is another skyscraper for offices fronted with a space decorated with plants. Further on is the Mechanic's Plaza with the Mechanic's Monument and benches. Beggars can be seen outside the stores, and sometimes homeless people sitting in the Mechanic's Plaza. Past the intersection with Battery Street is a public space, the Crown Zellerbach Plaza, with a skyscraper, a low round building for offices and a vast space with lawns and trees. There is a subway and BART exit. Past Sansome Street is a continuous row of buildings of different heights, from three to 21 storeys. The view is mainly dominated by two buildings of historical and artistic interest: the Flatiron Building – a ten-storey angular construction in the Beaux Arts style – and the 21-story Hobart Building in the Neoclassical style. The buildings are well maintained.

On their ground floors are offices or various kinds of stores. In this same stretch, on the sidewalk is a historical monument with a fountain at its base, and street peddlers sell food, drinks and flowers.

Apart from specific public spaces, whose design and furniture changes periodically, the urban furniture of the sidewalk is constituted, as along the other stretches of the street, by waste baskets and street lights with decorations, newspaper boxes and billboards.

The people who use this stretch are professionals, locals and tourists. The pace is moderate.

Perceptions are mainly visual, the most conspicuous sights being the Hobart Building and the skyscrapers. One also has a view of the 345 California Center, a white granite skyscraper with two towers at the top, which lies in a parallel street. Auditory perceptions mainly consist of vehicle noise.

Proceeding past the intersection with Montgomery Street, you encounter a public space, the One Post Plaza, with various kinds of restaurants at street level and on an underground level below it. At street level are a café, green plants and stairs that people sit on, a place for casual socialization. Behind the One Post Plaza you can see skyscrapers for offices. Further on, on the sidewalk in front of another skyscraper, are vases with plants and a street peddler selling food and drink. This stretch is concluded by the de Young Building, an historical eleven-storey building in mixed style. In front of it, in a small open space, is the historical Lotta Crabtree Fountain.

In the stretch after the intersection with Kearny Street one notices a continuous row of buildings, six to nine storeys high, prevalently of historical importance, with shops and chain stores on the ground floor. Here is also the Asian Art Center. Along this whole stretch of Market Street special care appears to be taken in the decoration of stores.

The most striking visual perceptions include the view of the Phelan Building and of the main facade of the Hearst Building on the opposite side of Market Street. Another sense that is stimulated in this stretch is taste, due to the presence of a store selling traditional Japanese sweets.

After the intersection with Grant Avenue one observes an angular building, eleven storeys high, in the Victorian style. It is the Phelan Building, which dominates the surrounding urban landscape. On the ground floor of the building are various kinds of shops and chain stores. One also notices a closed shop with several windows and street maintenance works on the opposite sidewalk. On the sidewalk one observes a subway and BART exit, bicycles leaning against the wall and a flower kiosk.

Proceeding after the intersection with Stockton Street, one encounters another angular building and the James Flood Building, in the Classical Revival style, with stores on the upper floors as well as the ground floor. On the sidewalk is a large gilt clock supported by a column and a podium. This stretch ends at the Powell district cable car turntable – where the historical cable car is rotated to start back in the opposite direction – and the Hallidie Plaza, with BART and subway exits on the underground floor. The Powell district cable car turntable, which lies at the intersection with Powell street, is busy with people lining up to take the cable car. On Hallidie Plaza one can see several street performers and peddlers. The people using this stretch of Market Street are mainly locals or tourists, with a high concentration of the latter near Powell street. The pace is moderate, at times sustained. The general sensation at these times is one of chaos.

As to visual perceptions, the most conspicuous are the Ferry Building on the north-east side and the hill on the opposite side, as well as the street maintenance works on the stretch after Grant Avenue, which also annoyingly engage the tactile and auditory senses. Other auditory perceptions include vehicle noise.

Powell to Van Ness, right-hand side

This stretch begins from the intersection with Mason Street, past the Hallidie Plaza. The first part is characterized by buildings of different heights with stores and fast food restaurants on the ground floor, a continuous row of recent two-storey buildings lacking a distinctive architectural style, and finally a building in the Classical style with various kinds of stores on the ground floor, of which some are closed. One also sees a Crazy Horse venue. From differences in the style of the buildings and stores one immediately perceives a sort of break of continuity here with the Powell–Embarcadero stretch, which on average is characterized by well-maintained buildings and a certain care in the decoration of stores. On the sidewalks are chess tables with several players sitting at them.

Figure 21.9
Photographic survey: Market Street, stretch with no adequate pedestrian crossings

Going on past the crossing with Taylor Street, one observes a continuous row of buildings, two to three storeys high. The first is angular with Classical-style decorations and a caféteria on the ground floor. On the ground floor of the buildings one notices various kinds of stores, some of which are closed. A long mural conceals renovation works on a low building.

Further on one observes the historical Renoir Hotel, a seven-storey building in the Neoclassical style, and beyond it the United Nation Plaza. This square is graced with fountains, sculptures and benches of contemporary design. It is crossed by a path leading to City Hall. On the floor of this path is a round granite plaque with the charter of the United Nations World Environment Day of 2005.

Following on, one observes the Art Institute of California and the historical Orpheum Theater, which dominate the urban landscape on this stretch.

Continuing past Hyde Street, one observes buildings two to four storeys high, in the Classical style or of recent construction. On the ground floors are stores of various kinds, fast food restaurants, bank offices and hotels. There is also a subway and BART exit.

After the intersection with Larkin Street, there is a small public space furnished with a round bench and a lawn in front of a recent low building with stores, offices and a caféteria. Following up is a skyscraper for bank offices.

Past Polk Street are three to five-storey buildings, mostly of recent construction. On their ground floors are closed stores and pubs, some with graffiti.

Urban furniture is sparser compared to the Embarcadero–Powell stretch. This stretch is also used by fewer people than the Embarcadero–Powell stretch. One mainly encounters locals and a few homeless people.

The pace of the square is calm to moderate.

Vehicles are the same as in the previous stretch, but there are some short stretches of bicycle lane and cyclists which can be seen on the sidewalks. Here street crossings are very wide, detracting from the sense of continuity of Market Street.

The urban green is mainly constituted by trees, which are found along the whole length of the street.

As to visual perceptions, notable sights include some artistic graffiti on the stretch past Taylor Street and other graffiti on a building past the intersection with Polk Street. Among other remarkable sights are the view of City Hall from the United Nations Plaza, that of the Hibernia Bank in the Beaux Arts style past the intersection with Jones Street, and that of the hill past the intersection with Polk Street. The most noticeable sound is that of the water of the fountains on the United Nations Plaza.

Van Ness to Castro, right-hand side

This stretch features a non-continuous row of buildings, one to seven storeys high, mainly of recent construction, except in its final part where they are characterized by a Neoclassical style. Among the buildings are two open parking lots. The ground floors are used for various kinds of stores, an art gallery and an antiquarian store. At the corner of a building one notices a street vendor selling flowers. There is also a subway stop.

Past the intersection with Franklin Street one observes a low closed building followed by a four-storey building with an Art Deco object store on the ground floor. Following on, past Rose Street comes a row of buildings, two to six storeys high, predominantly housing restaurants and hotels. Among these, the Gaffney Building in the Renaissance Revival style stands out especially.

Past the intersection with Gough Street is a continuous row of recent buildings, one or two storeys high, used as offices or stores. This stretch is concluded with an unused fenced space with uncultivated vegetation.

The stretch of Market Street after Octavia Boulevard features a Victorian style building next to a contemporary glassed one housing the Charles M. Holmes Campus of the Center. Next comes a large empty fenced space with land and uncultivated vegetation, and several three to four-storey buildings in the Victorian style, with stores on the ground floor.

Past the intersection with Laguna Street one observes a seven-storey building in the Revival style, with stores on the ground floor, followed by low recently constructed buildings for offices and stores. The stretch ends with a gas station and a parking lot.

Going on, the stretch from Duboce Street to Church Street is occupied by a large parking lot and a low recent building housing a department store. In this stretch there is a centre walk with palms in the middle of the carriageway.

After Church Street, Market Street is mainly characterized by a pleasant row of buildings in the Victorian style, or more recent but drawing on that style. They are mainly used as hotels and restaurants. Among these buildings are some parking spaces and at the end of the stretch an unpaved and unused fenced space.

After the intersection with Sanchez Street are some low recent buildings, followed by a row of Victorian-style buildings whose ground floors are mostly occupied by restaurants. At the beginning of this stretch one observes a flower vendor on the sidewalk.

Past the intersection with Noe Street and all the way to the end of the area under scrutiny, which ends with Castro Street, Market Street features buildings of various heights – from one to five storeys – and different styles – recent, Revival, Victorian. At the ground floor of the buildings are offices, restaurants and stores.

In the Van Ness–Castro stretch examined above, houses in the Revival or Victorian style are mainly in good condition and the ground-floor stores are carefully decorated. Although one loses the axis-sense in this stretch, in some parts of it there is an agreeable atmosphere. The initial part, instead, has an unstructured feeling to it. There is in general little urban furniture.

The pace is mainly calm, except at the intersections with Octavia Street and Noe Street, where it becomes sustained.

Here the carriageway becomes wider and the sidewalks narrower. The people who use this stretch of Market Street are mainly residents and tourists. Some homeless can be seen at the beginning of the stretch.

Transportation is the same as on the rest of Market Street, with a prevalence of cars, partly because this stretch intersects a freeway. As in the previous stretch, pedestrian crossings are very wide. Visual perception is stimulated by the coloured graffiti and writings on a building past the intersection with Van Ness Street, and by the hill and trees on other streets intersecting Market Street, which become increasingly visible as one approaches the intersection with Castro Street. Acoustic perception is stimulated by vehicle noise. Taste perception is stimulated by the food offered by various international food restaurants.

Fifth Street to Eleventh Street, left-hand side

This stretch begins, after the intersection with Fifth Street, with a row of buildings, one to 15 storeys high, of different styles: recent, Neoclassical and Revival. On the ground floor of these buildings are various kinds of stores, several of which are closed.

Past the intersection with Sixth Street is another row of buildings, one to six storeys high, in different styles: most were built in the early twentieth century, while others are more recent. Among the historical buildings here, the Furniture and Carpets building is especially conspicuous, partly thanks to the faux columns framing its facade. The ground floors are used for various kinds of stores, restaurants and hotels. Several of the stores are closed. One building is used as a cinema.

Figure 21.10
**Photographic survey:
Market Street, a
stretch between
Cyrill Magnin and
Eleventh Street**

Continuing past the intersection with Seventh Street, one observes a non-continuous row of buildings of various heights – two to approximately ten storeys – and styles. Recent buildings alternate with historical ones, among which the Odd Fellows Hall stands out with its classical features. On the ground floor one observes stores of various kinds, closed street-front rooms and, in the middle, an empty space fenced with opaque panels. Further on is a large half-round building used for residences and a subway and BART exit.

Going on, the stretches on either side of Eighth and Ninth street are characterized, respectively, by two buildings – a seven-storey historical one with classical decorations, housing a hotel, and a 15-storey modern one with a stepped facade, used for offices – and an 11-storey building housing the San Francisco Mart, which dominates the local urban landscape with its facade and Liberty-style portals. On the ground floor of the latter are stores of various kinds and a few closed stores.

As one goes on, past the crossing with Tenth Street one observes first a fenced space with uncultivated vegetation and then a twenty-one storey 'mono-lithic' reinforced concrete building housing offices, with a portico on the ground floor. On the ground floor are a fast food restaurant and stores of various kinds.

Continuing past Eleventh Street, one observes another eight-storey modern building housing offices. The state of maintenance of the buildings is decent. The pace is, in general, calm.

Over the whole stretch under scrutiny urban furniture is mainly limited to a few waste baskets and street lights. Transportation is mainly provided by cars, street-cars, buses and bicycles, as well as the above-mentioned subway and BART lines.

The stretch is very diverse, especially in its first part, which appears to be the one most used by pedestrians. Crossing the street is easier here than in the previous stretch, as on this side the street grid intersects Market Street orthogonally.

As regards perception, the most stimulated sense is vision, through views of the United Nations Plaza, the reinforced concrete building between Tenth and Eleventh and the hill from several points.

Eleventh Street to Castro, left-hand side

Up to the intersection with Brady Street, this street is mainly characterized by low buildings of recent construction, including one where cars are sold and others housing various stores, one an antiquarian's. Some closed stores can also be seen, and an open parking lot between Twelfth and Brady Street. There is also a subway exit.

Continuing past Brady Street, one observes two five-storey historical buildings in the Classical Revival style, one of which is used as a hotel, and two other buildings, one and two storeys high, with Classical-style facades. On their ground floors are various kinds of stores and a restaurant. Here the sidewalk becomes narrower.

After the crossing with Gough Street one observes two historical buildings with a parking lot between them and stores on the ground floor. They are followed by low buildings of recent construction used for commercial purposes. Past the intersection with Valencia Street, the street begins to slope slightly up. There is a four-storey building with no distinctive architectural character and then a freeway entrance, which causes a break in continuity. Past the freeway and Pearl Street, one observes one to three-storey buildings, mostly recent, with facades inspired by the Victorian style and stores on the ground floor.

Here, as in the previous stretch, the narrowness of the sidewalks creates a livable atmosphere that contrasts with the sense of dislocation created by the broad carriageway. After Guerrero street is a historical building with a facade of small bricks, followed by other more recent low buildings. Between some buildings are parking lots. Here double intersections make pedestrian crossings more difficult. After the crossing with Duboce Street are two buildings, one of which is historical, with a Classical-style facade. They are followed by a vast parking lot. Past the intersection with Dolores one observes a row of low buildings, mostly recent, with commercial activities on the ground floor. Following on, between Fourteenth and Church Street are some three-storey high Victorian-style buildings with stores on the ground floor. Past Church Street are historical two and three-storey buildings, as well as some more recent ones, not used or with stores on the ground floor. Before the intersection with Fifteenth is a large area occupied by a gas station.

Almost all the way from the intersection of Fifteenth to that with Sixteenth, Victorian-style buildings alternate with others that are more recently built, but whose facades draw on that style. On the ground floors are cafés or stores selling special products and novelty gifts. At the end of the row is a movable flower kiosk. Past Sixteenth one observes an empty fenced lot. After Noe Street is a continuous row of Victorian or more recent houses reproducing that style, with various kinds of stores or restaurants on the ground floor. The stretch ends with a gas station. Further on, at the intersection with Seventeenth, is a small space with chairs that often serves as a place for socialization.

There is scarce urban furniture. The state of maintenance of the buildings is decent, or even good, especially in the last stretch, where special care is taken in store decoration.

The pace is mainly calm, except at the intersection with the freeway. In many parts of the stretch between Van Ness and Castro, the narrow sidewalks and low Victorian-style buildings create an agreeable atmosphere.

Means of transportation are the same as observed in the other stretches, with a prevalence of cars due to the presence of gas stations, parking lots and the freeway entrance.

Few people, mainly locals, use the first part of this stretch. In the second part there are more people, again mostly locals, with a few tourists.

As to perceptions, the most stimulated sense is that of vision, through the view of Victorian houses on the opposite side of the hill, which becomes increasingly conspicuous as one approaches Castro. Auditory perception is stimulated by vehicle noise. Tactile perception is stimulated, albeit only slightly, where the street slopes up after Valencia Street.

Figure 21.11
Photographic survey: Market Street, a stretch with shops and Victorian houses

As regards our graphical survey, its main purpose was to transform the visual scene, rather than the pace or flow of people, into symbols. The most striking features of Market Street are the presence of different visual perceptions along the whole thoroughfare and the difference in post-seismic reconstruction in the Embarcadero–Powell stretch compared with the Powell–Castro stretch.

For the photographic survey we took about 400 pictures, due to the considerable length of the axis. The pictures are both general and detailed views of parts of the street, seeking to capture all its different aspects. Due to the height of the skyscrapers of the Embarcadero–Powell stretch, the pictures were taken from different visual perspectives in order to better frame the interrelations among urban elements and people. In the Powell–Castro stretch care was taken to capture the many historical buildings which, because of a state of low maintenance, appeared hidden. Finally, the video survey showed a mainly moderate pace in the various parts of the street and auditory perceptions mainly determined by vehicle traffic.

Phase 3: Analysis of traditional mapping

Market Street is one of the most important axes in San Francisco. It crosses the city transversally from north-east to south-west for about five kilometres, from Embarcadero to Twin Peaks hill, intersecting several districts. It was built by the engineer Jasper O'Farrell as part of his plan for San Francisco, as the widest street in the city. The 1906 earthquake damaged it severely. Its reconstruction was carried out in several stages. Today several renovation projects are under way, especially regarding its public spaces.

The street is about 36 metres wide. It has a broad four-lane carriageway, bicycle lanes in some stretches and two broad sidewalks. It is bordered for all its length with one or two rows of trees.

Various means of transportation serve Market Street. Notably, in the stretch from Embarcadero to Eighth Street there are subway and BART stops, while in the subsequent stretch, until Castro, there are only subway stops. There are also buses and streetcars, and cable car stops at Powell and California Street.

Market Street constitutes the limit between two differently oriented city sectors, both predominantly laid out in a grid plan. One runs from north to south, the other is aligned with the transversal orientation of Market Street itself. Where they meet in Market Street, these two sectors result in several street intersections forming spaces or small squares.

Buildings of historical interest observable on Market Street – almost all listed in the National Register of Landmarks or the National Register of Historical Sites – include: the Matson Building, the Pacific Gas and Electric Company Building, the Pacific Building, the Ferry Building, the Hearst Building, the Hobart Building, the Old Chronicle Building, 582–592 Market Street, the Union Trust Bank, 215 Market Street, 801–823 Market Street, 245 Market Street, the Phelan Building, 760–784 Market Street, 735 Market Street, the Flatiron Building, 540–548 Market Street, the Flood Building, 870–898 Market Street, the Garfield Building, 938–942 Market Street, the Call Building, 703 Market Street, the Orpheum Theater, 1192 Market Street, the Furniture and Carpets Building, the San Francisco Mart Building, and 1651–1657 Market Street. They were mostly built in the early-twentieth century in various forms of the Classical Revival style. There are also several houses in the Victorian style.

Historical monuments include the Historic Fountain, the Lotta Crabtree Fountain, the Liberty Bell Slot Machine Site and the Mechanics Monument. There are many skyscrapers on Market Street, including the McKesson Plaza, One Market Plaza and the First Market Tower.

Market Street also has a number of squares, especially on the Embarcadero–Powell stretch. These include the Justin Herman and Embarcadero Plaza, Mechanics Plaza, One California Plaza, Sansome Street and Crown Zellerbach Plaza, Market Street Plaza, One Post Plaza, Yerba Buena Lane, and United Nations Plaza and Fox Plaza in the Powell–Castro stretch.

The urban fabric, although laid out in a regular grid plan, shows different orientations. It is orthogonal to Market Street on the south-west side of the street, while it intersects it obliquely on the north-east side. There is a further change in alignment, although slight, on the north–south-west side, beginning at Duboce Street. On the side where the streets are perpendicular to Market Street, street crossings are single, while where there is a difference in orientation double crossings occur.

The grid plan of the area is outlined by several other axes intersecting Market Street, as well as Market Street itself. Of these, the one that most stands out in the city plan is Van Ness, which crosses San Francisco from north to south. Freeway 101 enters Market Street near the intersection with Valencia Street.

Urban green can be seen at several points. Besides the single or double rows of trees lining the sidewalks for the whole length of Market Street, there are green spaces in the public squares listed above. Market Street also reaches the Embarcadero area and thus offers glimpses of the sea at several points. Thanks to its position and a slight gradient, one also gets views of the hill.

When looking at the city plan at the territorial scale, the first consideration that comes to mind is that Market Street, with its size and transversal orientation, puts a strong stamp on the plan of San Francisco. Indeed, almost the whole city plan connects to Market Street.

The street also stands out for its gentle, constant gradient, which changes only in its last stretch. In this it differs from the many steep streets of this hilly city, such as Lombard Street.

At the territorial scale, besides Freeway 101 one also observes Freeway 80.

Market Street runs through several districts, with many historical buildings and landmarks, and some museums. The part of Embarcadero bordering on Market Street continues eastward and westward to several piers, notably Pier 39 with the Fisherman's Wharf.

In the Financial District, besides the buildings already mentioned above, one has a view of several skyscrapers, including the Transamerican Building and the 345 California Center. Through Third Street and Fourth Street, from Market Street one is within easy reach of several museums, including the San Francisco Museum of Modern Art (SFMOMA), designed by Mario Botta, and the Contemporary Jewish Museum, designed by Daniel Libeskind. Fourth Street also connects Market Street with the Yerba Buena Gardens, which have interesting sculptures and buildings.

Grant Avenue connects Market Street to China Town, with several interesting buildings including the Sing Chong Building. Going on towards the Civic Center, one observes the City Hall in the Beaux Arts style. In the Height Ashbury and the Mission district there is the Castro Theater, along with several houses in the Victorian style. In the Buena Vista Park district is Clarke's Folly, in the Victorian style. The Victorian houses in Alamo Square are also interesting.

As to the squares, those that most stand out in the city plan are the Union Square with its regular plan – also designed by O'Farrell as part of his plan for San Francisco – the Alamo Square and the Jefferson Square.

As to green areas and spaces, the most noticeable are the above mentioned Yerba Buena Gardens, the Union Square, the Twin Peaks hills, the Buena Vista Park and the Golden Gate Park.

The relationship of Market Street with the sea and the hill, which is already very close at the urban scale, becomes stronger at the territorial scale.

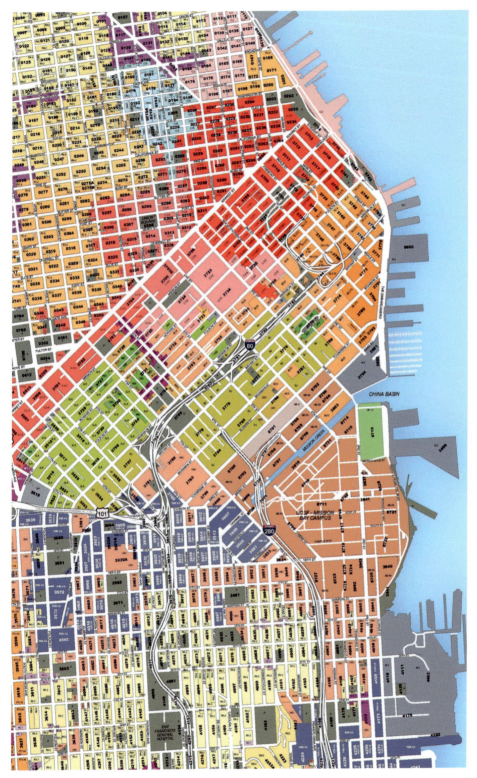

Figure 21.13
Traditional analysis:
planimetry of San
Francisco, May
2012. Detail with
Market Street.
(Source: Michael
Webster, San
Francisco Planning
Department)

Phase 4: Questionnaire for analysis

The questionnaire which consisted of ten questions that are listed below, is followed by a summary of the answers. The expected time to complete it varied between ten and 20 minutes.

0) Nationality, age

Passing through the study area:

1) What elements strike you most (people, things, etc.)?
2) Are there one or more elements that produce a particular sensation?
3) Is there any one element that brings to mind some moment that was important to you for any reason?
4) Are there any things that bother you?
5) Is there any one element that produces a strong sensation?
6) If you could change, improve or enhance anything, what would you do?
7) Is this area comparable to another area in San Francisco or elsewhere?
8) If so, why?
9) What is the symbol of San Francisco?
10) What is the symbol of Market Street?

The interviewees (about 25 in total) comprised locals, workers and visitors. Their countries of origin were the USA, Mexico and Europe. The language used was English. The age of the respondents varied between 23 and 60. We administered the questionnaire to people taking a break on benches in public places along the street. Almost all the interviewees showed interest in responding to the questionnaire.

Before describing comments to the questionnaire, it is worth pointing out that most of the people were interviewed in the stretch of Market Street between Powell and Embacadero, because it is more frequented and people there were more interested in answering the questionnaire. This detail is important, as some of the answers may reflect the fact that the questionnaire was administered in that specific stretch of Market Street.

As regards the first question, about what the most striking elements are, people typically indicated more than one element in their answers. For half of the people, mainly from the USA, regardless of age, the most striking elements were buildings, notably the Flatiron and Ferry buildings. As to the other half, for some it was the street cars and cable cars, for others the homeless, and for the rest the stores. Very few interviewees, mainly from Mexico, were most impressed by the businesses and professionals.

As to the second question, about elements producing a particular sensation, half of the interviewees indicated the homeless people. The other half answered that they were impressed by how busy the street is. A few of them added the adjective 'crazy'.

To the third question, about elements that bring to mind an important moment, this is the only question which all the interviewees answered negatively.

To the fourth question, about the things that cause the most annoyance, for half of the people, mostly from the USA, it was traffic. The other half, regardless of nationality and age, mentioned the dirtiness of the street and the disagreeable smells in some parts of it.

As to the fifth question, about elements producing a strong sensation, almost all the interviewees mentioned the kind of people one met on the street and the traffic.

When asked (question 6) if they would change, improve or enhance anything, half of the interviewees answered that they would have many spots along the street cleaned up. As to the remaining half, mostly composed of people aged 40–50, they said that they would improve the stretch of Market Street between Powell and Castro, since this is where the more typical restaurants, shops and general atmosphere are found. A small number of interviewees answered that they would address the problem of the congestion of Market Street caused by the various streets intersecting it.

As to the seventh question, if this area is comparable to any another area in San Francisco or elsewhere, people answered that Market Street is unique and there is no other place like it. A few – but we regard their observation as significant – emphasized this by specifying that this street is the only axis of San Francisco.

As regards the symbol of San Francisco (question 9), the interviewees gave different answers, and many gave more than one. In general, there were five kinds of answers. A first group of people said 'freedom', a second 'the Transamerican Building', a third 'the Ferry Building', a fourth 'the good weather, architecture, cable cars and the diversity of people', a fifth 'the Golden Gate Bridge'.

As to the question about the symbol of Market Street (question 10), the interviewees mainly gave three kinds of answers. For some, it was the contrast and at the same time the coexistence between the rich and the poor; for others the Ferry Building; and a third group gave multiple answers mentioning street cars and the presence of financial institutions and businesses.

Phase 5: Complex map of analysis

This stage involves elaborating the data collected to construct the system of symbols and draw up the complex map of analysis.

Constructing the complex map of Market Street was difficult due to the many items that needed to be highlighted. Different identities seem to characterize this thoroughfare. Its many components include: historical buildings characterized by both a good and scarce state of maintenance, historical monuments, skyscrapers, a significant amount of public spaces of different kinds in one part and a lack in another, visual perceptions of both sea and peaks, Victorian houses, a quiet – or almost absent – flow of people in one part and a moderate

Figure 21.14
**Market Street:
complex map
of analysis and
legend**

LEGEND

● **place of historical interest**
1- Southern Pacific Building, 2- Matson Building, 3- Pacific gas and electric company, 4- Mechanics monument, 5 -Hobart building, 6- Monadnock building, 7- Lotta Crabtree Fountain, 8- Hearst building, 9- Phelan building, 10- Flood Building, 11- Furniture ad Carpets building, 12- San Francisco Mart, 13 - 1649-1651 Market Street, 14- 1657 Market Street

◉ **place od historical and cultural interest**
1- Orpheum Theatre

◒ **place with business and residences**

○ **place with offices**

◎ **large commercial place**

⊛ **place with multiple use**

⊙ **place of traditional socialization**
1- Embarcadero, 2- Table for chess, 3- Marshall square, 4- space between Market and 17th street

⊛ **place of new socialization**
1- Shopping centre

● **place with high concentration of people**
1- cable car turntable

⬚ **closed place of commerce**

⊛ **public spaces**
1- Embarcadero Plaza, 2- Embarcadero Station Plaza, 3-One California Plaza, 4-Mechanics Plaza, 5- Market Plaza, 6- Sansome Street & Crown Zellerbach Plaza, 7- Post Plaza, 8- Yerba Buena Plaza, 9- Plaza betweem 4th and 5th Plaza, 10 - United Nations Plaza, 11- Fox Plaza

◉ **evocative place**
1- 2005 United Nations World Environment Day event paving

☐ **empty place**

▥ **food kiosk**

▨ **flower kiosk**

▧ **publicitary panels**

▦ **graffiti**

⊛ **historical shoe shine**

⊛ **live statue**

🎒 **hawkers**

▭ **historical mean of transport**
1- cable car

◆ **permanent visual perception**
1- Hill, 2- The Bridge and the sea, 3- Skyscrapers, 4- Ferry Building, 5- Hobart Building, 6- Transamerica Pyramid, 7-Hearst Building, 8-Phelan Building, 9 Murals, 10-Market cinema signs, 11- City Hall, 12- graffiti, 13- Victorian Houses, 14- Cable car

▽ **permanent taste perception**
1- international food cafeterias, 2-Japanes cakes shop

◺ **transient sound perception**
1- means of transport

👓 **chaos**

⋏⋏ **regular pace**

⋀⋀ **hectic pace**

🌳 **trees**

𝅥 **pigeons**

〜 **sea**

○ small size of symbol = presence of given element in slight percentage

◯ medium size of symbol = presence of given element in medium percentage

◯ large size of symbol = presence of given element in considerable percentage

n no-influential perception

p pleasant perception

a annoying perception

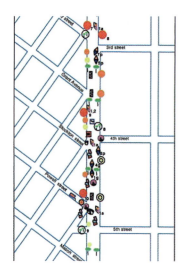

Figure 21.15
**Market Street: detail
of the complex map
of analysis**

or hectic pace in another, different ratios between the height of buildings and street, highway entrance points, signs of earthquakes, and so on. Thus the complex map of analysis represents more than a single place identity, which in one respect could be considered a problem, but in another could represent a good potential for the next stages of design.

To indicate a large store we used the symbol for a store, with a smaller circle within to indicate the large size. For the historical theatre we used the symbol of historical and artistic interest with an empty circle, in order to indicate an historical place connected to the culture of this street. To indicate the traditional cable car, a symbol with two large wheels was chosen placed in a rectangle evoking the historical means of transport. For an evocative and emblematic place we chose a square containing a circle with solid colour in its centre marking the symbolic value of the place. To indicate the symbol of graffiti a stylized image of a wall marked by graffiti was used. For the symbols representing the flower and food stalls we chose square symbols of different colours and contents referring to the shape of the booths and the goods on sale. We also created a symbol for chaos by showing elements of different shapes and colours within a contour of undefined shape to convey the idea of disorder. To indicate the billboards on the sidewalks, we used a square symbol enclosing a drawing evoking an advertisement poster. For public spaces, we used a green-area symbol inside a circle to indicate that here the green designates a place and not merely urban green.

Phase 6: Identification of identity resources

Identity resources were identified through observation of identity potential, problems and quality reported in the complex map of analysis.

One of the main problems of Market Street highlighted by our analysis carried out with PlaceMaker is its lack of continuity. Notably, the stretch from Powell to Embarcadero is very different from that from Powell to Castro. The reconstruction that followed the earthquake of 1906 focused especially on the Powell–Embarcadero stretch, where the historical buildings were restored or rebuilt, new buildings, including skyscrapers, were erected, and several public spaces were created. In the Powell–Castro stretch, instead, several buildings are in a state of insufficient maintenance, and some are defaced by non-decorative graffiti. The discontinuity between these two stretches of Market Street is accentuated by the wide street crossings found along the Powell–Castro stretch, which undermine the sense of continuity and axis.

Another issue is the scarcity of public spaces in the Powell–Castro stretch, which does not allow people to use it as actively as they could. The presence of many closed stores in some parts of this stretch, as well as several empty spaces covered with uncultivated vegetation or dirt floored, give it an aura of neglect that draws several homeless people.

Not least is the problem of vehicle traffic, which is quite intense in some parts, producing annoying levels of noise.

Finally, the most critical issue of Market Street is probably its lack of a strong identity capable of making it as attractive to locals and tourists alike as other places in San Francisco.

As to the potential of Market Street, our analysis highlighted several aspects. It is a broad street with wide sidewalks, except in its final part towards Castro, where it narrows down. The Powell–Embarcadero stretch is much used because of the presence there of the Financial District, the Ferry Building and the Embarcadero, as well as some large department stores.

The square in front of the Ferry Building is very large, but several parts of it are not used or used for stands sometimes arranged in a chaotic fashion.

In a way, the Embarcadero Plaza and the Hallidie Plaza are entrance gates to Market Street. The former has a primary role in providing access from the sea to the hillside. Although broad, it does not appear to be well designed, in spite of being graced by exquisite sculptures and fountains, benches and trees. It is mainly a transit place, occupied by street peddlers with their stands, which also extend into the stretch of Market Street between Drumm and Davis Street. The Hallidie Plaza is most frequented at the intersection with Powell Street, where street artists and peddlers gather.

The Powell–Embarcadero stretch has many other public spaces besides the ones just mentioned. Most, however, are underused, either for the lack of benches or because they are in shade most of the day, or because they do not afford interesting views.

There are several monuments that seem to go unnoticed and are in need of enhancement. These include Lotta's Fountain, the Plaque to Robert Frost and the Liberty Bell Slot Machine plaque.

Crossings and empty spaces on the one hand constitute a problem, but on the other could become the public spaces that are presently lacking in the Powell–Castro stretch.

Various views, including some very striking ones, could be exploited to better advantage. The skyscrapers, the Flatiron and the historical buildings are certainly interesting features in the urban landscape. The views of the Ferry Building on one side and the hill on the other are also remarkable. In the Powell–Castro stretch, too, there are agreeable views, such as that of the Hibernia Bank, that are not enhanced as much as they could be. The proximity of Market Street to several places, such as City Hall, is an important resource, which, if used wisely, would increase the attractiveness and utilization of the street.

In the Powell–Castro stretch there are several interesting historical buildings that are presently underused and poorly maintained.

Finally, our PlaceMaker analysis highlighted many qualities. First of all, the central position of the Market Street axis, which intersects many other axes of the San Francisco grid plan. Then there is the fact that Market Street is the only street in San Francisco connecting the sea to the hills. Furthermore, the street affords easy vehicle transit.

On both sides of the street are well maintained historical buildings included in the lists of the historical sites and landmarks of San Francisco. These lists also include the monuments and fountains. There are also historical buildings and Victorian houses not included in the lists, but which are nevertheless of historical interest. The Ferry Building has been well renovated and is well used, with restaurants and typical stores. Its space facing the sea provides a fine view of the surroundings.

As to the street itself, especially in the Powell–Embarcadero stretch it is constructed with good-quality materials and has mostly well-designed public spaces. Furthermore, Market Street is treed along its whole length and there are several green spots. Some stretches have bicycle lanes. Besides, there are two stops of the historical cable car, one on Powell, where the cable car turntable is, the other in California Street. These stops, besides allowing use of this traditional means of transportation, attract many people.

There are traditional shoeshiners in the Powell–Embarcadero stretch who give it local colour. In the Van Ness–Castro stretch there are stores with special products and various novelties, and international restaurants. If these were incorporated in a more welcoming context for pedestrians, they could increase the street's attractiveness. Finally, there are some museums and theatres.

Phase 7: Questionnaire for planning

The design questionnaire which we administered consists of a ten-point questionnaire concerning possible actions to be undertaken.

> 0) Nationality, age
> Passing through the study area:
> 1) Why do you come to this street?
> 2) What do you think about the quality of this place?

3) What do you think about the overall perception of Market Street as an axis?
4) What do you think about restoring historical buildings in the Powell–Castro area?
5) Have you noticed the historical buildings, the fountains and plaques, and the Victorian houses?
6) What about enhancing different characteristics of the street?
7) Did you feel threatened at any point?
8) What about creating new urban spaces and introducing more green spaces?
9) What do you think about designing new urban furniture in the Powell–Castro stretch in continuity with Powell–Embarcadero?
10) What do you think about improving pedestrian and cyclist mobility and circulation?

The interviewees (approximately 30 in total) were passers by in Market Street aged 30 to 60. Their countries of origin were the USA and Mexico. The language used for the interviews was English.

To the first question – 'Why do you come to this street?' – most interviewees replied that they came for work. This was the answer given by over half of the interviewees, independent of age or nationality. The rest answered for shopping or simply for a stroll. A small number said they were there to visit the city.

As to the question regarding the quality of Market Street, the answer was unanimous. All interviewees answered that the quality of the Powell–Embarcadero stretch is good, while that of the Powell–Castro stretch is generally not. Many of the interviewees, however, added that in the Powell–Castro stretch there are many interesting buildings, stores and restaurants.

To the question about the perception of Market Street as an axis, almost all gave a positive answer, especially the interviewees who worked on Market Street or had come there to shop. Some of the answers indicated an awareness of the historical value of the Market Street axis. A smaller percentage were not aware of how long the street actually is, and thought that the name Market Street only applied to the stretch of the street they were on.

To the question 'Have you noticed the historical buildings, the fountains and plaques, and the Victorian houses?' the interviewees gave rather different answers. While a significant percentage answered that they had noticed the presence of historical buildings, only very few had noticed the fountains, the sculptures and the Victorian houses on the Powell–Castro stretch.

To the question about whether it would have been worth enhancing certain characteristics of the street, the interviewees mostly gave an affirmative answer. Some, especially those who had taken less notice of the street's monuments, replied that they had no answer.

To the question about whether they felt threatened anywhere in the street, most of the people answered that they only felt threatened in the

Powell–Castro stretch. A few answered that they also felt threatened in the other stretch, especially on holidays.

All the interviewees agreed that it would be desirable to create new public spaces and introduce more green. Most of the interviewees added that what they especially would have liked is more public benches.

To the question regarding the designing of new urban furniture in the Powell–Castro area in continuity with Powell-Embarcadero, all the interviewees expressed their agreement.

Finally, all the interviewees found that it would have been a good idea to create a bicycle lane for the whole length of the street and improve pedestrian circulation. Many added that motor vehicle traffic should be reduced.

Phase 8: Complex map of project and design interventions

The final phase of PlaceMaker consisted in merging the data collected during the previous three phases (V, VI and VII) and drafting a project proposal.

Possible interventions to be taken include: reinforcing axis continuity; designing new urban characteristics, enhancing identity; creating connections; creating and enhancing public spaces; improving greenery; and improving mobility.

Reinforcing axis continuity

Market Street is one of the axes that place the strongest stamp on the urban fabric of San Francisco. Walking on Market Street today, while in the Powell–Embarcadero stretch one observes axis continuity, in the Powell–Castro stretch this continuity is lost, to the point that in some places it is very difficult to understand that we are still on the same street.

The first action to be taken to address this issue is to create a continuous design of urban elements, sculptures, etc. along the whole length of Market Street. The second action is to design illumination to highlight the axis from different angles and perspectives. The third action is to plan ways to diminish street-crossing distances at intersections in the Powell–Castro stretch and, wherever possible, to widen its sidewalks to the same width as those in the Powell–Embarcadero stretch.

Designing new urban characteristics

Although axis continuity must be conceived from the perspective of the street, certain features are susceptible of being further enhanced to add to the character of some stretches of Market Street, especially between Mid Market and Castro. Among these are some cultural features such as art galleries and antique furniture shops.

The first action is thus to create aggregations of functions and design new features for Market Street to allow frequenters and visitors to use this thoroughfare more often. The features we singled out with the PlaceMaker method, starting from Embarcadero, include: the sea and the piers, business centres and museums, stores for young people, art and antique shops, the civic and cultural centre and the Victorian centre.

The second action is to complete existing functions with new elements and integrate them with the new functions.

Enhancing elements of identity value

Market Street has several identity elements, and only some of these receive adequate attention, such as the Flatiron, Phelan, Food and Ferry Buildings.

Of these, only the last induces people to protract their stay in Market Street. The first action is thus to promote monuments, historical buildings and historical trades. These include Lotta's Fountain, the Plaque to Robert Frost, the Liberty Bell Slot Machine, the Victorian houses and the shoeshiners in the Powell–Embarcadero stretch. Besides, there are many historical buildings in the Powell–Castro stretch that are poorly maintained or not adequately promoted, such as the Carpet and Furniture Building – the second action.

The sea and the hill constitute two strong identity elements of Market Street, but are only really perceivable near the Embarcadero and Castro. Besides enhancing their actual visual perception – the third action – the sense of the vicinity of the sea and the hill can be reinforced by making them into a theme evoked in public spaces and by urban furniture.

The second action is to provide for the maintenance of historical and cultural monuments and buildings, in order to both safeguard their recognizability and beauty, and their rootedness in the memory of citizens and visitors.

The third action is to enhance visual perceptions. These constitute a part of the urban landscape of Market Street and hence need to be recovered and promoted as much as buildings and monuments. These perceptions include views of the Transamerican Building, the Ferry Building, the hill from the intersection with Powell Street as well as several other spots, the Main Bridge and the sea, City Hall, and the skyscrapers. Other views to be recreated are to be found especially in the Powell–Castro stretch, whose discontinuity and gaps detract from its identity potential.

Creating connections

The different orientations of the streets intersecting Market Street offer a strong potential for development.

The first action is to use the many intersections to create connections with monuments and interesting sites which are actually close by but not perceived as such, as in the case of City Hall.

The second action is to create connections between monuments, buildings, functions and spaces in the Powell–Castro and Powell–Embarcadero stretches.

Figure 21.16a
Market Street: complex map of design and legend

L E G E N D

Reinforcing Axis Continuity

1 - to create a continuous design
2 - to design illumination
3 - to diminish street-crossing distances

Designing new Urban Characters

1 - to create aggregations of functions
2 - to complete existing functions

Enhancing elements of identity value

1 - to promote monuments, historical buildings, and historical trades
2- to provide for the maintenance of historical and cultural monuments and buildings
3 - to enhance visual perceptions

Creating Connections

1 - to create connections with monuments and interesting sites
2 - to create connections between monuments, functions and spaces

Creating and Enhancing Public Spaces

1 - to create public spaces
2 - to make existing public spaces more liveable

Improving green

1 - to add more green in public spaces

Improving Mobility

1 - to improve pedestrian crossings
2 - to create a continuous bicycle lane
3 - to impose speed limits

Figure 21.16b
Market Street: detail of the complex map of design

Creating and enhancing public spaces

Here the first action is to create public spaces, especially in the Powell–Castro stretch, where they would help to improve walkability.

The second action is to make existing public spaces more liveable by adding benches and other structures to facilitate stops and the enjoyment of natural resources, such as natural light, or cultural ones, such as monuments or views of historical monuments or buildings, or of the cable car.

Improving greenery

To add more greenery in public spaces is an important improvement in order to balance the strong presence of buildings in the area and thus make the thoroughfare more liveable.

Improving mobility

The width of the street and sidewalks allows an adequate mobility project. The first action is to improve pedestrian crossings near bus stops, which are presently not receiving sufficient attention. Furthermore, to create adequate pedestrian crossings in the stretches with double street crossings, and at the freeway entrance.

The second action is to create a continuous bicycle lane to spare cyclists difficult cycling amidst cars and other vehicles.

The third action, finally, is to impose speed limits to reduce the acoustic pollution of the street.

Conclusion

Market Street is one of the main axes of San Francisco, and as such is especially interesting for its connections with various parts of the city.

The fact that it is the only city street directly connecting the hill to the sea surely constitutes a huge potential, to be taken into account in enhancement works. The project interventions proposed in the present study are: reinforcing axis continuity, designing new urban characteristics, enhancing identity, creating connections, creating and enhancing public spaces, improving greenery and improving mobility.

We have taken special account of the consequences of the 1906 earthquake and the subsequent rebuilding and development of Market Street. These actions were not aimed at rebuilding the axis as a whole according to a strong and distinctive plan, but only parts of it. Both our careful observation of the street and the questionnaires we administered bear witness to this. People mainly use Market Street in connection with their job or business. Only a minority uses it as a place for strolling, shopping and visiting interesting buildings.

In the Powell–Embarcadero stretch, in spite of the presence of public spaces, one observes a certain monotony, although it is livened up by views of historical and more recent buildings. In the Powell–Castro stretch, places are, as it were, 'on hold'. There are empty spaces, unused stores and buildings, and a certain discontinuity in the state of maintenance, architectural styles, building heights and functions. This discontinuity is toned down only in the last stretch, approaching Castro, where the presence of Victorian houses and quality stores and bars makes the spot mostly agreeable and liveable.

In our study of the whole axis, several features emerged that make Market Street suitable for specialization in different sectors. Starting from Embarcadero, we singled out the sea and the piers, the business centres and the museums, the stores selling articles for young people, the art and antique shops, the civic and cultural centres, and the Victorian centre. These places reflect specializations already present in Market Street or the adjoining streets, but unconnected or not clearly defined. For example, from the Financial District, Third and Fourth Streets provide easy access to several museums, including the SFMOMA, as well as the Yerba Buena gardens.

In any case, we see the promotion of specialization as part of a plan to reinforce Market Street's role as a single axis. Indeed, one of the nodal points is that of continuity, which is clear and perceivable in the Embarcadero–Powell stretch, but almost completely lost as one goes on towards Powell–Castro. This loss of axis continuity depends especially on the many intersections with other streets.

The above-mentioned actions are meant to restore the coherence of an urban fabric impacted by a significant seismic event, where the ensuing reconstruction, although it did not disrupt it, took little account of place identity. The actions we propose share the intent of making place identity the driving force in the promotion of Market Street, complementing the development actions currently under way in this thoroughfare.

Part III
Case studies

Section III
Enhancing place identity

The sustainability of any place depends on a number of factors which contribute to its liveability, quality and identity (Watson and Bentley, 2007; Carter *et al.*, 1993; Hague and Jenkins, 2005; Whyte, 1980). All over the world today, streets serving for the throughput and intersection of vehicles are increasing with respect to those available to pedestrians. As Fred Kent (2008) pointed out:

> Although many began as people-friendly streets that could be shared comfortably by pedestrians and motorists, most have evolved to accommodate an ever-increasing number of cars and trucks. While streets have become wider, sidewalks have become narrower. But no matter how much any street has been widened, it is never wide enough. Every time word gets out that a street has more room for cars, new traffic keeps coming until it's filled up again.

Indeed, streets are space in their own right and have an important role in the public realm. They have to be considered in their three-dimensional characteristics.

> Streets are not just a flat plane on which to travel, but a volume of space, a kind of large 'outdoor room', in which the surface of the street serves as a 'floor', and the surrounding buildings serve as the 'walls'. … James Kunstler notes that 'whether in garden at home, or on Main street, people like to feel sheltered and protected. We're attracted to arbours, pergolas, street arcades, even awnings'.[1]

> We enjoy spaces that are scaled appropriately for use by people, interpreting them as cozy, intimate, or safe. We feel invited to spend time there. When streets have poorly defined edges, large empty spaces, and are sized for cars and trucks instead of people, the space instead become isolating, intimidating, and even dangerous, encouraging us to move through it and leave it quickly, just as the vehicles are doing. Quality, safety, convenience, and interesting destinations are among the factors that determine how people choose to move around the city.[2]

Furthermore, pedestrian-intensive areas, in particular urban, cultural and histori-cal poles of attraction, increasingly bear the imprint of globalization, conveying messages which have developed in an uncontrolled manner and are aimed at conveying their users' patterns of thought and action. The presence of a dense mixture of contrasting elements and perceptions can detract from the image of a city and can contribute to creating urban decline and a chaotic atmosphere, including increased episodes of street crime (Alcantara de Vasconcellos, 2004; Appleyard, 1976, 1981; Appleyard et al., 1964; Fyfe, 1998; Hass-Klau et al.,1999; Urry, 1995; Zelinka and Brennan, 2001).

We present the results of experiments carried out in Oxford Street in London and Las Ramblas in Barcelona, where the process of globalization has already started and the effects on place identity may be observed, and in the Esplanadi area in Helsinki. These experiments were part of a series of case stud-ies carried out in pedestrian or semi-pedestrian thoroughfares in some major European cities. These three case studies are located in areas that are dimen-sionally and geographically quite different, but which share a central position and proximity to the historical centre of the city and represent symbolic places for citizens, tourists and users in general.

Oxford Street is an historical axis for car and pedestrian transit. In Oxford Street, many buildings of historical interest appear hidden by the shop-ping functions, and the annoying perceptions due to the huge volume of means of transport are decreasing the liveability.

Las Ramblas in Barcelona is an historical thoroughfare mainly for pedestrian use, even though the lateral streets are also for car transit. The intensive use by tourists is leading this vital place to lose its uniqueness in favour of globalized tourist demands.

The Esplanadi area in Helsinki, unlike the other case studies, is not affected by problems such as poor maintenance, the impact of globalization, chaos or a clear lack of liveability. The Esplanadi owes its interest as a case study to the fact that, although it has the potential for being one of the most symbolic and rep-resentative spots in the city, it is not as impressive and appealing as it could be.

The purpose of the case studies was to understand whether the present identity of these places is sustainable with their walkability and if there are critical points where it might be possible to think in terms of urban redesign enhancing identity, improving the quality of its image, walkability and urban safety (Carmona et al., 2003; Jones et al., 2008; Christensen, 1999; Forrester, 1969; Forrester and Snell, 2007; Gospodini, 2004; Massey and Jess, 1995). Accordingly:

> Better public spaces bring more people outside into shared activities, and build stronger communities. By creating destinations – tables and chairs near a favorite street vendor, a fountain that encourages play, or public ball courts – more people choose to spend time in the public realm. Well-designed and cared-for public spaces are a source of com-munity pride and often generate economic benefits.
>
> (Bain et al., 2012)[3]

Chapter 22

London
Oxford Street

Phase 1: Anticipatory analysis

The anticipatory analysis of Oxford Street is based on the imagined idea of London and the knowledge of other shopping streets in European cities. This analysis was supported by research conducted with the help of the internet using 'Oxford Street' as a key word. London is one of the most cosmopolitan cities in Europe: the image associated with this city has changed in recent years, becoming increasingly tied to that of an innovative, young and informal city.

The expectations for Oxford Street itself were as follows: it is a major commercial route in the heart of London, with substantial pedestrian and vehicle flows. It is a symbolic place for Londoners and for many visitors, whose function over time has remained unaltered. In architectural terms, there is a mix of both historic and modern buildings in a fairly good state of maintenance. The buildings will be four to five floors high and will form a continuous curtain. Mainly used for shopping, it is very easy to reach thanks to the various stops along bus and underground routes. There are also several fast-food outlets with their smells of street food and souvenir shops catering to different needs and tastes.

In Oxford Street, you will breathe a typical London atmosphere. It will be frequented chiefly during working and shop opening hours, while at other times it will be less busy. It will therefore be used especially by Londoners and tourists rather than by residents and professionals. The pace will be moderate and, at certain times of the day, hectic. The most hectic area will be close to Oxford Circus, the central axis where several roads converge. The perception of the typical British grey climate is attenuated by the presence of coloured shop windows and street furniture. There will be little or no presence of greenery.

Phase 2: Denominative and perceptive description

The description is carried out by dividing the road into two sections from Marble Arch to Oxford Circus[1] and from Oxford Circus to Tottenham Court Road, describing first the left-hand side and then the right-hand side, and showing first the denominative and perceptive survey and then the graphic, photography and video surveys.

Marble Arch to Oxford Circus left-hand side

Our observations/maps start at Marble Arch which borders Hyde Park. On the left-hand side there is an exit from the underground station with a currency exchange shop and a kiosk on the sidewalk for the sale of tickets for tourist buses.

The buildings form a continuous line, are of mixed age dating mainly to 1900 and are seven to eight storeys high; in the first part of the street the buildings are undecorated and in a fairly good state of maintenance. Department stores occupying whole buildings alternate with shops selling various goods, mainly clothing and footwear, and fast food outlets at street level. The signs for the bus stops, for the underground stations and those for pedestrians on the pavements are very clear and recognizable, and become an integral part of the urban landscape.

Signs of different types and sizes and the bright lights of the shops may be observed, bearing their names or products. Further on, a large corner building with a red brick facade, site of a large hotel, makes its mark on the street. Here starts a row of trees with canopy and trunk of average height. Several side streets intersect Oxford Street without breaking, at least in terms of visual perception, the continuity of this route.

The road section is made up of a central stretch with two traffic lanes (one in each direction) as well as two wide pavements for pedestrians, protected by railings close to the underground exits. The paving, mainly the same along the whole axis, consists of slabs of stone as regards the pedestrian walkway, and asphalt on the road surface.

There are three underground stations and many bus stops. People using this stretch consist mainly of locals, residents, professional people and tourists who form a crowd as they go in and out of shops, walking, stopping at fast-food outlets, waiting for the bus and distributing advertising outside shops. Furthermore, there are police officers and tourist guides who provide information about the city.

Transportation modes comprise double-decker buses, taxis, tourist buses, cars, a few bicycles and the underground. Street furniture is mostly made up of the same elements for all axes: modern double-height posts with double lamps to illuminate both persons and buses on the road, litter bins, telephone booths (including some typical red London booths), bus shelters and benches mainly in stone with very linear design.

Perceptions are most heightened in this part. First of all, there is acoustic perception due to the continuous noise made by public transport, in particular double deckers, taxis and cars, which, with their horns, braking, or simply their motion, produce high noise levels, suddenly interrupted when the traffic lights turn to red; steps and voices of passers by in all languages.

Figure 22.1

**Graphical survey: view
of Oxford street with
Selfridges department
store, double-decker
buses and the
Centrepoint skyscraper**

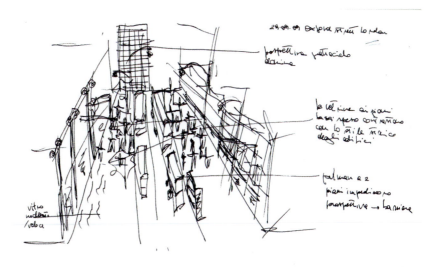

Table 22.1 **Detail of the denominative survey**

Place	Date	Time	Type	Constructed elements	Natural elements	Transport mode	People
Intersection with Orchard street	September	11:00		Historical buildings Shopping mall Lights of the mall	Trees	Double-decker buses Cars Bikes	Residents Locals Tourists
			Low, medium, high percentage	All high	Low	All high	Medium High Medium

Table 22.2 **Detail of the perceptual survey**

Place	Date	Time	Type	Smell p.	Taste p.	Sound p.	Touch p.	Visual p.
Intersection with Orchard street	September	11:00		Smog		Means of transport		Double-decker buses Historical buildings
			Low, medium, high percentage	Medium		High		High Medium
			Non-influential, pleasant, annoying, surprising perceived feeling			Annoying		Annoying Pleasant

Figure 22.2
**Photographic survey:
double-decker buses
create a visual barrier**

Figure 22.3
**Photographic survey:
historic buildings
behind Parklife**

Then there is visual perception, which is pleasing when referring to the turn-of-the century architecture such as that behind Parklife where buildings are in red brick with gable roofs, and again those with columns and wrought iron decorations such as those of the Selfridges department store, and the coloured lights of shops. Visual perception is also captured by the crowding of people and the double-decker buses: while the latter are a characteristic feature of London, on the other hand they impede views of the architecture, thereby constituting a real visual barrier.

The sense of smell is stimulated by vehicle emissions or smells from fast food. Taste is not particularly heightened, nor is touch, given by the presence of a flat pavement which, despite some interruptions due to roadworks, makes walking easy.

The south right-hand side, however, shows more discontinuity. The first part is characterized by the presence of a historic monument, Marble Arch.

After crossing Park Lane, the first stretch of Oxford Street is characterized by buildings of different heights, set back at varying distances, and open spaces. The first consists of an ornate twentieth-century building eight storeys high with ground-floor shops selling London souvenirs. Next, there is a low building, followed by a twentieth-century eight-storey red-brick building, followed again by an area enclosed by a low wall where a leisure centre called Parklife is due to open soon. The space is bordered by mainly turn-of-the-century red-brick historic buildings with sloping roofs, or gabled roofs, three to six storeys high, in a good state of upkeep.

Figure 22.4
Photographic survey: historic buildings with a fast-food outlet on the ground floor

Figure 22.5
**Photographic survey:
a visual perception of
historic buildings**

Continuing along Oxford Street, buildings of the same age and material are observed, some with bow windows and mansard roofs. The road section for this first stretch is the same as the right-hand side as regards the urban design. On the other side, a large number of souvenir shops are observed.

Further on, there are other historic buildings in red brick or light-coloured stone with ornate facades, mixed with modern buildings with architectural character of no particular interest. The neon signs of shops, while attracting the attention of the viewer with their variety of colours and shapes, tend to obscure the historic buildings. Kiosks selling clothing, fruit, ice cream and other goods are positioned at every intersection of Oxford Street with pedestrian side streets. At the end of this stretch one arrives at Oxford Circus. The four buildings in the Circus are arranged symmetrically like a cross and form a circular space intersected by Oxford Street and Regent Street.

The twentieth-century buildings with their columns, pilasters and ornate facades lend character both to the square, giving it an imposing appearance, and to the intersection itself. On the east side towards Regent Street an underground station exit is observed. There are building sites for the redesign of the square, and crossings at some points are congested. At street level, like the rest of the street, there are stores. At street corners free from the building site there are kiosks selling tickets and other products. The buildings here are six storeys high with mansard roofs.

The main perceptions occur at the auditory level: not only is there exposure to traffic noise, but also to site machinery.

Figure 22.6
**Photographic survey:
a kiosk at a pedestrian
road intersection**

Figure 22.7
**Stretch of the street
with a wide sidewalk**

Figure 22.8
Photographic survey: a stretch of Oxford street with contemporary buildings

Figure 22.9
Photographic survey: stretch of the street with a narrow sidewalk

There are also strong visual perception experiences due to both the views of the buildings and the site works, and that of All Saints Church on Regent Street with its circular colonnade.

Tactile perception is stimulated by temporary boards for pedestrians in the square. Here the road section narrows, the carriageway becomes two-lane, and the row of trees begins to thin out. Wooden benches and bus shelters are turned towards the pedestrianised part of the street. Also in this road section, historical buildings in the same style as the previous stretch alternate with modern buildings, with the latter being more numerous. The shops have goods of lower quality than the department stores along the first stretch.

Different visual perspectives are obtained, both of historical buildings which continue in the streets intersected by Oxford Street, the 35-storey skyscraper near Tottenham Court Road on the right-hand side and the tower with receivers on the left. There are clear road markings on the ground to regulate the passage of vehicles, but also to control the crossing of pedestrians. The floor of the platform is broken into three sections, one adjacent to the shops, with a smooth surface, and two of stone slabs.

This stretch of road has an exit from the Oxford Circus underground station, followed by an historic conical building with a facade with bow windows and a sloping, gabled roof. The block which follows consists of mostly modern five-storey buildings of no particular interest or character. All the buildings have ground floor shops selling various goods.

Due to the narrowing of the next stretch, Oxford Street takes on the nature of a street and no longer an axis. This stretch contains historical buildings, one of which is of special interest with its red-brick facade and frieze decoration, followed by a mix of historic and modern buildings. In the final stretch of Oxford Street, the buildings are mostly one storey. The shop signs and billboards are very different from one another, contributing to chaotic visual perception. In this final stretch there are fewer street-sellers on the side streets. The view of the 35-storey Centrepoint skyscraper dominates the road's central prospect. Here, the tension that makes this axis pulsate seems to be slacking.

Oxford Street terminates at the Tottenham Court Road underground exit, with Tottenham Court Road running perpendicular northwards, and Charing Cross Road southwards. As the new underground exit is still under reconstruction, it is surrounded by a building site. The pace is moderate to hectic. The senses that are most stressed at this point are auditory perception, from the voices of passers by, traffic and underground works, and visual, because in addition to the curtains of buildings and the Centrepoint skyscraper, there is the illuminated sign of the Dominion theatre that can be seen before arriving in Tottenham Court Road.

Figure 22.10
Photographic survey: the huge amount of people who typically walk in Oxford street

Figure 22.11
Photographic survey: view of Tottenham Court Road

With regard to the graphical survey, the sketches mainly served to transform the visual scene, rather than the pace or flow of people, into symbols. The most striking feature is the presence of vehicles which tend to obscure the prospect of the buildings and the sudden widening and narrowing of the road, leading to different experiences at street level. With regard to the photographic survey, about 400 images were taken during the inspections due to the considerable length of the axis.

The pictures are both general and detailed views of parts of the street, seeking to capture all aspects of the street which only at first glance may seem homogeneous. Finally, the video survey showed a mainly sustained moderate pace in the various parts and strong auditory perceptions.

Phase 3: Analysis of traditional mapping

Phase 3 is devoted to the traditional analysis carried out on cartography of both the city and territory.

Oxford Street is a mixed vehicle and pedestrian axis which crosses the centre of London for about two kilometres. The road, following the course of a Roman road, was laid by John Nash in the first half of the nineteenth century to connect the royal estates with the streets of Soho. Oxford Street runs as far westward as Marble Arch, which marks the beginning of Hyde Park and its well-known Speakers' Corner, and on the eastern side it stops at the axis formed by Tottenham Court Road and Charing Cross Road. Despite the different ratios between the walkways and the road pavement, the section is largely constant throughout its length.

Marble Arch is an arch in white Carrara marble, also designed by John Nash, with carved decorations which represent England, Scotland and Ireland. The arch, designed for the passage of the royal ceremony on The Mall to Buckingham Palace, was transported to its current location in the mid-nineteenth century.

Analysis on the urban scale shows a non-regular urban fabric and intersections in different directions. The roads that intersect Oxford Street are in some cases deep cuts such as Orchard Street, Regent Street, Wardour Street and Charing Cross Road, and in other cases constitute small roads that can give life or lead to wider areas, such as St Christopher's Place. The continuity of the axis is partially interrupted by Oxford Circus, a large area intersected by Oxford Street and Regent Street, which constitutes a sort of square thanks to the four corner buildings that surround and give shape to the space.

The history of the street dates back to the early 1700s, when it was called in various ways including Tyburn, Uxbridge, Oxford or Worcester Road.[2]

The continuous curtain of buildings that still distinguishes it underwent several facelifts before it reached its current style which, albeit mixed, may be mostly credited to the Victorian period. The continuity in building style is often interrupted by buildings of the late twentieth century. A large space between Orchard Street and Duke Street is configured as a void.

Figure 22.12
London planimetry: detail with Oxford Street
(Source: Ordnance Survey map 2009, © Crown copyright. All rights reserved. License number 100052898)

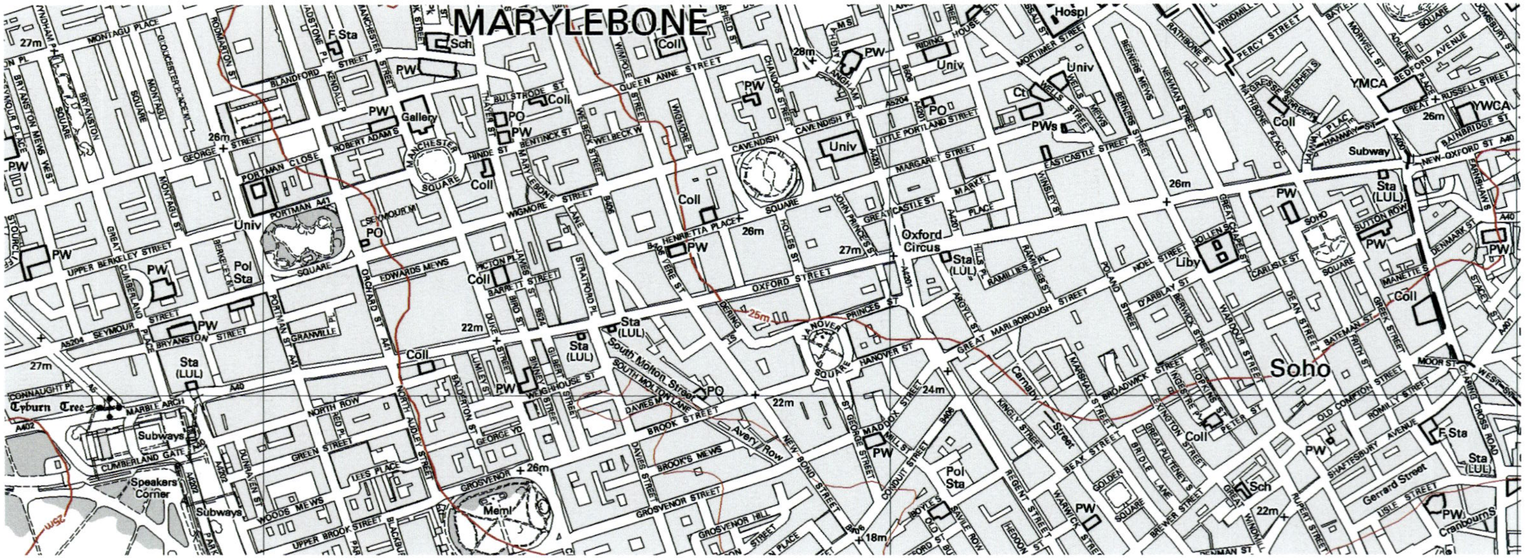

The presence of ground-floor retail businesses is now the main element of continuity along the street front. In addition to Oxford Circus, there are no open spaces except for some squares. There are no religious buildings. The presence of urban greenery is constituted by the row of trees along the axis for more than half the pedestrian pathway.

At the regional scale, we can observe that the presence of Oxford Street in the urban fabric of the historic centre is easily visible despite the different roads that intersect this axis and that seem to break its continuity. The squares that can be observed at this scale include: Portman Square, Grosvenor Square, Manchester Square, Cavendish Square, Hanover Square, Soho Square, Piccadilly Circus, Leicester Square, Trafalgar Square and Bedford Square. Buildings of cultural interest include in particular Marble Arch, the various historical buildings in Georgian and Victorian style, the British Museum and the National Gallery. Religious buildings include All Souls Church which can be seen from Regent Street. The most important urban park is Hyde Park, behind Marble Arch.

Phase 4: Questionnaire for analysis

The expected length of the questionnaire varied between ten and thirty minutes and consisted of eight questions listed below. This is followed by a summary of responses.

0) Nationality, age
Passing through the study area:
1) What elements strike you most (persons, things, etc.)?
2) Is there an element which brings to mind a particularly significant moment for you for any reason?
3) Are there any things which bother you?
4) Is there any one element which produces a strong sensation?
5) If you could change anything, what would you do?
6) Is this area comparable to another area of London or elsewhere?
7) If so, why?
8) What for you is the symbol of London?

The interviewees (roughly 30 in number) comprised locals, workers and tourists. Their countries of origin were the UK, Switzerland, France, Spain, Poland, Italy, India and Columbia. The language used was mainly English for local residents, workers and foreigners, except in the case of Italians when Italian was used. The age of respondents varied between 20 and 50 years.

The points at which we conducted the questionnaire were mainly near underground station exits, often used as meeting points and where people will remain for longer than at bus stops. Whilst not wanting the questionnaire to take up too much of their time, the interviewees showed an interest in responding. In general, we note that people responded by focusing on certain elements that they felt were particularly present in Oxford Street.

As regards the first question, the most striking elements, about half mentioned the crowds, while the other half, mostly young people regardless of nationality, were attracted by the number of different kinds of shops. A small percentage of foreigners, aged between 20 and 30 years, mentioned the architecture of the buildings.

The second question, concerning any element that brought to mind a particularly significant moment, almost all respondents said that they had no memory to be associated with Oxford Street. The rest of the respondents gave rather diverse responses, including some young people who mentioned their colleges and schools.

In response to the third question, whether there were things which bothered them, most mentioned the large crowds of people and noise due to the large number of vehicles that use the road all the time. Fewer, consisting mainly of locals aged between 40 and 50 years, said they were disturbed by the presence of pickpockets. In the fourth question about one or more elements that produce specific sensations, a small percentage said nothing, while a high percentage of people regardless of nationality and age mentioned the site, namely Oxford Street, in its entirety.

When asked if they would change anything, and if so what, most interviewees mentioned, albeit in different ways, elements at street level both with respect to the road itself and the sidewalk. Regardless of age or nationality, most said they would prefer a reduction in the number of vehicle lanes. The other respondents mentioned, with almost the same percentage, pedestrianization of the street and better organization of the sidewalk, while a small percentage were bothered by very different food prices at various points in the road.

When asked to compare the area to another part of London or another city, very different responses were given. Most mentioned places in London such as Regent Street and Covent Garden, due to the presence of many people and shops. A small number of interviewees responded with places in other cities. For example, one Italian compared Oxford Street to Via del Corso in Rome, again because of the presence of shops and people, and an Englishman to Time Square in New York, for the reasons above, including the presence of many advertising lights.

As regards the last question on the symbol of London, the majority regardless of age and nationality mentioned the fact it is an international melting pot. The rest provided quite diverse responses ranging from the Houses of Parliament, the London Eye, the London Transport symbol to Big Ben, from hard work to double-decker buses.

Phase 5: Complex map of analysis

The re-elaboration of the data collected in order to construct the systems of symbols and draw up the complex map of analysis is now carried out.

The place identity of Oxford Street is mainly due to: its old history – perceptible by the many historical buildings present along the thoroughfare; shopping

– which, with its functions, is increasingly hiding the history of this place; the pace which is rather hectic; and the flux of people – often sustained. Furthermore, dynamicity and the melting-pot effect makes this place unique and recognizable, even though the noise and smog caused by the means of transport mine its liveability and walkability. Accordingly, in addition to those of the basic PlaceMaker system, many symbols were created in order to represent the place identity of Oxford Street.

To indicate a large store we used the symbol for a store, with a smaller circle within to indicate the large size. For a store located in a large historic building, we used the symbol just mentioned with the red circle on the outside, to recall a place of historic interest. For the symbol of the 'place-street' we used a sign that refers to the paving and which inside has the symbol of a site of traditional socialization, in order to show how some parts within the road are used.

For the stalls we chose square symbols with different colours and contents, referring to the shape of the stalls themselves and what is on sale. For symbols relating to the typical phone booth, the multimedia information point and double-decker buses we used simplified shapes which directly recall the object itself. A special symbol was created for souvenirs and local products in order to emphasize the presence of globalized goods.

To indicate hawkers selling souvenirs a symbol with three coloured rectangles was chosen, the fan-shape suggesting the seller displaying his various wares. To indicate living statues a circle was chosen containing an irregular shape in movement suggesting the indefinite dynamic of the scenes being mimed.

To indicate a continuous throughput of people of different cultures the basic symbol of a busy pace was chosen, with additional colours suggesting the different cultures (Sepe, 2011).

Phase 6: Identification of identity resources

Analysis and the relative complex map with PlaceMaker indicated the basic elements and critical features in the area, and how to go about enhancing and using it in a sustainable fashion, creating a high-quality public space. From the analysis carried out with PlaceMaker, the problems of Oxford Street which emerged are primarily related to the practicability of the road which is not pleasing due to the perception of chaos and loud noise. Apart from the stress induced by the vast numbers of people walking at all hours and the sound of buses and cars, this road is exposed to high vehicle emission levels. Further, the red double-decker buses often follow close behind one another in both directions and in two lanes, thereby creating a real visual barrier.

The architecture of the buildings is also overwhelmed by their commercial function, which tends to hide from view entranceways and decorative elements in the facades. On the ground floor of buildings there are stores of varying quality and of every kind, in some cases occupying the whole building. At road intersections street vendors alternate with kiosks of different sizes selling goods, food, tickets and souvenirs.

LEGEND

● **place of historical and artistic interest**
1- Marble Arch, 2- Historical building

● **place with offices and residences**

◉ **large commercial place**

◉ **large commercial place in a historical building**

▢ **place of commerce selling local souvenirs**

▢ **place of commerce selling local and non-local souvenirs**

◉ **place of traditional socialization**
1- South Molton Street and Lane

✴ **place of new socialization**
1- Fast-food, 2-Store

🦋 **place of random socialization**

▦ **place-street**

▢ **empty place**

▥ **place of limit**
1- ParkLife barrier

▼ **permanent visual perception**
1- Marble arch, 2- Building of historical interest, 3- Historical buildings
with continuous façade on to the street, 4- Large bright sign, 5- All Souls
Church, 6- Skysraper, 7- Mast with receivers, 8- Dominion Theatre bright
advertisement, 9- Perspective buildings

▼ **transient visual perception**
1- Large advertisement panel , 2- Oxford Circus
building site

▭ **transient taste perception**
1- Temporary pedestrian crossing

◣ **transient smell perception**
1- Smell from fast food or cafeteria, 2- Smog, 3- Parfumes from
beauty shop

▽ **transient taste perception**
1- Typical fruit

◭ **transient sound perception**
1- Sounds from means of transport, 2- Noise from
construction sites

〽️ **continual flow of people of different culture**

〰️ **regular pace**

▲▲▲ **hectic pace**

▨ **food kiosk**

▨ **fruit kiosk**

◼ **tourist bus kiosk**

▨ **local e non local souvenir kiosk**

♟ **live statue**

@ **multimedia information point**

▤ **double decker**

▯ **Typical telephone box**

● **trees**

ﾉ **pigeons**

○ **small size of symbol = presence of given
element in slight percentage**

○ **medium size of symbol = presence of given
element in medium percentage**

○ **large size of symbol = presence of given
element in considerable percentage**

n **no-influential perception**

p **pleasant perception**

a **annoying perception**

Figure 21.13a
**Oxford Street: the
complex map of
analysis and legend**

Figure 21.13b
**Oxford Street: detail
of the complex map of
analysis**

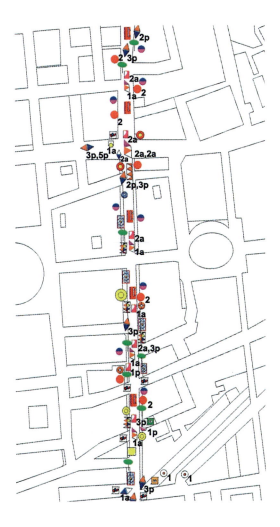

The presence of large numbers of people and the lack of seats and public spaces, as noted by some respondents, make the street a prime site for pickpockets who can act more easily in the chaos of the crowd.

With regard to its qualities, Oxford Street is for many Londoners and people from around the world a very representative thoroughfare in London, linked to the memory of this city. Many of the buildings lining the street are historic, in Victorian style and of good architectural quality, and form a continuous curtain although interspersed with more modern buildings.

With regards to the potentialities, despite the presence of many globalized chain stores, it is still possible to recognize that we are in London. The double-decker buses, the typical phone boxes, taxis and even the souvenir shops make it quite distinguishable. Thanks to its location and function, the street is experienced by thousands of Londoners, but also by tourists from all over the world who can find goods to cater for all kinds of tastes and needs. However, what this road is lacking is its historical importance; its architecture is giving up increasing numbers of elements to its trading function. Given that Oxford Street makes a very strong mark on London's historic fabric, as can be seen by a quick look at any map of central London, this is a fact which should not be overlooked. Looking carefully beyond the visual barrier created by people and vehicles we may observe several potential ways to restore historical dignity and liveability, as well as to improve the sense of security in its users.

Phase 7: Questionnaire for planning

With respect to Phase 7, we administered an eight-point questionnaire concerning possible interventions.

0) Nationality, age

Passing through the study area:

1) Why do you come to Oxford Street?
2) What do you think about the quality of this place?
3) Have you noted the historical buildings?
4) What do you think about making this street or part of it just for pedestrians?
5) Did you feel threatened at any point?
6) What do you think about restoring some buildings to become museums or serve some other cultural function?
7) What about planting more trees?
8) What about to insert here urban spaces?

The interviewees (approximately 30 in number) were passers by in Oxford Street and between 20 and 50 years old. Their countries of origin were the UK, France, Spain, Poland, Italy and Columbia. The language used for the interviews was mainly English for native speakers and foreigners, except in the case of Italians when Italian was used. Also for the project questionnaire it was necessary to find a place where people were more inclined to stop. Underground station exits were those considered most suitable since many people spend time at such exits there for various reasons. The questionnaire responses generally confirm the design ideas for this site.

The most frequent response to the first question on why they use Oxford Street was for shopping. The remainder, in particular respondents aged between 40 and 50 years, responded to work, while a further small percentage of those between 20 and 30 years old answered to meet friends.

As regards the second question, on what they think about the quality of the place, respondents generally said that they could not give a precise answer, as they had not paid particularly attention to quality. For a minority of respondents the quality was good.

In response to question 3, whether they noted that there were some historic buildings, half of the interviewees replied that they had noticed, some of them also added an opinion stating that they were very beautiful or interesting, while the other half said that they had not noticed them.

When asked (question 4) what they thought about pedestrianizing all or part of the street, the majority of respondents answered positively. Only a small portion responded negatively due to the doubt concerning the difficulties of implementation.

As regards the personal safety issue (question 5), they all replied that they had felt threatened at some point.

As regards the last questions on what they thought of buildings being used as museums or recovering their cultural functions, and the introduction of urban spaces, most respondents replied positively, while a small percentage said they could not give an answer. Finally, when asked what they thought about planting more trees, all the interviewees responded affirmatively.

Phase 8: Complex map of project and design interventions

As regards the last phase, the construction of the complex map of the identity project, the elements noted for redesign of Oxford Street take into account the different requirements both of the users and place elements. The interventions which emerged in the design phases of PlaceMaker are identified below. The interventions represented in the Complex map of design cover the road itself, the pedestrian walkways and the buildings.

The main objective is to make Oxford Street a 'place' rather than just a road, and somewhere to walk, stop, or attend a performance or a cultural event rather than using it only for shopping and then abandoning it like any space used for quick consumption.

The first intervention is to slow down vehicle traffic. With regard to the road surface itself, the first action that would restore Oxford Street to people is to pedestrianize it wholly or in part, apart from the intersection with Regent Street. As regards pollution, suitable speed limits could be set for vehicles and the four lanes reduced to two. In addition, a cycle lane should be created: travelling by bicycle is currently very difficult along Oxford Street, and some bicycle hire points should be inserted – such as in other parts of London – to encourage their use. By restricting the area for vehicles to two lanes the sidewalks can then be widened for easier, more enjoyable walking.

The second intervention is to reduce the human flow. Some actions will contribute to making walking more pleasant. The first is to insert benches along the street and quality public spaces in the pedestrian streets which intersect the axis, using Oxford street urban features and 'materials'. In the complex map of design several places are identified, including Duke Street, Vere Street and Binney Street, where small squares could be designed with seating, urban elements and points of historical information about Oxford Street and the historic buildings nearby.

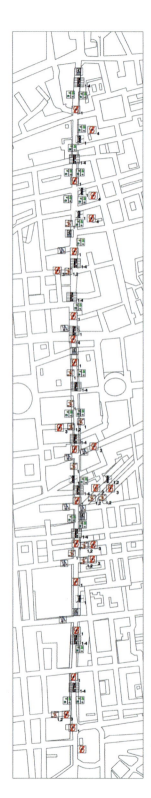

Figure 22.14a
Oxford Street: the complex map of design and legend

LEGEND

Slowing down vehicle traffic
1 - slow vehicle speed
2 - reduce the number of lanes
3 - pedestrianize all or part of the street
4 - add a cycle lane

Reducing the human load
1 - insert benches
2 - create breaks in adjacent new urban spaces

Improving urban attractivity
1 - change the road pavement
2 - ensure programmed maintenance of historical buildings
3 - create new public spaces
4 - insert cultural functions within historical buildings

Differentiating activities
1 - insert shops with quality local products
2 - include cultural activities

Giving identity to what is transitory
1 - create lightweight, multifunctional structures, with variable sizes with a commercial function to replace existing kiosks or stalls

Making more natural
1 - insert trees or plants

Virtualizing the itinerary
1 - Create virtual platforms with information on commercial and cultural activities on Oxford Street and relative locations with the help of interactive multimedia guides on mobile

Figure 22.14b
**Oxford Street: detail
of the complex map of
design**

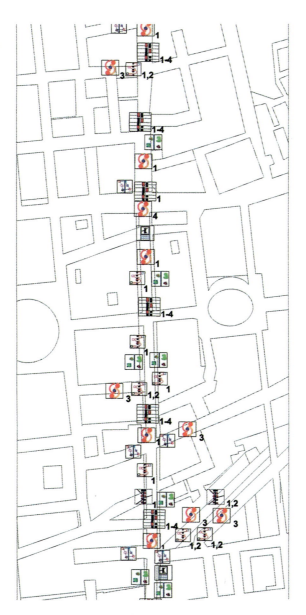

The third intervention concerns improving urban attractivity. Though many are in good condition, several are in a barely adequate or mediocre state. There could also be plans to recover some floors in buildings and convert them to serve as spaces for exhibitions and cultural events of various kinds. In this way people would not be in Oxford Street just for shopping, as evidenced by the responses to the questionnaire, but have cultural alternatives and other interests in the use of this road.

One possibility could comprise the buildings inside Parklife: the events in this space could also be of a cultural nature, stressing the London and Oxford Street history, for example using works by the nearby college of arts and design. The existing walkway could also be replaced by high-quality paving which would be more pleasing to the touch and sight, in order to raise the commercial level of the street and not encourage street vending, low-quality shop windows and goods, and so forth. The use of measures regulating shop signs and billboards would complement the design of the road.

The fourth intervention is to differentiate business. In this regard, there would be space for historic shops stocking quality products that call to mind the traditions in London and the UK, of textiles, footwear, umbrellas, tea, etc., whose history could be explored in specially created museum spaces. The proximity to the college of arts and design is an important element in this direction.

The fifth intervention is to give identity to the transitory. Since the presence of kiosks is in fact part of Oxford Street and passers by take undeniable pleasure in using them, the existing kiosks could be replaced with light ones in structure and form, so that they become an integral part of the route as added value and not as an element of disorder.

The sixth intervention is to improve nature. Along Oxford Street rows of trees are placed discontinuously. The introduction of trees where they are currently absent, paying due attention to the space for their root systems and relative urban furniture to contain them, or of plants where trees cannot take root, would undoubtedly create a more liveable space.

The final intervention is to create a virtual route through satellite media guides accessible with the use of mobile phones. Visitors could thus be steered to discover not only shops but also historic buildings, cultural activities and less crowded parts of the itinerary.

Oxford Street could in this way become a 'place' – rather than just a thoroughfare – of historical, rather than just commercial, interest. It could become pleasant and attractive to walk along, with minimal stress, enjoying clean air and various kinds of interesting activities.

Conclusion

This case study shows that the attractiveness of this place is in its vitality and its characteristic to be an historical place where many elements are present. On the other hand, the street shows various problems. The main issues observed include: the presence of many double-decker buses and the other means of transport, the globalized and non-traditional stores, the mass of people using the site, poor liveability in the area and the feeling of insecurity. In addition, the street is viewed only as a place for shopping. There is a lack of public spaces in which to have a break and sit, and the street's economic and commercial function is accentuated to attract visitors. However, the use of Oxford Street, which has long represented a major historic axis for Londoners, concerns residents as well as tourists.

To slow down vehicle traffic, to slow down the human flow, to restore and enhance historic buildings, to differentiate business, to give identity to the transitory, to improve nature and to create a virtual route were the interventions which were identified.

Indeed, as observed in the questionnaires, the attractiveness of this place is given not only by its commercial function, but also by the undoubted atmosphere of history and tradition, albeit about to be overwhelmed by globalization. People come here attracted by the shops, but at the same time by the added value which lies in the beauty of the buildings which, though at times hidden by shop windows, inevitably helps enhance the atmosphere of this place.

As it emerged in the sixth phase, a greater diversity of activities with the inclusion of places for cultural events also associated with the nearby college of arts and design would certainly benefit liveability.

Finally, designing suitable small public spaces – within the places surveyed during the analysis phases – together with the other design orientations, would have the effect of creating a 'place' rather than just a road, reducing congestion and slowing down the human flow along the street.

Chapter 23

Barcelona
Las Ramblas

Phase 1: Anticipatory analysis

Prior to carrying out the initial site inspection, we were aware of Las Ramblas as one of the city's most symbolic sites. It is a long, broad avenue, with traffic flow along two sides and a tree-lined walkway in the middle; the perfect place for a casual stroll. Las Ramblas bisects the historical quarter and the Barrio Gòtico (Gothic quarter). It is very popular with tourists and full of vendors of souvenirs and local produce. Along the two carriageways we can see some historical shops and businesses. We also expect that there are many fast-food outlets catering for the tourists, producing smells which mingle with the traditional ones and giving an overall impression of disorder. The walkway is on the level, and the paving induces no particular tactile sensations. The trees and the proximity of the sea ensure the presence of birds. The sea does not make a strong impact, or at least does not contribute to the feel of Las Ramblas. The proximity of the historical centre, on the other hand, does have a strong impact, in terms of architecture and the people frequenting the area. The predominantly warm weather, frequently bright and sunny, also influences the atmosphere of this thoroughfare.

Phase 2: Denominative and perceptual description

The study area comprises a broad, lengthy street, Las Ramblas, with a dense tree-lined thoroughfare running down the middle, devoid of public benches except for a short stretch off Placa Catalunya, and on either side two carriageways with wide pavements. In spite of these pavements there is no doubt that most pedestrians are attracted to the central tree-lined thoroughfare, which is thronged with people at all hours of the day and night. Each stretch of Las Ramblas has a name and presents a particular urban townscape, especially in the central section covering Rambla de Canaletes, Rambla dels Estudius, Rambla de Sant Josep, Rambla de Caputxins and Rambla Santa Monica. The buildings that characterize Las Ramblas are in different styles dating from different eras, mainly of a high architectural quality which sometimes attains excellence, although not always in a good state of conservation. For the most part they stand six or seven storeys high, comprising a predominantly unbroken facade along the two carriageways.

Our analysis starts from Rambla de Canaletes and finishes at Rambla Santa Monica, with the results of the surveys being presented stretch by stretch.

In the first stretch, Rambla de Canaletes, the central pedestrian zone is broad. The tree-lined perspective dominates perceptions, excluding the lateral carriageways from the field of vision. A tall structure ornamented with friezes and lamps marks the beginning of this stretch and is used by passers by to sit or lean on.

Then come the access points of the metro station. Just beyond them there are seats on both sides of the thoroughfare where people can pause and watch the comings and goings. Here the pace is quite rapid but discontinuous. Further on there is a kiosk for tourist information and some living statues miming different scenes and street performers, to attract the attention of passers by. In some cases the 'statues' wait for a donation before embarking on their routine.

Table 23.1 **Detail of the denominative survey**

Place	Date	Time	Type	Constructed elements	Natural elements	Transport mode	People
Rambla de Sant Josep	May	10:00		Flower stalls	Trees		Tourists Living statues
			Low, medium, high percentage	Medium	Medium		High Medium

Table 23.2 **Detail of the perceptual survey**

Place	Date	Time	Type	Smell p.	Taste p.	Sound p.	Touch p.	Visual p.
Rambla de Sant Josep	May	10:00			Flowers	Voices of people		Perspective of people Historical buildings
			Low, medium, high percentage		Medium	Medium		High Low
			Non-influential, pleasant, annoying, surprising perceived feeling		Pleasant	Non-influential		Annoying Pleasant

Figure 23.1
**Graphical survey:
Rambla dels Estudius**

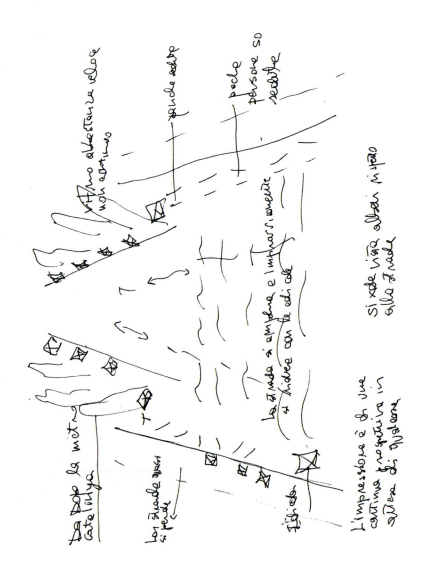

Figure 23.2
Photographic survey: Rambla de Canaletes, seats for people staying and watching

Figure 23.3
Photographic survey: Rambla de Canaletes, living statues

Figure 23.4
**Photographic survey:
Rambla des Ocells,
stall selling animals**

Next is the Rambla dels Estudius, also known as des Ocells, where there is a break in the line of trees and the carriageways predominate, together with the buildings lining them. Here, too, mime artists present their scenes. Along the lateral carriageways tall buildings adorned with friezes alternate with others whose facades are not decorated, in a good state of conservation, making for an attractive urban townscape.

Along the right-hand carriageway we see the historical pharmacy at the corner of Via Bonsucces and beyond it some fast-food outlets. Continuing along the left-hand carriageway we see a building with a colonnade, and on the right-hand side the baroque church called Eglesia de Betlem followed by the concourse with the building of the Liceu. A characteristic feature of the Rambla dels Estudius are the stalls selling birds and small animals, all along the central thoroughfare. When the stalls are closed the carriageways dominate perceptions with traffic noise, whereas when they are open it is the sounds made by the birds and animals and the voices of onlookers which prevail, blotting out the traffic noise. The stalls are interspersed with streetlamps where one can usually see bicycles parked. Here the overall perspective culminates in a single point and does not run in a straight line: we have the impression that people crowd together and become confused with the line of trees.

The central section becomes narrower and the lateral carriageways broaden out. This is where Rambla de Sant Josep begins, and flower sellers' stalls dominate the scene. Here too the stalls are interspersed with streetlamps and the carriageways occasionally impinge on perception. Looking ahead the press of people is even denser and the backdrop of buildings is largely concealed. Along the left-hand carriageway we see souvenir shops; on the right-hand side perception is arrested by a large publicity hoarding covering up building work.

Figure 23.5
**Photographic survey:
Rambla de Sant Josep,
the Boqueria Market**

Then there is the Palau de la Virreina in Rococo style, housing an office providing information on current events in Barcelona. Beyond this on the right-hand side there is the old covered market called the Boqueria with its elegant facade, offering characteristic glimpses of fruit and vegetable stalls, a magnet for residents and tourists alike.

Past the market there are more fast-food outlets, and further on the Antigua Casa Figueras with its traditional Escribà pastryware and yet another fast-food outlet.

Figure 23.6
**Photographic survey:
Rambla de Sant
Josep, stall selling
flowers**

Figure 23.7
**Photographic survey:
Rambla de Sant
Josep, Palau de la
Virreina**

Figure 23.8
Photographic survey: Rambla de Sant, detail of the Josep Antigua Casa Figueras

This is the only stretch in which the trees are planted in raised beds; where the flower sellers' stalls end, the trees thin out and come to an end. The right-hand side culminates in the modern theatre and two more fast-food outlets. The left-hand carriageway is characterized by a modern building with a large L-shaped open space providing a view through to the bell tower of the Church of Santa Maria del Pi. This is followed by a concourse with an old residence adorned with eye-catching sculptures of dragons and umbrellas making for a distinctive urban backdrop. As we go on we look down a long straight cross-street with old-fashioned lighting down the street fronts to a bell tower. In this stretch, near the fast-food outlets, we are assailed by food smells.

This is the central section of the whole Las Ramblas, characterized by an image by Miró reproduced on the walkway and, a little further on, two access points for the metro station Liceu. Here the prevailing perception is one of chaos on account of the numerous intersections for both pedestrians and traffic. On the left-hand side after the image by Miró we come across the first open-air cafés, and on the right-hand side more living statues featuring particularly original scenes.

The next stretch is Rambla de Caputxins. The first part of this pedestrian area is characterized by the open-air cafés on both right and left. Ahead rises the tall monument of Christopher Columbus. Along the left-hand carriageway there is a building with a colonnade giving access to the old Placa Real; then comes the Placa del Teatres with its statue of Frederic Soler, a gathering place for pigeons. On the right-hand carriageway we see a street leading up the hill and the Hotel Oriente. This stretch of Las Ramblas is characterized by the booths of painters, at first on the right-hand side and then along both sides. People pause to buy or merely inspect the pictures, or to have their portrait or caricature painted. Here the Rambla is curving. The prospect changes and in the distance we can see the cable car line. One prevailing acoustic perception here is the wind; the trees and urban features gradually thin out.

At the beginning of the last stretch, the Rambla Santa Monica, the thoroughfare once again becomes straight and broad. There are open-air cafés on both sides, and the acoustic perception of wind is still quite marked. The long-range view features the statue of Christopher Columbus and the cable car. On the left there is the Dressanes metro station. There are fewer people here, and the pace quite rapid. There is a general sense of dispersion, as if the tension had been relaxed. Along the left-hand carriageway there is an underground car park and beyond it the way into the old waxworks museum.

On the other carriageway there is the Church of Santa Monica and Santa Monica cultural centre; at the crossroads a broad street leads off, dominated by a sky-scraper. Along the central pedestrian zone of Las Ramblas, where the painters' booths come to an end, there is an 'empty' space given over at weekends to a craft market. A modern fountain on the right serves as a meeting and resting place. The view moves from the towering statue of Christopher Columbus on to the street leading to the harbour with palm trees, making for a perception characterized by lack of definition and dispersion.

For the graphic relief, graphic-perceptive sketches were made of some of the places considered significant for the analysis, accompanied by a few notes and preliminary indications concerning the symbols to be used in constructing the final map. The sketches were useful in order to comprehend some of the urban dynamics of Las Ramblas, the different components of the visual perspectives and the flux of people.

Figure 23.9
Photographic survey: Rambla de Sant Josep, fast food

Figure 23.10
**Photographic survey:
Rambla de Sant
Josep, the Miró
painting**

Figure 23.11
**Photographic survey:
Rambla de Caputxins,
booths of painters**

Figure 23.12
**Photographic survey:
Rambla de Santa
Monica, view of
the Christopher
Columbus statue**

For the photographic relief some 200 photographs were taken along the different stretches of this thoroughfare, recording all the elements which may contribute to the analysis. Many pictures were useful to note elements that are difficult to observe by a typical passer by because of the large amount of people and urban factors which often make the urban scene chaotic.

Finally, the footage shot for the video survey had the dual function of recording data concerning both pace, often sustained, and acoustic perceptions, including the voices of people, the sounds of birds and animals from the kiosks, and traffic noise.

Phase 3: Analysis of traditional mapping

The study area comprises a long, slightly curving axis of variable width. Known as Las Ramblas, this traverses the historical centre of Barcelona from Placa Catalunya to Placa de la Porta de la Pau with the statue of Christopher Columbus, dividing it into two parts.

The name Ramblas probably derives from the Arab word *raml* to indicate the bed of a covered river. In the nineteenth century, the city walls were destroyed and in place of the river, which was then drained, a boulevard was built. Las Ramblas comprise a tree-lined walkway in the middle with traffic flow along the two sides. There are no areas of vegetation bordering on Las Ramblas, only visible further off. The north-eastern area of the historical quarter, away from the sea, is characterized by irregular, winding streets and blocks, with a concentration of historical buildings round Placa de Sant Jaume, whereas the

Figure 23.13
Traditional analysis: Barcelona planimetry, detail showing Las Ramblas and the surrounding quarters (Source: Barcelona Town Hall cartography, 2004)

north-western area is more regular and features many historical buildings. The main elements of interest to emerge from our analysis on the urban scale include: places of historical and cultural interest such as the Reial Acadèmia de Ciències i Arts, the Mercat de la Boqueria, the pavement on the central stretch with a mosaic by Joan Miró, the shop decorated with an Art Deco dragon, the Gran Teatre del Liceu, the Palau Guëll in the Carrer Nou de la Rambla, the Centre d'Art Santa Mònica and the Christopher Columbus statue; public squares with both regular and irregular outlines; urban voids; axes; and striking sightlines.

On the territorial scale we observed, in addition to the confines of the study area, its position with respect to the city, its topography (set on an area of flat land within the city), the presence of urban areas going back to Gothic times, public squares outside the study area, buildings of historical and artistic interest, the hills and the sea as viewed from the study area.

Phase 4: Questionnaire for analysis

The questionnaire is designed to take between 10 and 30 minutes to complete. The questions are listed below, together with analytical summaries of the answers provided.

    0)   Nationality, age.

As you walk through the study area:

1) What are the elements which strike you (people, things, etc.)?
2) Are there one or more elements which produce a particular sensation?
3) Is there an element which brings to mind a particularly significant moment for you for any reason?
4) Are there any things which disturb you?
5) Is there an element which causes a strong sensation?
6) If you could change something, what would it be?
7) Can you compare this area to another area in this city or elsewhere?
8) If so, why?
9) What is the symbol of this city?

The people interviewed, mostly tourists – from Spain, France, Austria, Chile, Denmark and USA – and passers by aged between 25 and 65, generally responded quite readily to all the questions. The language used was English.

    From our summary of the replies the elements of particular significance include: the general atmosphere, the variety and multitude of people who pass through at all hours of the day and night, the cafés with tables in the openair, artists, flowers, the architecture, trees, the general feeling of happiness and goodwill.

    The most significant elements which produced a particular sensation were: the old covered market of la Boqueria, the enormous throughput of people, the living statues, the building with the sculptures of dragons and umbrellas, the mosaic fountains, all arousing positive sensations apart from the living statues, which for some people introduce a note of sadness.

    The elements recalling a particularly significant moment were: the stretch of Las Ramblas alongside the sea, with its hint of holidays; the statue of Christopher Columbus, with various reminiscences including the discovery of America; strolling along Las Ramblas took some people back to schooldays; and the various fine buildings and also the trees could evoke people's hometowns.

    Among the things which were disturbing: traffic, noise, the attempts of some beggars to get money from passers by, bad smells, disabled beggars, the lack of benches to sit down on, the overall sensation of insecurity, the continuous throughput of people, making it impossible to keep Las Ramblas clean.

    Among the elements causing a strong sensation: the statue of Christopher Columbus, the atmosphere, the flowers, the throng of people from all over the world.

    Things interviewees would like to change include: removing the stalls in which animals are sold, eliminating traffic along the carriageways, making them pedestrian zones too, introducing more benches, encouraging local businesses in place of commercial chains and improving security.

The study area was compared to: the Kartnerstrasse, Vienna, for the similar crowds out for a stroll; the Paseo Aumada, Santiago, Chile, another broad pedestrian thoroughfare with a craft fair on Saturdays and Sundays; Central Park, New York, with its artists, etc; the pedestrianised streets in Denmark, viz. Copenhagen, where one can stroll; Malaga and Puerta del Sol in Madrid, for the general atmosphere.

Finally, the following elements were considered symbolic of Barcelona: the harbour, the sea, the statue of Christopher Columbus, the Sagrada Familia, Las Ramblas, Placa Catalunya, the architecture of Gaudì, Miró's paintings, Parco Guell.

Phase 5: Complex map of analysis

The analysis of Las Ramblas made it possible to identify and represent on a complex map the current identity of this place and establish whether this is sustainable with walkability.

Indeed, the huge amount of both urban and non-urban elements makes it difficult to recognize the salient traits of Las Ramblas identity. Place identity here seems to concern above all the central walkway rather than the lateral carriageways: this pedestrian concourse features a constant change of urban scene, with a continuous throughput of passers by who often become an active part of the scene. Each stretch is characterized by a dynamic mix of history, culture, business and entertainments (see on the map, symbols including: place of historical and artistic interest, evocative place, place with multiple use, live statue, birds, flowers and painters kiosk).

At some points the confusion of hybrid elements introduced from the side streets and in some stretches of the central walkway make the identity not sustainable, creating perceptions of danger among passers by.

The symbols of the basic scheme were updated according to the different surveys carried out and the peculiarities of Las Ramblas.

For an evocative place we chose a square with a coloured circle inside to characterize the place's symbolic value. For a place possessing multiple values, we chose a circle with different colour arrows pointing outwards, to indicate the various different values offered by the site.

For the stalls of flowers and birds and the painters' booth we chose square symbols with different colours and contents, referring to the shape of the stalls themselves and what is on sale.

For the living statues we chose a solid circle with an irregular shape in movement within it, indicating the indefinite and dynamic nature of the scenes mimed (Sepe, 2009b).

To symbolize the constant throughput of people of different cultures we used the symbol of rapid pace embellished with different colours to represent the various cultures. Finally, for the symbols of the natural elements, such as those of the sea, the trees and pigeons, we used the stylized real reference image.

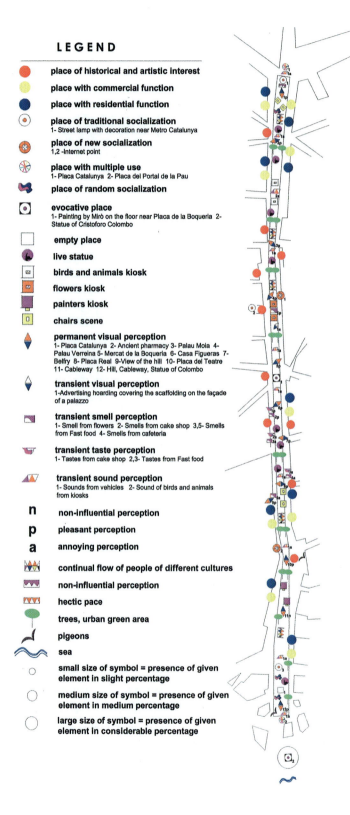

LEGEND

🔴 place of historical and artistic interest

🟡 place with commercial function

🔵 place with residential function

⊙ place of traditional socialization
1- Street lamp with decoration near Metro Catalunya

✳ place of new socialization
1,2 -Internet point

✳ place with multiple use
1- Placa Catalunya 2- Placa del Portal de la Pau

🎗 place of random socialization

◉ evocative place
1- Painting by Mirò on the floor near Placa de la Boqueria 2-
Statue of Cristoforo Colombo

☐ empty place

🟣 live statue

▦ birds and animals kiosk

▦ flowers kiosk

▮ painters kiosk

0 chairs scene

🔺🔻 permanent visual perception
1- Placa Catalunya 2- Ancient pharmacy 3- Palau Moia 4-
Palau Verreina 5- Mercat de la Boqueria 6- Casa Figueras 7-
Belfry 8- Placa Real 9-View of the hill 10- Placa del Teatre
11- Cableway 12- Hill, Cableway, Statue of Colombo

◇ transient visual perception
1-Advertising hoarding covering the scaffolding on the façade
of a palazzo

▨ transient smell perception
1- Smell from flowers 2- Smells from cake shop 3,5- Smells
from Fast food 4- Smells from cafeteria

👅 transient taste perception
1- Tastes from cake shop 2,3- Tastes from Fast food

🔺🔼 transient sound perception
1- Sounds from vehicles 2- Sound of birds and animals
from kiosks

n non-influential perception

p pleasant perception

a annoying perception

🔺🔺🔺 continual flow of people of different cultures

🔻🔻🔻 non-influential perception

🔺🔺🔺 hectic pace

🌳 trees, urban green area

🕊 pigeons

〰 sea

○ small size of symbol = presence of given
element in slight percentage

○ medium size of symbol = presence of given
element in medium percentage

○ large size of symbol = presence of given
element in considerable percentage

Figure 23.14a
**Las Ramblas: the
complex map of
analysis and legend**

Figure 23.14b
**Las Ramblas: detail of
the complex map of
analysis**

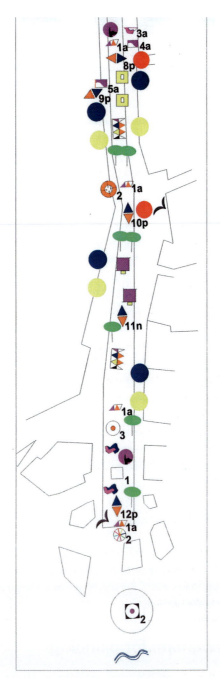

Phase 6: Identification of identity resources

The detection of the identity resources resulting from the complex map of analysis emerged to the greatest extent in the central pedestrian avenue rather than in the side streets.

The main critical points, as it was observed in the previous section, are found in the mix of hybrid elements coming from some stretches of the side streets and from some areas of the central avenue which make identity not entirely sustainable, creating, as shown in the phase 2 description and questionnaire responses, and in the complex map of analysis, perceptions of unease and the sensation of a lack of safety amongst passers by.

In contrast, dynamicity, agreeable atmosphere, variety of functions and uses along the route and the presence of historical buildings are the fundamental qualities. Indeed, along the central area, the visitor finds more characteristic urban scenes and it is here that strollers congregate in a continuous, sustained flow, often becoming an active part of the urban scene itself.

However, the potential of Las Ramblas derives above all from the mix of user needs and the places themselves. Tourists are on the lookout for entertainment, the possibility of taking time out on public benches; they do not want to be harassed by traffic noise nor live in fear of snatched handbags or wallets. The locals want to use the area without having to cleave their way through the crowd, they do not want to see litter on the ground, they want to be able to use their bikes and cars to move around, and, just like the tourists, they too want to be able to sit down occasionally and feel safe. The street artists need free spaces to improvise, where they can exhibit their skills freely in mimed scenes and games, but also in paintings, caricatures and other things of this kind. The itinerant sellers need room for their stalls, where they can sell small pets, flowers, souvenirs, newspapers, postcards and posters. The buildings flanking Las Ramblas also deserve a prominent role due to their artistic merit and their function as a testimony of times gone by, but they also need ongoing maintenance and appropriate use. The historic shops and emporiums look to their own survival and the continued sale of their typical products, but they too have architectural worth and attract with their window displays. The fast-food outlets seek to meet the rapid feeding requirements of the enormous crowds of passers by, at times also utilising sidewalk space with tables and large trash receptacles. The publicity blurbs, shop signs and various types of lighting seek to enhance products and outcompete their rivals. The harbour, with its statue of Christopher Columbus set in the midst of all this, claims a role of its own. Finally, the trees clamour for their own Lebensraum and constant nurturing.

Phase 7: Questionnaire for planning

We administered a 14-point questionnaire concerning possible interventions aimed at: enhancing the image of Las Ramblas and identifying its place identity; improving the walkability of the central and lateral pedestrian routes; and creating a major perception of safeness.

0) Nationality, age.

As you walk through the study area:

1) What do you think about the quality of this place?
2) Do you think that the presence of too many people, street sellers, open air cafés and restaurants, etc. diminishes the benefits of this place and its perception?
3) Do you think it might be preferable to decongest the central pedestrian route?
4) Do you think we should create a lane for cyclists?
5) Do you think traffic-calming measures should be included?
6) What about redesigning or recovering the paving, differentiating the different sections? Did you notice that there is a painting by Miró drawn on the pavement?
7) Do you think that there are now enough public benches?
8) Do you think that mobile platforms might be useful for street artists and sellers?
9) Do you think that shops with typical products and quality souvenirs should be recovered or enhanced?
10) Do you think that the current mix of shop signs and illuminations and advertising posters creates visual chaos?
11) Do you think that the current upkeep of buildings is sufficient?
12) What do you think about creating an urban furniture for protecting the trees?
13) Do you think multimedia guides might be useful to lead the visitor to discover particular spaces, elements and perceptions of this place, especially at less crowded times?
14) Do you think that some or all of these measures if adopted would make the identity of these places emerge more clearly and make the route not only more walkable but also safer, or do you only think a greater police presence is required?

Interviewees were area users: tourists from the USA, France, the UK, Italy, Germany and Finland, and local people, with an age range from 30 to 65. The language used was English.

All questions were mostly answered willingly and without reticence. The responses provided supported in most cases the hypothesis of the project explained below. The only discordances were in responses to two questions: 'What about redesigning or recovering the paving, differentiating the different sections? Did you notice that there is a painting by Miró drawn on the pavement?' – which most interviewees had difficulty answering because they had not noticed the pavement because of the enormous flow of people; and the last question – some people interviewed thought that both measures were important, some that a liveable place is more important, others a good system of surveillance.

Phase 8: Complex map of project and design interventions

As regards the last phase, the construction of the complex map of the identity project, the elements identified for redesign of Las Ramblas take into account the different requirements both of the users and place elements.

Interventions which were designed are based on the construction of the places according to their tangible and intangible characteristics. All the factors noted during the different phases were put into play in order to ensure that the complexity of this place is not reduced: spaces, architecture, people, transient perceptions, permanent perceptions, urban events, relationships and rhythms. The symbols were created using simple geometric shapes related to the idea of the proposed interventions.

Decongesting the routes, restoring old activities, enhancing elements of historical, cultural and identity value, harmonizing urban furniture, giving identity to what is transitory, respecting nature, and virtualizing the path are some of the interventions which, if duly integrated, should prove beneficial.

The principal need is to decongest the central pedestrian avenue by means of a series of micro-interventions that could include the following: enhancing the cultural resources of lateral carriageways; creating suitable urban furniture; designating the side streets as limited traffic areas; creating a cycle track; and applying traffic calming measures at the intersections and points of major traffic convergence.

The second intervention for Las Ramblas is restoring traditional activities, enhancing and/or recovering typical historic shops, some of which could link up with the specialities of the goods on sale in the stalls: for example the shops in the part of Las Ramblas where painters work could sell canvases, brushes, paints and books on painting; the shops in the area where small pets are on sale could sell cages, special pet beds and other gadgets; the area with flowers could sell gardening tools, books on gardening, etc. Another possibility is the insertion of quality souvenir shops referring to these speciality goods.

We then propose to enhance elements of historical, cultural and identity value. This means providing for the maintenance and enhancement of the historical buildings – which, for example, in the last stretch of Las Ramblas has been less thorough – and also eliminating graffiti. Furthermore we suggest enhancing some elements and perceptions which are representative of its identity, including, for example, the azulejo of Carrer de la Portaferrissa, the Miró painting on the pavement, the statue of Christopher Columbus, some decorated elements of old urban furniture and visual perception of the Guell Palace.

Another need is to harmonize urban furniture. We first suggest the re-planning of the pavement by differentiating the various areas of the central avenue and the side streets, enhancing the area with the painting by Miró in the central point of Las Ramblas, the terminal stretch with the statue of Christopher Columbus and the landmarks in the area. Furthermore, we propose designing a unitary urban furniture project, which is both harmonic with already existing furniture of historical value and useful for the various functions. This should include: benches for a brief rest; rubbish receptacles also in the vicinity of the fast-food outlets; coordinated shop signs, lights, and publicity panels and advertisements, above all as regards the side streets.

Continuing in this sense it is important to give identity to what is transitory, creating small mobile platforms for street artists and vendors. In this way, anyone could have their own recognizable space, harmonic with the place, and chaos could be eliminated from the urban scene.

Another fundamental intervention is to respect nature. The trees of Las Ramblas are necessary for their quality image and for the balance of this urban and environmental ecosystem. The trees are now increasingly used as objects to support tools useful for artists, street vendors, etc. It is important to create a suitable space for such articles and that trees and their ecosystem are duly respected.

A last intervention involves virtualizing the path by going online with the creation of multimedia guides. The various peculiarities of Las Ramblas can be presented and made more user friendly by means of multimedia guides via satellites accessible for example from mobile phones. In this way visitors can be steered towards alternative, personalised and less crowded routes which they can follow with the help of multimedia texts and maps (Sepe, 2010b).

Conclusion

This experiment shows that the beauty of this place is precisely in its dynamism – which probably comes from its history, from the fact that there was a river here – and its character as a place where many events occur.

What is interesting is that Las Ramblas do not attract because they are a place of contemplation, such as a piazza with important architecture, or a landscape.

The multitude of people come here because they are attracted by the atmosphere and the harmony of buildings, history, places, things, mix of people, activities, nature and perceptions that Las Ramblas offer and in which visitors feel involved.

All the actions of the project that were designed for Las Ramblas – decongesting the routes, restoring old activities, enhancing elements of historical, cultural and identity value, harmonizing urban furniture, giving identity to what is transitory, respecting nature and virtualizing the path – are aimed at safeguarding the quality of this place and its atmosphere through interventions that link past, present and future sustainably. The dynamicity, history and variety of activities are the main elements to protect, preventing places being subject to the demands for occasional, rapid consumptions of objects and feelings. This could lead to a slow but inevitable deterioration of places and a consequent lowering of the level of security.

The proposed interventions would ensure greater balance in the set up of spaces and organization of the various activities, and it would act as a dissuader to additional fast-food chains, would pressure those already in place to

Figure 23.15
Las Ramblas: the complex map of design and legend

L E G E N D

decongesting routes
1- enhancing the cultural resources of lateral carriageways
2- creating suitable urban furniture
3- designating the side streets as limited traffic areas
4- creating a cycle track
5- applying traffic calming measures at the intersections and points of major traffic convergence

restoring traditional activities
1 - enhancing or restoring typical historic shops with handicrafts producing local products, including high-quality goods
2 - restoring old shop signs and windows

enhancing elements of historical, cultural and identity value
1- providing for the maintenance and enhancement of all the historical buildings of the route, also eliminating graffiti
2 - enhancing some elements and perceptions which are representative for place-identity

harmonizing urban furniture
1- re-planning the pavement by differentiating the various areas of the central avenue and the side streets
2 - designing a unitary urban furnishing project, harmonizing with element of historical value already existing and differentiating them according to their various uses

giving identity to what is transitory
- creating lightweight multifunctional structures where artists, hawkers, living statues and others can create their own fluid, dynamic spaces

respecting nature
- creating a suitable space for trees and green areas

virtualizing the path
- creating multimedia guides with multimedia texts and maps to orient visitors towards the discovery of historical, cultural and perception details along the routes and with information about the history and identity of the places.

conform and the whole thoroughfare will appear less chaotic and more liveable. All the actions, if integrated, could improve walkability and the quality of the overall image.

The various areas of Las Ramblas should be marked out more decisively, combating the worst effects of globalization and improving the beneficial effects of place identity. It would also allow more accurate control of the area and provide a greater feeling of security for tourists, passers by and place users, enhancing and rendering sustainable the identity of this place.

Chapter 24

Helsinki

The Esplanadi area

Phase 1: Anticipatory analysis

The study area of the Esplanadi is a representative site for the city of Helsinki, culminating in the harbour. It is a pedestrian park-street, with traffic flow along either side; not particularly extensive it owes most of its popularity to it being a green area, where people can take a stroll in summer, and to the characteristic shops along the carriageways – the design showroom by Alvar Aalto, quality souvenir shops and high-fashion boutiques. The weather is cold and wet most of the year, and for many months the city lives immersed in almost permanent darkness, while in the summer months the sun does not set at all or only late and briefly. We also expected the park to be used above all in summer. The pace of users is not very rapid, and changes according to the light and weather conditions. The harbour, where the Esplanadi ends, offers a characteristic panorama with the sea, the fish market, the islands, the vegetation and seagulls.

Phase 2: Denominative and perceptual description

The study area comprises the whole Esplanadi park from Erottaya Square down to the harbour, including the carriageways bordering it – the Pohjesplanadi and Etelesplanadi side streets. Surveys began in Pohjesplanadi, followed on the opposite street, Etelesplanadi, and concluded in the central stretch where the park is located.

At these latitudes it is dark most of the year, with the midnight sun in summer. For practical reasons it was decided to carry out the inspection in the summer, while of course a complete analysis would also require data from the periods with just a few hours of daylight. The Esplanadi is a park-street with carriageways on either side, Pohjesplanadi and Etelesplanadi. The urban layout is grid-like, with crossroads cutting through the park to allow traffic flow. Each section of the park has a statue standing in the middle, apart from one area which has a tall sculpture made of leaves and branches.

The street's backdrop is formed by an almost unbroken line of buildings of good architectural quality and condition, mostly ranging between five and seven storeys in height, while close to the harbour some two- and three-storey buildings are also found. These buildings mostly date back to the late nineteenth and early-twentieth centuries, with some more recent constructions; a number of facades are decorated with flower motifs. The wrought iron street lamps mounted on some of the facades have a characteristic design. Some institutions have their headquarters here, including the Transport Ministry on the Etelesplanadi, a European Union centre and the Helsinki City Hall on Pohjesplanadi.

Pohjesplanadi is home to high-quality souvenir shops, fashion boutiques and top class hotels. The most characteristic stretch is the one leading on to the harbour, where every morning in Kauppatori Square there is a market for fish, fruit and vegetables, and local craftwork. You can also buy cooked fish from stalls in the harbour, some with chairs and tables so that you can eat and drink in the open air, or indeed on wooden boats along the quayside.

In the harbour you can board ferries for destinations close at hand, such as the island of Suomenlina, or more distant, such as Estonia. From the port you can also see a sailing ship, the island of Suomenlina, a cathedral and other buildings.

Table 24.1 **Detail of the denominative survey**

Place	Date	Time	Type	Constructed elements	Natural elements	Transport mode	People
Esplanadi Park final stretch	July	10:00		Statue	Trees Grass	Cars	Locals
			Low, medium, high percentage	Low	Medium Medium	High	Medium

Table 24.2 **Detail of the perceptual survey**

Place	Date	Time	Type	Smell p.	Taste p.	Sound p.	Touch p.	Visual p.
Esplanadi Park final stretch	July	10:00	Type	Grass		Means of transport		The harbour Historical buildings The Cathedral Ships
			Low, medium, high percentage	Low		Medium		Medium Low Low Medium
			Non-influential, pleasant, annoying, surprising perceived feeling	Pleasant		Annoying		All pleasant

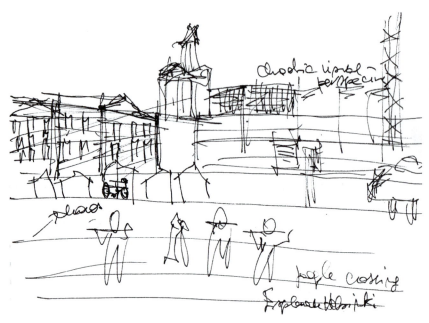

Figure 24.1
**Graphical survey: a
perspective showing
the chaotic crossing
between the end
of the park and the
waterfront**

The Etelesplanadi features distinctive paving, some buildings of high architectural quality, and a showroom by Artek, the manufacturer of Alvar Aalto's furniture, but it is not as busy as its counterpart. Two very well stocked tourist information offices, one with tables and chairs outside, are situated along Pohjesplanadi and Etelesplanadi.

The whole itinerary is provided with city maps showing you *where you are*. There is a constant passage of city sightseeing coaches. There are no signs of globalization, no glaring neon billboards, internet cafés or fast-food outlets: in fact, perhaps the most striking feature of this area is that it has resisted the trappings of 'globalized' identity. Nor, on the other hand, is it particularly Finnish: it rather has a Northern European overall feel.

The park attracts many visitors, especially on fine days, when the benches along the lawns and the pleasing decor make it a very agreeable spot. You can sometimes see people drinking alcohol on the benches. Both in the park and in the side streets many people go about by bicycle. In the last section of the park, towards the sea, there is a concert hall, a sort of pavilion fronted by benches where concerts are held throughout the year, making it a focal point for visitors to the park. During the concerts the music can be heard in the streets, and in Pohjesplanadi in particular there are open-air cafés where people can sit and listen to the music. In the park there are a number of typically Finnish kiosks selling ice creams and refreshments, and also, closer to the sea, flowers, fruit and vegetables. The area where the park borders the harbour is rather confused in terms of both visual and acoustic perceptions: there are tram lines, a fountain, and refreshment kiosks with tables and chairs. Great attention has been paid to urban decor both in the park itself and in the side streets, laid out with seats, modern and traditional street lamps, and tubs of flowers. The pace of users is always moderate and slower in the park.

Close to the harbour perceptions are somewhat chaotic and the pace is quicker. In terms of visual perceptions there are fine views of the railway station building, Helsinki Cathedral, the harbour with the market square, the islands and ships, and the park with its vegetation. The most pleasant and typical acoustic perception is the cry of the seagulls heard above all near the harbour but also all over the area. You also hear people's voices, the sound signal of the traffic lights, and the noise from cars and means of transport, the latter constant and at times annoying. The prevailing tactile sensation comes as you walk through the park, on the old paving stones of Etelesplanadi and as the itinerary slopes up towards Erottaja Square and downwards to the harbour. The senses of taste and smell are aroused by the food on offer in the cafés and restaurants and also by the fish (notably salmon) on sale in the market square. In general, the itinerary offers a pleasing overall perception, sometimes interrupted by the rain that falls in Helsinki for many months of the year; an impression of dispersal is only felt at the beginning and end of the itinerary, where there are two areas of urban void.

For the graphic survey, graphic-perceptive sketches were made of the places considered significant for the analysis, accompanied by a few notes and preliminary indications concerning the symbols to be used in constructing the final map. Useful sketches were realised at the edges of the Esplanadi, where critical points were highlighted. Furthermore, different fluxes of people within the three parts of the area were noted.

Figure 24.2
Photographic survey: perspective of the waterfront from the Esplanadi park

Figure 24.3
Photographic survey: Kauppatori, stalls in the harbour

Figure 24.4
Photographic survey: Kauppatori, boats with vendors selling cooked fish

Figure 24.5
**Photographic survey:
Erottaja Square**

Figure 24.6
**Photographic survey:
perspective of the Park**

Figure 24.7
**Photographic survey:
perspective of the park**

Figure 24.8
**Photographic
survey: view of
Pohjoiseplanadi**

Figure 24.9
**Photographic
survey: view of
Pohjoiseplanadi with
the Café Esplanad**

Figure 24.10
**Photographic survey:
perspective of
Etelesplanadi**

For the photographic survey, some 150 photographs were taken along both the Esplanadi and the lateral streets, recording all the elements which could contribute to the analysis. In particular, the relationships between the three parts of the itinerary and between the three parts and the lateral streets were observed. Selected photographs of some of the features of the Esplanadi area are shown on preceding pages and below. With respect to the video survey, the pace – which is sustained only in the critical points of the area – was highlighted. Furthermore the sound of seagulls and the noise of traffic and pedestrian crossings were noted.

Figure 24.11
Photographic survey: view of the Cathedral from the square

Phase 3: Analysis of traditional mapping

Our analysis of traditional maps showed that the area has a markedly regular layout, with a straight axis that bisects streets at right angles, forming crossroads within the park that offer design opportunities.

The old Helsinki was half destroyed by a fire at the beginning of the 1800s. The main feature that survives is its grid plan, dating back to the 1700s. Johan Albrecht Ehrenström's town plan of 1814 extended the old urban fabric northward and southward from the new capital. The plan singled out some main arteries, where the most important public buildings, planned by Carl Ludwig Engel, were erected. A distinguishing feature of Ehrenström and Engel's plan – which determined the current appearance of the area under study as well as Helsinki as a whole – is that urban planning and building went hand in hand in total harmony.

The central part of the town area is level, with slight changes in altitude in its initial and final stretches. Here lies a large rectilinear park, the Esplanadi, opened in 1812. The park is delimited on either side by two streets, the Pohjesplanadi and the Etelesplanadi. These streets and the park together form a single broad axis leading to the port and the fish market square.

At the urban scale, we singled out the following elements of interest. The layout is regular, with continuous building rows interrupted only by street crossings. The principal axis bordering on the area is Mannerheimvägen, which connects to both Pohjesplanadi and Etelesplanadi. Secondary axes include Lonnrotsg, the south-westward continuation of Pohjesplanadi. The interesting historical buildings, predominantly in the Neoclassical style, are on Pohjesplanadi and Etelesplanadi. They include the Swedish Theatre, designed by Engel himself, the Presidentinlinna (Presidential Palace) and the Kaupungintalo (Town Hall) on Pohjesplanadi. Other noticeable features are the regularly shaped Erottaja Square and the irregular Kauppatori (Market Square). An examination of the map suggests that interesting views can be enjoyed of the port and the sea from the park, and of the park itself from Market Square.

At the territorial scale, what stands out is the central position of the study area within the city, the regularity of its street grid, its nearness to the historical centre and the level topography of the area.

The main axis is Mannerheimvägen, secondary ones include Kasarmikatu and Lonnrotsg. The main square just outside the area is Senaatintori (Senate Square). Nearby parks include the Vanha Kirkkopuisto (Old Church Park) and the park around the Uspenski Cathedral on Katajanokka Island. Observable buildings of art historical interest include those around Senate Square, notably the Valtioneuvoston Linna (Senate Building), the Lutheran Cathedral, the University, the Library, and the Tuomiokirkko/Suurkirkko (Helsinki Cathedral), all designed by Engel between 1820 and 1850. Also noticeable are the Amos Andersonin Taidemuseo, the Helsingin Vanha Kirkko (Old Church of Helsinki) and the Uspenski Cathedral. An examination of the map suggests that the most interesting views are those of the Tuomiokirkko/Suurkirkko and of the sea.

Figure 24.12
Traditional analysis: planimetry of Helsinki with the Esplanadi area

Phase 4: Questionnaire for analysis

The planned duration of the questionnaire is between 10 and 30 minutes and it consists of the questions listed below. There follows a reasoned summary of the answers obtained.

0)   Nationality, age
Passing through the study area:
1)   What elements strike you most (persons, things, etc.)?
2)   Is there one or more elements which produce a particular sensation?
3)   Is there any one element which brings to mind a moment important to you for any reason?
4)   Are there any things which bother you?
5)   Is there any one element which produces a strong sensation?
6)   If you could change anything, what would you do?
7)   Is this area comparable to any other area of this city or elsewhere?
8)   If so, why?

People interviewed were users of the area, in particular tourists from Finland and locals, aged between 20 and 50. The language used was English, interviewees were generally very willing to answer the questions, but did not wish to spend too much time on the interview.

Review and synthesis of the answers obtained produced the following observations.

The elements interviewees found most striking were the Cathedral and the square surrounding it, the Esplanadi park and the fish market.

Elements producing particular sensations in most interviewees were the park's statues and the historic buildings of the Pohjesplanadi. Local inhabitants in particular remarked on the trees and flowers whereas the young mentioned the music drifting out from the music pavilion.

The things which almost all interviewees found most bothersome and distracting were the ongoing road repair works and building maintenance in the Pohjesplanadi and Etelesplanadi. Non-locals and younger respondents remarked on the sad countenance of some people strolling through the park. If they could change something, most people said they would try and cut down noise from repair and maintenance works in the Pohjesplanadi and Etelesplanadi.

None of the interviewees were reminded of areas similar to this with the exception of one person who compared the study area to the Gamla Stan in Stockholm.

Phase 5: Complex map of analysis

The information by the different surveys were here synthesized in order to catch the place identity.

The first observation is of a general nature. As we have noticed before, although the Esplanadi area is representative of the city, it cannot be regarded as typical of Finland, being rather classifiable as more generally Northern European. This consideration calls for a complex identity discovery operation. The distinctive appearance of the area is probably due to its Neoclassical buildings, which although of remarkable historical interest are not specifically recognizable as Finnish.

The place identity which is represented in the map emerged from the different characteristics that were identified in the three parts of the area.

In the Esplanadi area there is a greater throughput of people off the central walkway, largely on account of the institutional headquarters and superior shops located on the side streets, making them attractive to passers by.

The part of the area most characteristic is the one towards the harbour comprising the fish market. In the park, the presence of benches makes it a place more suited to sitting than strolling and the pace is generally quiet. Furthermore, there are not enough elements of attraction such as the music pavilion.

With regards to the symbols specifically created for the complex map concerning this case study, for an evocative place we chose a square with a coloured circle inside it to characterize the place's symbolic value. For a place possessing multiple values, we chose a circle with different colour arrows pointing outwards, to indicate the various different values offered by the site. For the symbols representing the flower, fish, fruit and vegetable stalls and the handicraft stands we chose square symbols of different colours and contents referring to the shape of the booths and the goods on sale.

For the symbols of natural elements, such as in particular those related to the sea, seagulls and pigeons we used the real reference image, but stylized.

Phase 6: Identification of identity resources

The detection of the identity resources resulting from the complex map of analysis was carried out observing criticality, potential and quality concerning the place identity.

As regards criticality, being one of the most representative areas in the city, our area is well maintained, even though road works can be observed in places. Problematic spots are found at the border between the park and Market Square and, to a lesser degree, between the park and Erottaja Square. The former is extremely chaotic due to the casual organization of the market. The street is busy with lorries bringing products to the market, many cars and buses, which block off the view of the sea. Erottaja seems less chaotic, but conveys a similar impression of a place lacking design.

The park, although well maintained, could be improved in several ways. The presence of benches makes it a place more for lingering than for walking through. However, some parts of the park have become a drinking haunt for some people. Furthermore, the appearance of the people frequenting it is somewhat sad, and this impression is borne out by some of the answers to the questionnaire. One of the reasons for this, climate issues aside, might be the scarcity of meeting places or places providing occasions for social contact in the park.

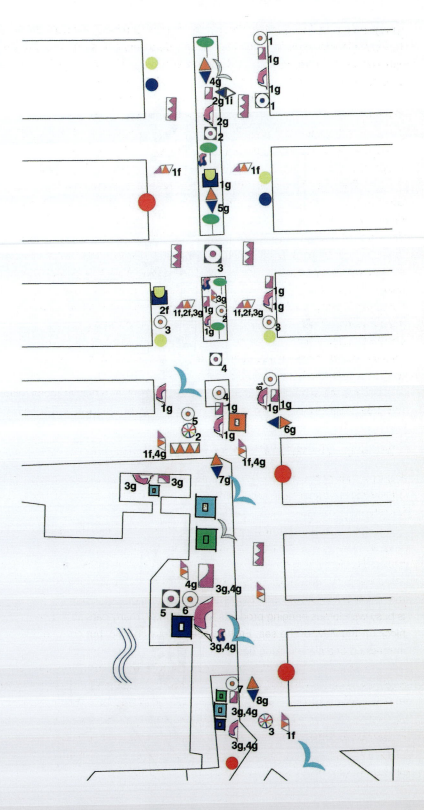

Figure 24.13a
Esplanadi area: complex map of analysis, detail

287

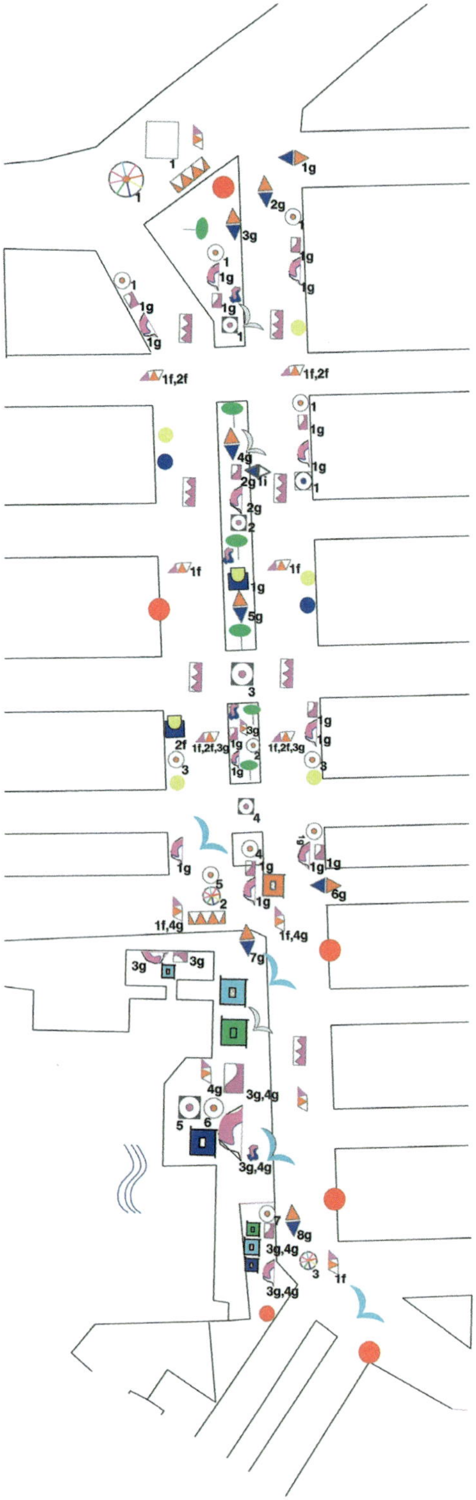

Figure 24.13b
**Esplanadi area:
complex map of
analysis**

Figure 24.13c

**Esplanadi area:
complex map of
analysis, legend**

L E G E N D

● space of historical and artistic interest

● space with commercial function

● space with residential function

◉ **space of traditional socialization**
1- Cafe's 2- Music pavilon with open space and
cafeteria 3- Tourist Information 4- Eatieres kiosks 5-
Fountain 6- Market square 7- Ancient covered market

✳ **place with multiple use**
1- Erottaja 2- Kauppatori 3- Paavarantiontori

🔖 **space of random socialization**

◉ **evocative place**
1,3,4 - Bronze statue 2- Bronze statue and
foliage statue 5- Market square

◉ **emblematic place**
1- European Union office

▢ **empty place**
1- Space around Erottaja

▣ flowers kiosk

▣ fish kiosk

▣ fruit and vegetable kiosk

▣ handicraft box

▲ **permanent visual perception**
1- Railway station building 2- Stockman department
store 3- Swedish theatre 4-5 Park 6- Cathedral 7-
Market square, sea, sailing ship, ships, Suomenlina
island 8-Uspenski Cathedral

◆ **transient visual perception**
1-Advertising hoarding covering the scaffolding on
the façade of a building

◩ **transient smell perception**
1- Smells from cafés and cafeteria 2- Smells from
kiosks 3- Smells from boats which sell fish 4-
Smells from fish and fruit and vegetables market

◡ **transient taste perception**
1- Tastes from cafés and cafeteria 2- Tastes from
kiosks 3- Tastes from boats which sell fish 4- Tastes
from fish and fruit and vegetables market

◿ **transient sound perception**
1- Sounds from means of transport 2- Music sounds 3-
Sounds from traffic lights 4- Sounds from seagulls

n no-influential perception

p pleasant perception

a annoying perception

〰 medium pace

〰 hectic pace

🌳 trees, urban green

〜 sea

〰 seagull

〰 pigeons

○ **small size of symbol = presence of
given element in slight percentage**

○ **medium size of symbol = presence of
given element in medium percentage**

○ **large size of symbol = presence of given
element in considerable percentage**

Furthermore, in some parts of the park, especially near the entrance and at the back, stands selling flowers and food, and picnic tables are set up without any semblance of order, generating a sensation of chaos. Finally, the noise from the streets flanking the park is quite loud and annoying.

As regards potential, the Esplanadi has it in abundance, being an extensive green area connecting the financial district with the sea and located between two important shopping streets. The currently available attractors fostering socialization, such as the music pavilion and the adjacent café, meet the needs of the tourists and younger people, but not of all locals. Furthermore, the nearness of the sea and the views this nearness affords are not exploited to full advantage.

The Etelesplanadi side is less attractive than the Pohjesplanadi one, notwithstanding the presence of some fine public buildings, the elegant Savoy restaurant designed by Alvar Aalto, and the Artek shop selling design products by Alvar Aalto. As regards quality, the analysis we performed indicates that the greatest flow of people occurs externally to the central portion, and is especially concentrated on the Pohjesplanadi, where the nearness of the historic centre, the presence of imposing institutional buildings, large hotels, stylish big-name emporia and quality souvenir shops, all well maintained, and cafés with sidewalk tables make it more attractive for visitors.

The most characteristic part of the Esplanadi is that around the harbour, that is, the fish market plaza. Other noteworthy features are that all historical buildings display good quality and the urban furniture has a unique design.

The above considerations indicate that the area should be enhanced to make the most of its image and identity resources, to make the park area usable for all age groups, and to improve the Etelesplanadi sector, the fringes of the study area, and views of the sea.

Phase 7: Questionnaire for planning

We administered a questionnaire to users of the place about the identity resources identified in the sixth phase.

0) Nationality and age

Passing through the study area:

1) What do you think about the quality of this place?
2) Did you notice the historical buildings?
3) Did you notice the Artek shop or the interior design of the Savoy restaurants?
4) What do you think about setting up attractions in the park suitable for different ages and kinds of people, and to meet different needs?
5) What about increasing recreational activities such as music concerts or folk festivals using the area comprising the park, Etelesplanadi and Pohjesplanadi as a cohesive whole?
6) What about improving public spaces at the edges of the park, near Erottaja Square and Market Square?

7) What about improving the park green with more attractive and inter-active gardens, partly to be designed by architects selected by an international competition?

8) What about enhancing views of the sea?

9) Did you feel threatened anywhere in the area?

The questionnaire was administered to tourists, both foreign – English and Germans – and Finnish, and to resident and non-resident locals. The interview-ees were aged 20 to 70. The language employed was English. The questionnaire, which the 30 interviewees had no problem answering, took about 20 minutes to complete. The park was one of the most suitable areas to administer the ques-tionnaire, since there people slow down their pace and are hence more willing to take the time to answer.

To the question, 'What do you think of the quality of this place?' the interviewees, independent of age or nationality, replied that it is good, mention-ing in particular the buildings and the park architecture and gardens.

The interviewees had actually already answered the second question, 'Did you notice the historical buildings?' in their answer to the previous question. We nevertheless posed the question to understand whether the interviewees were expressing a general judgment or were aware, for example, that some of the buildings had been planned by Engel. Among the locals, most had noticed that the buildings are in the Neoclassical style, and some also mentioned Engel. Most of the non-local interviewees had noticed the historical buildings, especially on the Pohjoisesplanadi. A small number answered affirmatively, but without pro-viding further details.

As to the third question, most of the locals were familiar with the Savoy restaurant, but not with the fact that its interior was designed by Alvar Aalto, although they knew him as a famous architect. More precisely, half of the locals knew about Aalto's role in designing the Savoy, while the other half did not. As to the non-local interviewees, independent of age or nationality, only a small per-centage knew about the interior of the Savoy or of the Artek store.

To the fourth question, 'What do you think about setting up attractions in the park suitable for different ages and kinds of people, and to meet different needs?' the interviewees mostly gave a positive answer, especially younger peo-ple and the elderly. A smaller percentage replied that the park was fine as it was. In their answers, the locals and the Finns in general often referred to climate issues as an element to be taken into special consideration in any renovation plan.

To the fifth question, regarding increasing recreational activities such as music concerts and folk festivals in the park, the interviewees answered posi-tively, independent of age or nationality. The locals were especially interested in Finnish festivals and folk dances.

To the sixth question, 'What about redesigning public spaces at the edges of the park, close to Erottaja Square and Market Square?' the locals replied positively, especially as regards the part of the park towards Market Square, which they perceived as chaotic. The non-local interviewees, independent of age or nationality, were unable to give a precise answer.

As to the seventh question, about the creation of more attractive gardens, half of the interviewees answered that the gardens were already pleasant and well designed as they were. The other half asked for further clarifications about the question. After being told that the idea was to create gardens in some of the less attractive parts of the park, partly through international competitions, they answered positively.

As to the eighth question, about the enhancement of sea views, most of the interviewees answered affirmatively. The locals, in particular, underscored the importance of the sea as a symbolical element of the city.

Finally, to the ninth question, 'Did you feel threatened anywhere in the area?' all the interviewees answered that they usually felt safe there.

Phase 8: Complex map of project and design interventions

In this phase, we laid down project proposals to enhance place identity. What we propose is a set of closely interconnected actions to improve the three parts of the Esplanadi area as a single axis, as well as the perception of this axis as a 'gate' to the sea.

Improving urban attractivity

Improving urban attractivity is to be implemented in several actions.

The first action is that of enhancing the port and sea, making the most of the nearness of the port and the sea, both in the park and in the two streets flanking it, by designing spaces and urban furniture inviting people to stop or look. This step is important insofar as it highlights what is one of Helsinki's strong identity elements, to which the park should serve as a gate of sorts, or, at any rate, provide privileged access.

The second action goes in the same direction. It consists of redesigning the edges of the park, that is, the urban space between the park and Market Square – which is presently chaotic but nevertheless representative, partly because of the presence of street peddlers selling typical products – and between the park and Erottaja square, where the somewhat neglected Swedish Theatre by Engel stands.

The third action is designing small public spaces to enhance the character of the Etelesplanadi stretch, which is presently less distinctively characterized than the Pojiespanadi stretch.

Connecting places

This is one of the most important interventions to be undertaken to allow the area to be perceived as a cohesive whole. It comprises two main steps. The first is to introduce small public spaces to connect the park with its lateral streets. The second action is to place more emphasis on connections with nearby places of interest, such as Senaatintori (Senate Square), the Vanha kirkkopuist park, and the Amos Andersonin Taidemuseo.

Improving urban furniture

Taking account of Helsinki's major design tradition, as reflected by the presence in this area of the Artek shop and of the Savoy with its interior designed by Alvar Aalto, this action has the dual purpose of promoting the place and projecting a strong identity image.

To this end, the first action is to set up design objects drawing on local tradition in public places, partly as a means to evoke urban furniture and decorations designed by Aalto as found in the shop on the lateral streets. The second action is carrying out a lighting project covering the whole park in order to improve its illumination during the dismal dark months.

The third is to create some light temporary structures for exhibitions in the three sections of the area, in order to allow it to be used to better advantage and perceived in its continuity.

Differentiating and introducing new activities

This intervention mainly concerns the park and involves setting up activities here for different kinds of users to allow it to be used more extensively during different periods of the year. The setting up of such activities, in conjunction with the cultural and commercial activities in the lateral streets, would contribute to the more general intent of reinforcing the perception of the park and the streets on either side of it as a single axis. The first action is to introduce games such as chess, checkers or bowls, to be included in newly planned green zones, or set up in already available spaces in the park. This first action would be carried out especially for the benefit of the elderly, who have more free time on their hand, and of lovers of open-air games in general.

The second action is to set up playground areas with wooden recreational equipment for children. Children and their parents already use the park, but setting aside some areas and recreational equipment for them would increase everybody's enjoyment of it.

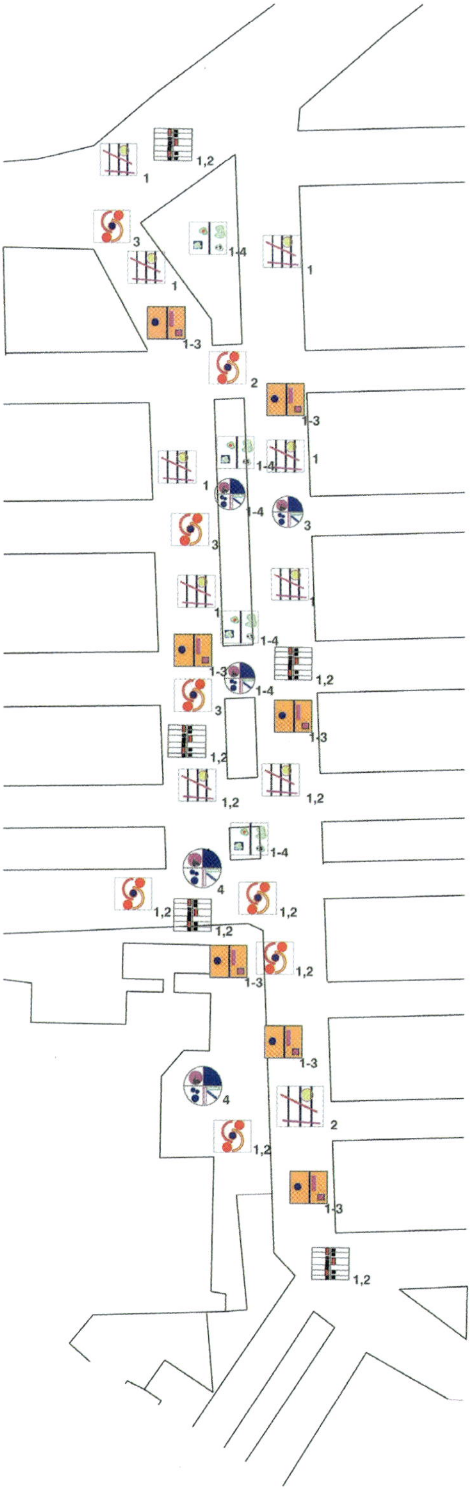

Figure 23.14a
Esplanadi area: complex map of design

Figure 23.14b
Esplanadi area: complex map of design, legend

L E G E N D

Improving urban attractivity

1 - to enhance the port and sea
2 - to redesign the edges of the park
3 - to design public spaces in Etelesplanadi stretch

Connecting places

1 - to introduce connective public spaces
2 - to create connections with nearby places of interest

Improving urban furniture

1 - to set up design objects drawing on local tradition in public places
2 - to carry out a lighting project covering the whole park
3 - to create temporary structures for exhibitions

Differentiating and introducing new activities

1 - to introduce games in the Park
2 - to set up playground areas
3 - to set up temporary exhibitions
4 - to improve entertainment

Introducing traffic regulation measures

1 - to reduce traffic
2 - to reduce annoying noises

Improving green

1 - to create didactic gardens
2 - to call a competition for the garden design
3 - to add plants with bright colours and unusual scents
4 - to rearrange the currently present kiosks

The third action is to set up temporary exhibitions. These exhibitions should be suitable for open spaces and designed to create a continuity between the three sections of the area. The fourth action is that of improving entertainment by organizing traditional street performances, as are already held, for example, at Christmas time, and enriching the programme in the park's House of Music to expand the use of this space during the year.

Introducing traffic regulation measures

Especially at the edges of the park bordering on Mannerheim and the port, chaotic traffic detracts from people's enjoyment of the area. Two actions could be taken to address this issue. The first would be to reduce traffic with appropriate measures, especially at the points most used by public transportation. The second would be to reduce annoying noise. The traffic lights, for example, emit rather loud signals that are so noticeable as to make this one of Helsinki's characterizing elements. The reduction of noise and traffic could help to improve the liveability of the lateral streets.

Improving greenery

Although green is strongly present in the park, a more dynamic use of it could increase its attractiveness. The first action would be to offer plants for sale directly in the park. Some of the less decorative garden areas could be replaced with 'didactic' gardens using native plants and shrubs with strong scents and bright colours, with labels showing their names, available for purchase on the spot. Such an activity would be an element of strong interactivity, especially in the brighter months. The buyer, whether a local or a tourist, would thus be able to bring back home part of the garden and make it live on elsewhere. The second action is to call a competition for the design of a part of the garden, to be planned in the winter months and carried out in the summer months, choosing year after year a new theme harmonising with the characteristics of the place. The third action is to add plants with bright colours and unusual scents, and also pleasing to the touch, or yielding edible fruit – such as strawberries – to stimulate visitors' olfactive, visual, tactile and gustative senses, and waterworks in the fountains to stimulate their auditory sense. The fourth action is to rearrange the currently present kiosks to fit with the new activities in the park.

Conclusion

Over the past few years, Helsinki has been improving its image, and investing on the regeneration of neglected areas, public spaces and housing. It is important to undertake actions in the Esplanadi area because it is one of the most representative in the city. The nearness of the historical centre and of the port make it a highly attractive area. This calls for more attention to the needs of various kinds of users.

Our case study shows how the identity of this place can be enhanced by reorganizing spaces and activities, and reinforcing already present cultural resources and the continuity of the park with its two lateral streets.

In this case, urban improvement action is not called for to address issues such as overcrowded streets or polluting vehicle traffic, or the maintenance of streets and buildings. As our analysis has shown, the area has spots with multiple assets, but, as in the case of the Erottaja, next to empty spots that are not exploited to full advantage. Likewise, places for socialization are abundant on the Pohjesplanadi but scarce inside the park and on the Etelesplanadi. The kiosks are arranged in a chaotic and random way, especially on the side of the park near the port, one of the most representative spots in the area.

In the Esplanadi area, the aim of our project is especially to improve public spaces, and hence needs to be fleshed out at a more detailed scale. The purpose of the actions we propose is, above all, to improve the connections between the three parts that make up this place, so that each part may contribute to improve the other, adding to the value of the public space as a whole and making the most of the place's natural and cultural resources, as well as its commercial resources.

The improvements we propose take account of children's need for playgrounds and the elderly's need for recreational activities also offering opportunities for socialization, such as chess or bowls. They also strive to meet the demands of residents and locals for agreeable places to stop, and of tourists, who are often pressed for time and could find in the attractions of the park a reason to slow down and relax.

Conclusion

Towards a sustainable place identity

The changes that are occurring as a result of mutations in interpersonal and inter-generational relationships, globalization and new technologies have led to the phenomenon of homogenization of territorial specificities, but by the same token have also prompted further discussion concerning the importance of identity of place. Present-day urban conditions appear rich in differentiation with regard to the times and ways in which the city is used, for the new typologies of spaces and the changing in the modalities of use of those already existing.

In some cities the observable transformations are perfectly evident; in others, where the changes are less visible, we can see mutations in the installation of the infrastructure system, internet networks, and so on... To investigate the various transformations we started from the concept of place, in the sense of a space endowed with unique characteristics that make a fundamental contribution to the city's identity, and from the identification of those features which can help us understand the complexity and approach the various questions presented in this volume.

The identity of the places we have referred to relies on the dual characters of 'individuality and uniqueness', involving both stability and dynamism. This is not just a question of the physical and implicit make-up but becomes a resource for designing sustainable places.

The elements and places we have investigated have enabled us to identify new materials which, together with those of the city as it has been consolidated, make up the 'text' of the contemporary city, making it possible to identify genesis, typology, characteristics and effects on the territory.

It is observed that some transformations which are apparently internal to the territory, such as mutation in the ways of living in the home, or others that are practically invisible, such as modalities of access to and navigation of the internet, have tangible effects on the territory. As a matter of fact, mutations in the ways of understanding the household as well as interpersonal relationships translate into different ways of requesting and designing dwellings, neighbour-hoods and cities; while, in the case of the internet, one click with the mouse, for example to purchase a product, followed by a sequence of further clicks, can be transformed into a physical transportation of merchandise which is anything but invisible, with perfectly tangible effects on the territory.

Other elements of transformation which apparently seem to be external to the city, for example the new urban containers such as multiscreen cinemas or huge shopping centres, have arisen alongside freeways, but now tend more and more to be located inside the urban centres, modifying spaces and habits. At the same time high-speed trains, superhighways and motorways have been changing the appearance of the contemporary city. They have assumed new functions which have empowered the role of the break stop. Infrastructures have become not only centres where goods are distributed and services are offered, but also places for entertainment and spending free time.

Still further transformations, although apparently less invasive, such as the smells from fast-food outlets, the feel of plastic objects, the sight of publicity hoardings on the facades of buildings undergoing renovation work, have produced very obvious changes in perception of the territory. Furthermore, video surveillance cameras, metal detectors and new technologies connected to the planning of new museums, shopping malls and other urban containers create places able to pilot masses of people. These systems constitute tools for surveying, as well as for violating privacy, providing guidance and changing habits.

The serial visions of Gordon Cullen and the maps produced by Kevin Lynch, which are the basis for placemaking, need to be updated in order to represent the current characteristics of the fragmentariness and simultaneity of the contemporary city.

In order to identify, represent and project the complex transformations in the contemporary city, transversal and multi-level methods of analysis and design are being elaborated and experimented with, together with hypertexts, maps and software capable of representing and making legible the urban complexity that confronts us today.

This volume has surveyed some of the leading new methodological approaches, illustrating their principles and applications. My studies of the typologies of approach and the aspects linked to territorial analysis has prompted me to develop one further type of approach, styled complex-sensitive, as the framework for the PlaceMaker method and the case studies presented here.

The PlaceMaker method was derived from the need to identify the elements and places that are the components of contemporary identity, many of which do not figure in traditional cartography, and the principles for their planning and enhancement.

The flexibility of the PlaceMaker method, as is apparent in the various case studies we have illustrated, enables it to be used in widely varying contexts and for a range of objectives. The investigation protocol can serve as a guide to be adapted and reinforced at some points, according to the characteristics of the place and the intended purposes.

The innovative aspect of this method consists, on one hand, in the integration of different modalities and instruments for obtaining the information required to render objective and measurable even those elements which are subjective and ephemeral, and in the construction of the complex map which sums up, by means of a graphic system of symbols and the relevant key, the data obtained; and on the other hand in exploiting the complexity of the data obtained to construct the planning guidelines.

The method relies on software that makes it possible to speed up the processes of operation, updating and elaboration of the data, and also to draw up dynamic, interactive maps able to render the complexity of the places investigated. Current progress is leading to the production of software able to perform all the significant operations of data acquisition in situ with the use of multimedia tablets. Navigation by a user who is not the operator can be effected with the use of tablets or smartphones so as to constitute personalised routes through the places, extend the replies to the questionnaires to ensure a participative action in both public and private sector projects, and display the projects in external contexts offering the possibility of multimedia interaction by users, visitors, etc.

The case studies we have illustrated have highlighted areas in Europe, the USA and Japan. PlaceMaker was designed to be used to identify elements and places able to solicit cultural transformations and be of use in constructing a sustainable project where place identity constitutes the principal resource to be taken into consideration. The pilot schemes we have illustrated were designed to present different examples in terms of features and size of the area analysed, representative of particular aspects and thus generalisable with respect to specific questions, so as to identify the current identity to be safeguarded, reconstructed and promoted in order to enhance it.

As regards preserving place identity, the two case studies we presented were differentiated not only geographically and dimensionally but also for the topics involved: the Trevi–Pantheon route in Rome and the South Broadway thoroughfare in Los Angeles (CA).

For the Trevi–Pantheon route in Rome the study focused on questions related to anthropic risk and mass tourism in historic centres. The Trevi–Pantheon route, due to its recent pedestrianization, which is leading to uncontrolled commercialization to satisfy the needs of mass tourism, has decreased in quality and perception of place identity. The case study detected the identity of the places in question as well as their characteristics and potential, and identified cultural sites and appropriate activities in order to mitigate the impact of mass tourism and provide sustainable and integrated fruition and enhancement of the site.

In the early-twentieth century South Broadway in Los Angeles was the main commercial street in Los Angeles and one of the prime theatre districts. Following the Second World War, with the rise of multiscreen cinemas and shopping malls, the financial district moved south-east of downtown Los Angeles, and the area went into a slow decline. This situation of disuse transformed the image of South Broadway, 'concealing' its historical tradition devoted to the cinema. The experiment identified the identity resources and proposed design interventions able to make the historical tradition of this place re-emerge, reinterpreted according to the new needs.

With respect to reconstructing place identity, the two case studies we presented, although different in typology and dimension, share issues related to post-seismic reconstruction.

In Kitano-cho we examined an unusual area, an historic district in Kobe which, like the whole city, was struck by a violent earthquake in 1995 and subsequently reconstructed. Analysis of this case study involved recognition of the complex identity that has followed reconstruction, assessing the extent to which the earthquake still affects the current reality, and reviewing the actions required for harmonising sustainable rebuilding with the protection of place identity.

In the case of Market Street in San Francisco, the only city street directly connecting the hill to the sea, the rebuilding and development after the 1906 earthquake were aimed at reconstructing only parts of it, with special emphasis on the Financial District. The actions proposed therefore aim to make place identity the driving force in the promotion of the whole of Market Street, complementing the development actions currently under way in this area.

Concerning enhancing place identity, case studies were carried out in pedestrian or semi-pedestrian thoroughfares in three major European cities – Oxford Street in London, Las Ramblas in Barcelona and the Esplanadi area in Helsinki – which are dimensionally and geographically quite different, but share a central position and proximity to the core of the city and represent symbolic places for citizens, tourists and users in general. The aim of the experiments was to ascertain whether the current identity of the places is compatible with their walkability and liveability, and whether there are critical points where a sustainable urban design process may be developed to conserve and enhance their identity, and improve their image together with walkability and safety.

The case studies gave rise to 12 principles for place identity enhancement, created from a reasoned set of blueprints for the various experiments carried out using the original PlaceMaker method. The purpose of these principles which are illustrated below is to provide urban planning guidelines for the construction and enhancement of sustainable place identity.

Indeed, although the concept of place identity is intended as a set of characteristics in a positive sense, it is also possible that these features will not prove to be sustainable or consonant with the history and culture of the place itself. Indeed, the set of characteristics may involve, for example, shops whose appearance disfigures the ground floors of buildings and prevents appreciation of an urban thoroughfare, but which nonetheless make that location recognizable. A further example might be the set of elements in a public space which make that place distinctive but which people in that neighbourhood do not use since it fails to give them a sense of belonging.

Principles for place identity enhancement

1 Respect for place identity should be considered sine qua non within the framework of planning tools on a different scale

Respect for place identity lends quality to a project. Place identity should thus be an essential aspect of urban planning tools, making it a fundamental requisite for project sustainability. Since the components of place identity are often intangible, and the boundaries unspecified, the planning tools have to be considered both on the urban and territorial scales in order to obtain the overall quality of the place in question.

2 Place identity has to be determined with ad hoc methods

Place identity is a complex concept that requires identification of the various factors and elements which make up a place. There are many such elements forming place identity, increasingly compromised by the acceleration of urban change and globalization. In order to make identification as thorough as possible, ad hoc methods have to be used both to detect such complexity and specify guidelines for design.

3 Identity resources of a place have to be protected and enhanced so as to give the place in question a distinctive character

In order to counter the standardization of places which tends to make sites increasingly similar to one another, it becomes ever more necessary to protect identity resources. A site should have elements that make it unique and recognizable. In order to be sustainable, an urban project must be integrated with the identity of places.

4 Proper enjoyment of the physical characteristics and natural beauty of the place should be considered a priority

We need to create liveable places that foster the enjoyment of the elements that make up the history and culture of the place through projects which stimulate knowledge and sustainable use. By the same token, it is necessary to promote the enjoyment of all natural resources which are part of that place.

5 Attention to context is to be understood from a social, environmental and urban perspective

The context of a place has characteristics not only related to its architecture, urban form and culture, but also to the people who live there, and its environment, understood as natural resources. For sustainability in its broadest sense, respect of all these components is required.

6 The maintenance of buildings, roads and public spaces should be programmed

Roads and public spaces have to be maintained in the same way as buildings. Programmed maintenance should be performed periodically in order to ensure constant quality of public spaces as well as buildings within.

7 **Places should perform functions which do not cause intensive use that can damage site quality**

Monofunctional uses can cause damage to place identity. An example of this is the case of pedestrian thoroughfares of historical importance, which are used only for business. Combined uses of places should be aimed for, provided they do not compromise place identity.

8 **Local businesses should be enhanced**

The intensive use of sites by mass tourism leads to businesses that result in rapid consumption of places at the expense of their culture. It is instead necessary to promote quality local businesses to ensure residents put down roots where they live.

9 **Users of a site should be questioned about place identity during both the survey and design phases, taking different needs into account**

Site users, the prime recipients of urban transformation projects, should be interviewed at various stages in the transformation process of an area, with particular attention to the identity of the place in question. The project will thus be more likely to succeed since various needs will have been taken into consideration.

10 **Place identity should be monitored periodically**

Given the great acceleration of the rate of urban change, it is important that place identity be periodically monitored in order to understand evolution and change in time and prevent identity being compromised.

11 **Vehicle use in areas with heavy pedestrian throughput should be avoided or slowed down**

In emblematic thoroughfares and historical centres the use of private vehicles is an annoyance factor. In this respect, in such places vehicle speed should be slowed down with appropriate traffic calming measures, or private vehicles should be banned altogether. The use of bicycles and dedicated lanes should where possible be encouraged.

12 **The safety of users is paramount**

The users of streets and public spaces in general need to be protected. In this respect, projects should ensure safety both as regards possible collisions with vehicles, with appropriate separation between the different types of flows, and as regards possible criminal acts, encouraging mixed uses of the places in question during different times of the day.

The 12 principles aim to provide a checklist which a project has to satisfy in order to enhance the identity of the place in question, making sure, however, that place identity is sustainable and is not used for the sole purpose of rapid consumption of intangible heritage.

The principles should be considered not as static but as dynamic, in keeping with the increasingly rapid rates of change in a place that continually lead to expanding the scope of the concept. These principles in their present form may thus be constantly updated to allow not only for changes in the contemporary city but also for new procedures and requirements in site design.

Notes

Introduction

1 *See also* Madanipour, 1996, 2003 and Urban Design Group, 2002.
2 Author's translation from Italian text.
3 Author's translation from Italian text.
4 Lynch, K. (1976), *Managing the Sense of a Region*, Cambridge, MA and London, England: MIT Press; *see also* Vale, L.J. and Warner, S.B. jr (eds) (2001), *Imaging the City*, New Jersey: Centre for Urban Policy Research.

1 The concept of place

1 *See also* Bachelard, 1969.
2 Aristotle in his Physica defines the concept of place as 'the innermost motionless boundary of what contains'. *See* Edward Hussey (1983), *Physics: Books III and IV*, Oxford: Oxford University Press.
3 For the concept of Khora refer to Plato's dialogue *Timaeus*.
4 Cf. Heidegger, M. (1962), *Being and Time*, trans. by John Macquarrie and Edward Robinson, London: SCM Press. *See also* Heidegger, 1969.
5 *Ecumene* is the relationship between humanity and the inhabited world. The feminine noun derived from the Greek *oikoumene* (ghê), namely 'inhabited earth': defined as a relation, ecumene indicates not only the Earth as inhabited by humanity, which is deployed in symbolic and technical topologies, but also 'humanity itself insofar as it inhabits the Earth, which exists in the concrete space-time of its geograms' (translated by the author from the French text by Berque *et al.*, 1999, pp. 58–59: Ecoumène. 'Relation de l'humanité a l'étendue terrestre. Ce mot féminin vient du grec oikoumene (ge), "terre habitée". Définie comme relation, l'éecoumene est non seulement la Terre en tant qu'elle est habitée par l'humanité, c'est-à-dire déployée en topologies d'ordre symbolique et technique, mais encore l'humanité en tant qu'elle habite la Terre, c'est-a-dire qu'elle existe dans l'espace-temps concret de ses géogrammes').
6 Translated by the author from the French text by Berque *et al.*, 1999, pp. 48–49: Chora/topos. 'Il possède nécessairement un coté matériel, physique et écologique, mesurable, donc commensurable à d'autre lieux. Cette dimension quantitative l'apparente au topos aristotélicien et à la Stelle heideggerienne: tel un récipient, c'est la limite externe d'un chose dans l'espace universel d'un environment objectivé. D'autre part, le lieu relève non moins nécessairement d'une dimension immatérielle, pénoménale et sémantique, non measurable, donc incommensurable à d'autres lieux. Cette

dimension qualitative et singulieère l'apparente à la chora platonicienne et à l'Ort heideggerien: c'est la condition d'existence de la chose au sein du monde sensible. Ces deux aspects du lieu se conjuguent trajectivement dans le réalité de l'écoumène: chaque lieu est non seulement un topos mais encore une chora, et réciproquement'.

7 *See also* Hayden, 1995.
8 Cited in Carmona *et al.*, 2003, p.93; *see also* Barthes, 1967 and Choay, 1986.
9 Cited in Carmona *et al.*, 2003, p.93.
10 'In this sense, the building, the monument, and the city become human things par excellence; and as such, they are profoundly linked to an original occurrence, to a first sign, to composition, permanence, and evolution, and to both chance and tradition. As the first inhabitants fashioned an environment for themselves, they also formed a place and established its uniqueness.The comments of the theoreticians on the framing of the landscape in painting, the sureness with which the Romans repeated certain elements in their building of new cities, acknowledging in the locus the potential for transformation – this and many other facts cause us to intuit the importance of certain artifacts; and when we consider information of this type, we realize why architecture was so important in the ancient world and in the Renaissance. It shaped a context. Its forms changed together with the larger changes of a site, participating in the constitution of a whole and serving an overall event, while at the same time constituting an event in itself. Only in this way can we understand the importance of an obelisk, a column, a tombstone.' (Rossi, 1984, p.106)
11 Cited in Bonnes and Secchiaroli, 1995, p.173.

2 Place identity

1 Cited in Watson and Bentley, 2007, p.3.
2 Cited in Southworth and Ruggeri, 2010, p.498.
3 Author's translation from the Italian text.
4 Author's translation from the Italian text.
5 Author's translation from the Italian text.
6 Author's translation from the Italian text.
7 Amundsen (2001), cited in Hague and Jenkins, 2005, p.13.
8 *See also* Hayden, 1995.

3 New spaces for living

1 As observed by Towers (2005, pp.101–102) with respect to the elderly and disabled: 'Self-evidently not all disabled people are elderly. Still less are all the elderly disabled. Nevertheless, it has long been recognized that many people do become incapacitated in various ways as they advance into old age and that their homes need to be designed to meet these changing needs. ... While the flexible design of all housing is a desirable aim, multi-storey forms are particularly suitable for housing the elderly. For most elderly people their space needs are modest and, with a need to increase housing densities, these can most easily be met in blocks of flats. Many elderly do not have the mobility to cope with gardening or the energy to manage external maintenance, and flat living relieves them of these demands. Most importantly, perhaps, living off the ground creates much higher security. Ground level dwellings have windows and front and back doors which can be breached by intruders – a

monitored by security cameras. In larger blocks, security and surveillance can be reinforced by concierge staff.'

2 'The needs of most young people can easily be met by general-purpose housing. Like many elderly people, though, they neither want nor need the responsibilities of home and garden maintenance and are well suited to living in multi-storey flats. While many of the young will continue to find homes in the wider community, two new forms of housing have emerged in recent years specifically tailored to ease the transition into adult lifestyles: *Foyers* and *Caspar*. *Foyers*. These emerged in France in the immediate post-war period. They provided basic accommodation for young single people backed up by common services. The *Foyer* idea did not come to Britain until the 1990s. Their first aim is to provide a safe haven for young people in housing need. Residents stay for a limited period and during this time they are able to develop the social skills necessary to support themselves. *Foyers* provide high-quality accommodation in self-contained rooms or flats. Communal rooms are provided for recreation and training sessions. Most *Foyers* are newly built but they could easily re-use existing buildings adapted for their purpose. *Caspar*. The Rowntree Foundation developed this concept and its full name spells out its purpose – city-centre apartments for single people at affordable rents. Unlike *Foyers* they are not intended for young people in need of training and support. They aim to provide for people who can afford a sizeable cost rent but who wish to live in accommodation which is fully serviced and readily available on a short-term basis. They are intended to be located within easy walking distance of the work and leisure opportunities of urban centres.' (Towers, 2005, pp.101–2)

3 Author's translation from Italian text.

4 'The objects in daily use for the purposes of housing, clothing and feeding ourselves need to be continually translated into a current idiom. Thus the objects, constructions and products that express habitation constitute for Lefebvre a partial system which may be the house, the city or the agglomeration. Each element contributes to the creation of the "social text" and at the same time is expressed by means of a language made up of words and phrases. In this way the distribution of the living space is manifested through the description of single objects and modes of behaviour together with their respective occurrences, rhythms and durations' (Lefebvre, 1966, cited in Viganò, 1999, pp.28–29, translation by the author). *See also* De Certeau, 1984.

4 Urban containers

1 *See also* Zukin, 2010.

2 Cited in Carmona *et al.* 2010 (second edition), p.129.

3 Cited in Carmona *et al.*, 2003, p.105. *See also* Gottdiener, 2001, 2003.

4 'Sometimes branded identities derive from the success of a location based entertainment (LBE) project, but in other instances they represent the imposition of pre-existing consumer and show business brands (such as Nike, Universal, Coca-Cola, ViaCom) on leisure sites in the expectation of creating a profitable "synergy". Another option is the rising popularity of "naming rights"; the sale of corporate names for sports stadiums and arenas and concert halls' (Hannigan, 1998, p.3). *See also* Anholt, 2010.

5 'Typically, an UED project will contain one or more themed restaurants (the Hard Rock Cafe, Planet Hollywood, the Rainforest Cafe), megaplex cinema, an IMAX theater, record (HMV, Virgin, Tower) and book (Barnes and Noble, Borders) megastores and some form of interactive, high-tech arcade complete with virtual reality games and ride simulators. Large, publicly sponsored projects might also include an aquarium, sport stadium and/or arena, live theater and a science museum.' (Hannigan, 1998, p.3–4)

6 'Without a doubt, a major inspiration has been the Disney model, not just because it has been widely imitated but also because a number of Disney "imagineers" (designers) have migrated to other entertainment and real estate companies and projects where they bring their "Magic Kingdom" sensibility. Increasingly, as motion picture and amusement park technologies merge to produce a new generation of attractions, the space between authenticity and illusion recedes, creating the condition of "hyperreality" described by such postmodern writers as Umberto Eco and Jean Baudrillard. Furthermore, Fantasy City is postmodern insofar as it represents a "collage" (Dear, 1995, p.30) or "gigantic agglomeration" (Soja 1989, p.246) of themed attractions, more closely connected to global commerce than to one another.' (Hannigan, 1998, p.4). *See also* Soja 1996.

7 'It's common sense taken to the level of brand marketing. Every place is potentially a brand. In every way as much as Disneyland and Las Vegas, cities like Paris, Edinburgh and New York are their own brands, because a consistent, clear image has emerged of what each place looks like, feels like, and the story, or history it conveys.' (Sircus, 2001, p.127)

8 As regards the Touristic-Historic City, *see* Ashworth and Tunbridge, 1990.

9 Author's translation from Italian text.

10 *See also* Tiesdell *et al.*, 1996

5 Networks and infrastructures

1 As pointed out by De Souza e Silva (2006, p.267), Deleuze and Guattari (2002) identify a framework in order to understand the idea of mobile networks through the relationship between the nomad movements and the 'spatiogeographic aspect of the war machine' through three kinds of 'spatiogeographic nomadic movement'. 'The first is related to points and paths of the nomadic network. Although a nomad is not ignorant of points, he or she focuses on paths, on the movement that happens between these points. In a nomadic network, the points are subordinated to the paths. Nomads also go from point to point, but as a mere consequence of their trajectories. "The life of the nomad is the intermezzo" (p.380). Nomadic spaces are, following Deleuze and Guattari, smooth spaces, which means that the paths that determine nomadic movement are also mobile and easily "effaced and displaced with the trajectory" (p.381). A nomad does not occupy predefined routes and paths: He or she constructs his or her own while moving through space.'

2 As observed by Bauman (2004, p.25), 'in the words of Andy Hargreaves, professor of education and a uniquely perceptive observer of the contemporary cultural scene: in Airports and other public spaces, people with mobile phone headset attachments walk around, talking aloud and alone, like paranoid

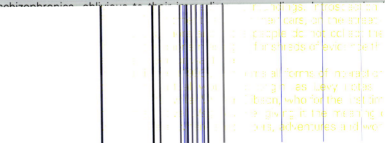

agree to have his or her location tracked by imaHima. There is also the possibility of contacting a stranger whose profile matches the user's request if he or she allows himself or herself to be contacted by an unknown person. However, whereas traditional instant messaging displays on computer screens simultaneously connected users, independent of their physical locations, imaHima connects people within a close radius in physical space. There are currently 250,000 active imaHima users in Japan who access the service through i-mode and wireless application protocol phones (imaHima, 2005). The popularity of these gadgets, devices and applications in Japan provides evidence that mobile phones are used not only to communicate with people who are distant but also to socialize with peers who are nearby, sharing the same physical space, even if they are not at eye-contact distance. Finding people to socialize in cyberspace has always been critical in multi-user environments on the fixed Internet. Mobile internet users also look for people with whom to socialize. The difference, however, is that mobile networks help find people in public places. In the hybrid-spaces logic, mobile phones do not take users out of physical space, as has been suggested by many scholars who have studied mobile devices such as voice communication technologies (Gergen, 2002; Plant, 2001; Puro, 2002).' (de Souza e Silva, 2006)

5 Author's translation from Italian text.
6 Author's translation from Italian text.
7 'But urban public space is not merely un-private – what's left over when everyone walls off their private domains. A space is genuinely public, as Kevin Lynch once pointed out, only to the extent that it really is openly accessible and welcoming to members of the community that it serves. It must also allow users considerable freedom of assembly and action. And there must be some kind of public control of its use and its transformation over time. The same goes for public cyberspace, so creators and maintainers of public, semipublic, and pseudopublic parts of the online worlds – like the makers of city squares, public parks, office building lobbies, shopping mall atriums, and Disneyland Main Street – must consider who gets in and who gets excluded, what can and cannot be done there, whose norms are enforced, and who exerts control. These questions, like the complementary ones of privacy and encryption, have become the foci of crucial policy debates.' (Mitchell, 1996, p.125)
8 Author's translation from Italian text.

6 New places of perceptions

1 As Mcpherson (2006, p.99) states: 'There is a considerable body of research which recognizes landscape as engaging other senses (Tuan 1993; Soini 2001; Thwaites 2001), including work on "soundscapes" and "smellscapes" (Porteous 1985; Porteous and Mastin 1985; Wrightson 2000; Hedfors and Berg 2003). This sort of sensory landscape research often utilizes a quite static visual conception of landscape to frame the research and give order to the data. In this "sensory landscape" literature there is a tendency to treat the senses as largely discrete sensory registers, to assume that sense perception is a rational, relatively objective process and to treat smells and sounds as static. This allows researchers and practitioners to map (impose a visual order) onto these "sensescapes" (Tuan 1993; Soini 2001; Thwaites 2001). However such approaches ignore the integrated nature of environmental perception. "Whilst it is possible to identify the apparent dominance of a specific sense in a given situation, on closer analysis all geographical experiences are made up of a complex of sensuous information combining activities of the sense organs, the body and its limbs, and mental processes (memory and expectation, analysis and evaluation)"'. (Rodaway 1994, p. 35)

2 'Take an electroperception. The city is a vast, dense area of electrical energy fields and waves estimated to be 100 million times stronger than 100 years ago. Urban life systems cannot operate without electricity; an electrical shutdown will bring the city to a halt. The accumulative cocktail of magnetic and electrical fields generated by power transmission lines, pylons and masts, mobile phones, computers, televisions and radio, lighting, wiring and household appliances can seriously interfere with the subtle natural balances of each cell in our body. These massive currents criss-crossing the urban environment are unseen, unfelt, unheard, without taste or smell, yet they operate upon us, albeit at a subconscious level.' (Landry, 2006, p.40)

3 'Although contributing to the richness of experience, non-visual dimensions of sensation and perception are often underdeveloped and underexploited. Lang argues that concern for the "sonic environment" should – in specific settings – focus on increasing the positive, e.g. birdsong, children's voices, the crunching of autumn leaves. He argues that an environment's "soundscape" can be orchestrated in much the same way as its visual qualities by the choice of materials used for the surfaces of the environment and the nature of objects within it" (1994, p.227). Positive sounds – waterfalls, fountains, etc. – can make negative sound like traffic noise.' (Carmona et al., 2003, p.88)

4 *See* Porteous, 1977, 1985, 1990, 1997

5 'Events that take place in urban space or in the doors and windows on ground floor at a distance of up to 100 meters (110 yards), we can also get close up and bring all our senses to bear. From the street, we can only experience with difficulty events that take place higher up in buildings. The higher up, the more difficult it is to see. We have to move further and further back to look up, distances become greater and greater, and what we see and experience diminishes.' (Gehl, 2010)

6 Pergola (1997, p.84) mentions the format of publicity posters, which in Europe and America is strictly related to the available hoardings, whereas in Japan there is a veritable explosion of formats of every shape and size. The messages are built around associations of ideas in order to put across some of the product features, endowing them with 'that cultural surplus value which determines the economic value in the society of communications and is represented by what features in the imagery of publicity'. (Author's translation from Italian text)

7 See the images of the sound mapping for the centre of Boston and acoustic diagrams for Nakamise, Asakusa, Tokyo, published in Barbara, 2000, pp. 170–171.

8 As Landry (2006, p.56) asserts: 'The sound of commerce is the sound of movement: packing, unpacking boxes, plonking crates on top of each other, shouts, self-advertising, the rustling of paper, trolleys, forklift trucks and their high-pitched whining. Markets are a sound and smell cliché, but compelling and ubiquitous. They have a rich sound colour and variations coming more

iconic nature of smells linked with places. "La Défense has its own particular smell, rather mineral, neutral, typical of a place given over to the service industry. If instead you walk through the cosmopolitan quarter of Barbès and go into the large Tati store, your nose will undoubtedly be caught unawares by the strong smells of spices and aromatic waters emanating from the African shops … that odour is reassuring for a group of individuals, providing them with a cultural continuity in space and time. Whether they are good or ailing, disquieting or reassuring, this ID card of the quarter represents the intimate, on-going city which affects our emotions".' (Barbara and Perliss, 2006)

10 'Let's move from the crusty smell of fast food to the antiseptic non-smell of electrical goods. Think of non-smelling computers, televisions and radio equipment, where only the rubbery connections exude a tiny whiff. However, changes are on the horizon to control our smell environment comprehensively. The Japanese communications ministry is investing large resources in creating the first 3D virtual reality television by 2020 to change the way we watch TV. It is proposed to have several thousand smells so as to create any mood. If that is frightening, consider that Las Vegas casinos already pump the smell of money on to the gambling floors: dry, sweaty, sweet.' (Landry, 2006, p.67)

11 Author's translation from Italian text.

12 As Landry (2006, p.43) states: 'Clearly planners and developers deal with sensory elements, but often with insufficient thought, subtlety or care. Even worse, sensory awareness is strongly manipulated in the world of shopping malls and destination marketing without an ethical aim. The purpose is for people to spend more so "nice" smells and good sounds direct and guide people. At the very least we should know what is happening – that, for instance, the smell of bread is pumped out in supermarkets, as is the smell of turkey at Christmas.'

13 Author's translation from Italian text.

14 An appreciation of air temperature is the property of nerve endings which can detect changes of a few tenths of a degree Centigrade. The blind can distinguish up to a dozen air speeds (Rapoport, 1977). These senses become important environmentally chiefly in terms of contrast, as when one moves from the blinding light of a street to the dark coolness of an alley or church, from hot, dry city centre to cooler, moister sea-coast or park, or from the windy to the protected side of a tall building (Porteous, 2006, p.38).

15 Author's translation from Italian text.

7 Monitored places

1 *See also* Oc and Tiedsell, 1997, 2000.

2 Patton (2000) also observed that: 'Uses and actions are often constrained by public places that are functionally defined for particular purposes. In the case of the homeless, parks are often legislated as places for recreation or leisure, not sleeping or bathing. The rights of presence, use, and action are further limited by restrictions on the appropriation and modification of places and the disposition of the given rights … By appropriating an area of a public place, a person temporarily excludes others from using that particular place. A picnic may be acceptable where a market stall is not. Individuals are generally not authorized to permanently modify public places (as in the case of graffiti). And lastly, since rights to public space are granted by the collective, individuals may not dispose of, trade, or revoke a person's rights to public space without the authority of the collective. Public places are public goods that ideally reflect a congruence between those who use the place and those who are responsible for it. Since the public place is by definition accessible to all, responsibility for that place and the decision-making that shapes it should similarly be broadly accessible.'

3 Still citing Bellotti: 'By making people aware of their observation, people will be better able to read the social context and thereby control their behaviours accordingly. In public areas, "designers must rely on users' exercising behavioural rather than technical control over information they give out." From the designer's perspective, "Behaving as though one is on public display is certainly trustworthy, low-effort, learnable, and low-cost." Feedback reduces the ambiguity of public places under surveillance, enabling people to better read the social context. With a better sense of who has a disembodied presence in the place and how one's actions are dissociated from it, people will be able to control their behavior so as to protect their privacy.' (Patton, 2000)

4 Satellite images as well as video camera surveillance have many other uses, which can have different kinds of consequences. Among these, catastrophes due to natural as well as human causes have always modified the appearance of places, cities and territories. In the era of globalization, places of destruction and conflict have become scenarios which thanks to sophisticated technology can be 'consumed' sitting comfortably in front of the television. The reduction of infinite richness in the representation of territories and the characteristics that these kinds of images transmit can dramatically mutate human relations and exchanges, and the places they belong to. Their representation may cause negative effects on the natural capacity of recuperation of life relationships as well as rebuilding new territories of socialization. Contemporary conflicts carried out with more and more sophisticated and penetrating tools and modalities constitute just one of the examples of how destruction is caused and determined.

8 Placemaking: origins and changes

1 On the concept of placemaking *see also* Friedman, 2010.

9 The virtual approach

1 The virtual approach has also led to other results, including a different way of conceiving citizen participation in the process of local construction. For example, TimeZone, an architectural research group, creates virtual communities living in a three-dimensional network yet interconnected with the real areas, with the aim of helping neighborhoods in intrinsic social and economic difficulty which are launching programs of social and urban rehabilitation. In the three experiments 'Second Time Zone' – St. Ouen, Pantin and Kobe – the citizens of these districts are involved in the composition of the true image of their area, in the virtual rehabilitation of degraded architecture, or that have had to change their original function, and

15 The method

1 *See* Chapter 17 devoted to the sustainable place identity index.
2 *See also* Viganò (1999, p.28): 'Surveying as you are walking means deconstructing: naming objects, saying what you see on different scales, at different levels of abstraction; it implies reducing the city to its basic elements. Thanks to the survey you can get closer to the material quality of the territory, the outcome and deposit of practices and cultures which in the course of time have characterized consolidated theories or practices .... Surveying means dealing with "places" according to the definition given by de Certeau, and to go on from this to "spaces" in the sense of "frequented places". The main points of reference for an investigation of the modes of use of the contemporary space and the role of the various elements in the representation of collective image-making are the studies of Benjamin on the passages of Paris, Krakauer on the streets of Paris and Berlin; Lefebvre, Raymond and others on the pavillonnaire in Paris; de Certau on daily urban frequentation; and more recently, Roncayolo on the boulevard-promenade in Marseilles and Host on the promenade in Geneva. Their chief interest lies in the attempt to describe the city and the different life styles starting from the forms that characterise the places; to build up a picture of the spaces that collates, without being determinist, rhythms of use, habits, physical qualities; to come up with an accurate study of the individual materials and styles of inhabiting them, using them, renewing them, deforming them, modifying them; to avoid separating words from things.' (Author's translation from Italian text)
3 Carmona *et al.* (2003, p.88) pointed out: 'Perception (sometimes, confusingly referred to as "cognition") concerns more than just seeing or sensing the urban environment. It refers to the more complex processing or understanding of stimuli. Ittelson (1978, from Bell *et al.*, 1990, p.29) identifies four dimensions of perceptions, which operate simultaneously: cognitive, involves thinking about, organising and keeping information. In essence, it enables us to make sense of the environment; affective, involves our feeling, which influence perception of the environment – equally, perception of the environment influences our feelings; interpretative, encompasses meaning or associations derived from the environment. In interpreting information, we rely on memory for points of comparison with newly experienced stimuli; evaluative, incorporates values and preferences and the determination of good or bad.'

Part III Section I Preserving place identity

Introduction

1 Many projects, including those of Los Angeles Conservancy and Bringing Back Broadway, are carried out in order to give back the past splendor and place identity of this thoroughfare.

Part III Section II Reconstructing place identity

Introduction

1 See *Safer Homes, Stronger Communities: A Handbook for Reconstructing after Natural Disasters*, published by the World Bank in January 2010.
2 *See* http://www.amra.unina.it with respect to the Italian post-seismic reconstructions. *See also* Mazzoleni and Sepe, 2004 and Sepe, 2005a.

3 'The great 1906 earthquake and the fire that it caused resulted in about 3,000 deaths. The worst building damage occurred on "made land": artificially filled areas created on former marshes, streams and bay. Wood-frame buildings in the South of Market area, and brick buildings downtown, were especially heavily damaged. Large ground displacements in the filled ground along the Bay damaged utilities.' (http://www.sfplanning.org/ftp/general_plan/I8_Community_Safety.htm)

4 http://www.sfplanning.org/ftp/general_plan/I8_Community_Safety.htm.

5 As regards the current projects concerning Market Street, *see* http://www.bettermarketstreetsf.org.

Part III Section III Enhancing place identity

Introduction

1 Kunstler, 1998, cited in Bain *et al.*, 2012.

2 Bain *et al.*, 2012.

3 Barcelona Town Hall is currently analysing this area with the aim of improving its quality and to provide for its management, consulting the different stakeholders involved (Ajuntament de Barcelona, 2008). The main task is to analyse this place and its peculiarities from all points of view: from the urban, to the economic and cultural, from mobility to safety.

22 London Oxford Street

1 There is a subtlety here: for it may be that the completion of work in Oxford might have the effect of the results of the experiment even though the significant length of Oxford Street would not appear to be

2

References

Abrams, J. and Hall, P. (eds) (2006), *Else/where: Mapping. Cartographies of networks and territories*, Minnesota: University of Minnesota Design Institute.

Agre, P.E. and Rotenberg, M. (2001), *Technology and Privacy: The New Landscape*, Cambridge, MA: MIT Press.

Alcantara de Vasconcellos, E. (2004), 'The Use of Streets: A reassessment and tribute to Donald Appleyard', *Journal of Urban Design*, 9(1): 3–22.

Amin, A. and Graham, S. (1997), 'The ordinary city', *Transactions of the Institute of British Geographers*, 22(4): 411–429.

Amundsen, A.B. (2001), 'Articulations of identity: A methodological essay and a report on Askim and Tidaholm', *NoordXXI Report*, 19.

Anholt, S. (2010) *Places: identity, image and reputation*, Basingstoke: Palgrave Macmillan.

Appleyard, D. (1976), *Planning a Pluralistic City*, Cambridge, MA and London: MIT Press.

Appleyard, D. (1981), *Livable Streets*, Berkeley: University of California Press.

Appleyard, D., Lynch, K. and Myer, J. (1964), *The View from the Road*, Cambridge, Massachusetts: MIT Press.

Arefi, M. (1999), 'Non-place and placelessness as narrative of loss: Rethinking the notion of place', *Journal of Urban Design*, 4: 179–193.

Ashworth, G.J. and Tunbridge, J.E. (1990), *The Touristic-Historic City*, London: Belhaven Press.

Augé, M. (1995), *Non-places: An introduction to an Anthropology of Supermodernity*, London: Verso.

Augé, M. (1999), *Disneyland e altri nonluoghi*, Torino: Bollati Boringhieri.

Ayeni, O.O., Saka, D.N. and Ikwuemesi, G. (2004), 'Developing a multimedia gis database for tourism industry in Nigeria', proceeding of *ISPRS*, Istanbul.

Bachelard, G. (1969), *The poetics of Space*, London: Bacon.

Bacon, E. N. (1974), *Design of cities*, London: Thames & Hudson.

Bain, L., Gray, B. and Rodgers, D. (2012), *Living Streets: Strategies for Crafting Public Space*, New Jersey: Wiley.

Banerjee, T. and Loukaitou-Sideris, A. (eds) (2010), *Companion to Urban Design*, London and New York: Routledge.

Banerjee, T. and Southworth, M. (eds) (1990), *City Sense and City Design*, Massachusetts: MIT Press.

Barajas, D. (2003), *Dispersion*, Rotterdam: Episode publishers.

Barbara, A. (2000), *Storie di architettura attraverso i sensi*, Milano: Bruno Mondadori.

Barbara, A. and Perliss, A. (2006), *Invisible Architecture*, Milan: Skira.

Barthes, R. (1967), *Element of Semiology*, New York: Hill and Wang.

Bauman, Z. (1998), *Globalization: The Human Consequences*, Oxford: Blackwell Publishing.

Bauman, Z. (1999), *In Search of Politics*, Standford: California Stanford University Press.

Bauman, Z. (2004), *Identity: Conversations with Benedetto Vecchi*, Cambridge: Polity Press.

Bellotti, V. (2001), 'Design for Privacy in Multimedia Computing and Communications Environments'. In Philip E. Agre and Marc Rotenberg (eds), *Technology and Privacy: The New Landscape*, Cambridge, MA: MIT Press.

Belsky, E.S., Bogardus Drew, R. and McCue, D. (2007), 'Projecting the Underlying Demand for New Housing Units: Inferences from the Past, Assumptions about the Future'. Joint Center for Housing Studies of Harvard University, Working Paper W07-7. November 2007.

Bentley, I. (1999), *Urban Transformations: Power, People and Urban Design*, London: Routledge.

Berque, A., Conan, M., Donadieu, P., Lassus, B. and Roger, A. (1999), *Mouvance: Cinquante mots pour le paysage*, Paris: Éditions de la Villette.

Boeri, S. (1997), 'Eclectic Atlases'. In *Documenta X, Kassel*, Documents 3, Documenta Kassel, Editore Cantz, Germany.

Boeri, S. (2003), *USE: Uncertain State of Europe*, Milano: Skira Editore.

Boeri, S. (2011), *The Anticity*, Roma-Milano: Laterza.

Boissevain, J. (ed.) (1996), *Coping with Tourists: European Reactions to Mass Tourism*, Oxford: Berghahn Books.

Bonnes, B. and Secchiaroli, G. (1995), *Environmental Psychology: A Psychosocial Introduction*, London: Sage.

Bosselmann, P. (1998), *Representation of Places: Reality and Realism in City Design*, Berkeley: University of California Press.

CABE (2001), *Better Places to live: by Design – A companion Guide to PPG*, London: Thomas Telford.

CABE and DETR (2000), *By Design: Urban Design in the Planning System – Towards Better Practice*, London: Thomas Telford.

Calabrese, F., Reades, J. and Ratti, C. (2010), 'Eigenplaces: Segmenting space through digital signatures', *IEEE Pervasive Computing*, 9: 78–84.

Calvino, I. (1995), *Sotto il sole giaguaro*, Milano: Mondadori.

Canter, D.V. (1977), *The Psychology of Place*, New York: Palgrave Macmillan.

Carmona, M. (2001), *Housing Design Quality: Through Policy, Guidance and Review*, London: Spon Press.

Carmona, M., de Magalhaes, C. and Edward, M. (2001), *The Value of Urban*

Chapman, D. and Larkham, P. (1994), *Understanding Urban Design, An Introduction to the Process of Urban Change*, Birmingham: University of Central England.

Choay, F. (1986), *Urbanism and semiology*. In M. Gottdiener and A.P. Lagopoulos (eds), *The city and the sign: an introduction to urban semiotics* (160–175), New York: Columbia University Press.

Christensen, K.S. (1999), *Cities and Complexity*, Thousand Oaks, CA: Sage Publications.

Ciorra, P. (1997), 'Autogrill. Spazi e spiazzi per la socialità su gomma'. In P. Desideri and M. Ilardi, *Attraversamenti. I nuovi territori dello spazio pubblico*, Genova-Milano: Costan & Nolan.

Cosgrove, D. (2001), *Apollo's Eye. A Cartographic Geneaology of the Earth in the Western Imagination*, Baltimore: The Jons Hopkins University Press.

Costanzo, M. (2006), MVRDV: Works and Projects 1991–2006, Milan: Skira.

Crang, M. (1998), *Cultural Geography*, London: Routledge.

Croxford, B., Penn, A. and Hillier, B. (1996), 'Spatial distribution of urban pollution: civilising urban traffic', *Science of the Total Environment*, 189–190: 3–9.

Cullen, G. (1961), *Townscape*, London: Architectural Press.

Cunningham, F.F. (1975), 'The human eye and the landscape', *Landscape*, 20: 14–19.

Dawson, J. and Lord, D. (1985), *Shopping Centre Development: Policies and Prospects*, London and New York: Routledge.

Dear, M. (1995), 'Prolegomena to a postmodern urbanism'. In P. Healey, S. Cameron, S. Davoudi, S. Graham and A. Madanipour (eds), *Managing Cities: The New Urban Context*, Chichester: John Wiley, 27–44.

De Certeau, M. (1984), *The practice of everyday life*, Berkeley: University of California Press.

Denis, C. and Daniels, S. (1988), *The Iconography of Landscape: Essay on the Symbolic Representation, Design and Use of Past Environments*, Cambridge: Cambridge University Press.

Desideri, P. (ed.) (2001), *ExCity*, Rome: Meltemi.

Desideri, P. and Ilardi, M. (1997), *Attraversamenti. I nuovi territori dello spazio pubblico*, Genova-Milano: Costan & Nolan.

De Souza e Silva, A. (2006), *Mobile Technologies as Interfaces of Hybrid Spaces*, Thousand Oaks: Sage.

Dibbell, J. (1999), *My tiny life: Crime and passion in a virtual world*, New York: Owl.

Dickens, P. (1990), *Urban Sociology: Society, Locality and Human Nature*, Hemel Hempstead: Harvester Wheatsheaf.

Donath, J.S. (1997) 'Inhabiting the virtual city: The design of social environments for electronic communities'. Unpublished doctoral dissertation, Massachusetts Institute of Technology. Retrieved 28 November 2005, available at http://judith.www.media.mit.edu/Thesis/ Thesis/Contents.html.

Donofrio, M.E. (2010) 'Preserving the Neighborhood Theatres of William Harold Lee', Masters Thesis, Pennsylvania, PA: University of Pennsylvania.

Dovey, K. (1999), *Framing Places: Mediating Power in Built Form*, London: Routledge.

Easterling, K. (1999), *Organization Space: Landscapes, Highways, and Houses in America*, Cambridge, MA: MIT Press.

Eco, U. (1968), *The City and the Sign*, New York: Columbia University Press.

Edgington, D.W. (2010), *Reconstructing Kobe: The Geography of Crisis and Opportunity*, Vancouver: University of British Columbia Press.

Entrikin, J.N. (1991), *The Betweenness of Place: Towards a Geography of Modernity*, Baltimore: John Hopkins University Press.

Erikson, E. (1959), *Identity and the Life Cycle*, selected papers, New York: International Universities Press.

Evans, B., McDonald, F. and Rudlin, D. (2011), *Urban Identity: Learning from Place*, London and New York: Routledge.

Fainstein, S. (1994), *The City Builders: Property, Politics and Planning in London and New York*, Oxford: Blackwell.

Farè, I. (2003), *Nuove specie di spazi*, Napoli:Liguori

Forrester, J.W. (1969), *Urban dynamics*, Cambridge, Massachusetts and London, England: MIT Press.

Forrester, J. and Snell, C. (2007), 'Planning inclusive and sustainable urban regeneration: Balancing a visitor-based economy with local needs in the city of York, UK', *Journal of Urban Regeneration and Renewal*, 1(1).

Frers, L. and Meier, L. (eds) (2007), *Encountering Urban Places – Visual and Material Performances in the City*, London: Ashgate.

Friedmann, J. (2010), 'Place and place-making in cities: A global perspective', *Planning Theory & Practice*, 11(2): 149–165.

Fuller-Seeley, K.H. (2008), *Hollywood in the Neighborhood: Historical Case Studies of Local Moviegoing*, Berkeley: University of California Press.

Fyfe, N. (1998) (ed.), *Images of the Street: Planning, Identity and Control in Public Space*, London: Routledge.

Gandelsonas, M. (1991), *The Urban Text*, Cambridge, MA and London: MIT Press.

Gausa, M. (2002), *Housing*, Barcelona: Actar.

Gausa, M. *et al.* (2003), *The Metapolis Dictionary of Advanced architecture*, Barcelona: Actar.

Gausa, M., Guallart, V. and Muller, W. (2003), *Hicat: HiperCatalunya, Research Territories*, Barcelona: IAAC/Generalitat de Catalunya.

Gehl, J. (1971), *Life between Buildings: Using Public Space*, New York: Van Nostrand Reinhold.

Gehl, J. (2001), *Life Between Buildings: Using Public Space*, Copenhagen: Arkitektens Forlag.

Gehl, J. (2010) *Cities For People*, Washington: Island Press.

Gehl, J. and Gemzoe, L. (1996), *Public Spaces Public Life – Copenhagen*, Copenhagen: Danish Architectural Press.

Goffman, E. (1959), *The Presentation of Self in Everyday Life*, New York: Anchor Books Doubleday.

Gospodini, A. (2002), 'European cities and place-identity', *Discussion Paper Series*, 8(2): 19–36.

References

Gunn, C.A. (2002), *Tourism planning*, New York: Routledge.
Hague, C. and Jenkins, P. (eds) (2005), *Place Identity, Participation and Planning*, Abingdon: Routledge.
Halbwachs, M. (1992), *On collective memory*, Chicago: The University of Chicago Press.
Haldrup, M., Larsen, J. and Urry J. (2004), *Performing Tourist Places*, Aldershot: Ashgate.
Hall, P. (1988), *City of Tomorrow: An Intellectual History of Urban Planning and Design in the Twentieth Century*, Oxford: Basil Blackwell.
Hall, T. (1998), *Urban Geography*, London: Routledge.
Hall, P. and Preston, P. (1988), *The Carrier Wave: New Information Technology and the Geography of Innovation*, London and New York: Unwin Hyman.
Hannigan, J. (1998), *Fantasy City: Pleasure and Profit in the Postmodern metropolis*, London: Routledge.
Harvey, D. (1985), *Consciousness and the Urban Experience*, London and Baltimore: Johns Hopkins University Press.
Harvey, D. (1989), *The Urban Experience*, Oxford: Blackwell.
Hass-Klau, C., Crampton, G., Downland, C. and Nold, I. (1999), *Streets as Living Space: Helping Public Spaces Play their Proper Role*, London: Landor.
Hauptmann, D. (ed) (2001), *Cities in transition*, Rotterdam: Publishers Rotterdam.
Hayden, D. (1995), *The power of place: urban landscapes as public history*, Cambridge, MA: MIT Press.
Hayward, R. and McGlynn, S. (eds) (1993), *Making Better Places, Urban Design Now*, Oxford: Architectural Press.
Healey, P. (2010), *Making Better Places*, New York: Palgrave Macmillan.
Heidegger, M. (1962), *Being and Time*, New York: Harper & Row.
Heidegger, M. (1969), *Identity and Difference*, New York: Harper & Row.
Hillier, B. (1996), *Space is the Machine*, Cambridge: Cambridge University Press.
Hillier, B. (2007), Space is the Machine: A configurational theory of architecture, London, UK: Space Syntax.
Hillier, B. and Hanson, J. (1984), *The Social Logic of Space*, Cambridge: Cambridge University Press.
Hillier, B. and Stutz, C. (2004), 'New methods in Space Sintax', *Urban Design*, 93: 2–33.
Hillier, B., Leaman, A., Stansall, P. and Bedford, M. (1986), 'Space Syntax', *Environment and Planning B: Planning and Design*, 13: 147–185.
Hillman, J. (1990), *Planning for Beauty*, London: RFAC.
Horan, T.A. (2000), *Digital Places: Building Our City of Bits*, Washington: Urban Land Institute.
Indovina, F. (ed) (2006), *Nuovo Lessico Urbano*, Milano: FrancoAngeli.
Jacobs, A.B. (1993), *Great Streets*, Cambridge, MA: MIT Press.
Jacobs, A. and Appleyard, D. (1987), 'Towards an Urban Design Manifesto: A prologue', *Journal of the American Planning Association*, 53: 112–120.
Jacobs, J. (1961), *The Death and Life of Great American Cities: The Failure of Modern Town Planning,* London: Peregrine Books.
Jha, A.K., Barenstein, J.D., Phelps, P.M., Pittet, D. and Sena, S. (2010), *Safe Homes, Stronger Communities: A Handbook for Reconstruction after Natural Disaster,* Washington DC: The International Bank for Reconstruction and Development/The World Bank.
Jones, P., Marshall, S. and Boujenko, N. (2008), *Link and Place: A Guide to Street Planning and Design,* London: Landor Publishing.

Kaika, M. and Swyngedouw, E. (2000), 'Fetishizing the modern city: The phantasmagoria of urban technological networks', *International Journal of Urban and Regional Research*, 24: 120–138.

Kaika, M. and Swyngedouw, E. (2010), 'The urbanization of nature: Great promises, impasse, and new beginnings'. In G. Bridge and S. Watson (eds), *New Companion to Urban Studies*, Oxford: Wiley-Blackwell.

Kajalo, S. and Lindblo, A. (2010), 'Formal and informal surveillance and competitiveness of shopping centers: a structural equation modelling approach', *Proceedings of ASBBS*, 17(1).

Kent, F. (2008), *Street as place. Using streets to rebuild Communities*, New York: Project for public spaces.

Kim, A.J. (2000), *Community building on the Web*, Berkeley, CA: Peachpit.

Knox, P.L. (1984), 'Styles, symbolism and settings: the built environment and imperatives of urbanised capitalism', *Architecture et comportment*, 2: 107–122.

Knox, P. and Martson, S.A. (1988), *Places and Regions in a Global Context: Human Geography*, Upper Saddle River: Prentice Hall.

Koolhaas, R. (1994), 'Generic City'. In *S,M,L,XL*, New York: Monacelli Press.

Koolhaas, R., Boeri, S. and Kwinter, S. (2001), *Mutations*, New York: Actar.

Krier, L. (1984), 'Houses, places, cities', *Architectural Design*, 54: 7–8.

Landrove, S. (ed) (1997), *Nuevos territorios nuevos paisajes*, Barcelona: Macba.

Landry, C. (2006), *The Art of City Making*, London: Earthscan.

Lanzani, A. (2003), *I paesaggi italiani*, Roma: Meltemi.

Lassus, B. (1977), *Jardins imaginaires*, Paris: Les Presses de la Connaissance.

Lawrence, R.J. (1987), *Houses, Dwellings and Homes: Design, Theory, Research and Practice*, New York: Wiley.

Lefebvre, H. (1991), *The Production of Space*, London: Basil Blackwell.

Levy, P. (1999), *Collective Intelligence*, Cambridge, MA: Perseus Books.

Lo Piccolo, F. (ed) (1995), *Identità urbana: Materiali per un dibattito*, Roma: Gangemi.

Losasso, M. (ed.) (1997), *La casa che cambia*, Napoli: Clean.

Losasso, M. (2011), 'Eco-innovative products and green economy prospects for the construction industry', *Il Progetto sostenibile*, 30.

Lynch, K. (1960), *The image of the city*, Cambridge, MA: MIT Press.

Lynch, K. (1972), *What Time is This Place?* Cambridge, MA: MIT Press.

Lynch, K. (1976), *Managing the Sense of a Region*, Cambridge, MA: MIT Press.

Lynch, K. (1981), *A theory of Good City Form*, Cambridge, MA: MIT Press.

Macpherson, H. (2005), 'Landscape's ocular-centrism – and beyond?' In B. Tress, G. Tress, G. Fry and P. Opdam. *From Landscape Research to Landscape Planning: Aspects of Integration, Education and Application*, Dordrecht: Springler.

Mazzoleni, D. and Sepe, M. (2004), 'Safeguarding of urban and landscape identity in post-earthquake reconstructions in Italy: Methodology of the analysis and first results'. In G. Manfredi, M.R. Pecce and A. Zollo (eds), *Proc. of the Workshop on Multidisciplinary Approach to Seismic Risk Problems*, Napoli: CRdC AMRA.

Mello, P. (2002), '*Metamorfosi dello spazio, Annotazioni sul divenire metropolitano'*, Torino: Bollati Boringhieri.

Migliorini, L. and Venini, L. (2001), *Città e legami sociali: Introduzione alla psicologia degli ambienti urbani*, Roma: Carrocci Editore.

Middleton, R. (ed) (1996), *The Idea of the City*, London: Architectural Association.

Miller, N. (2003), *Mapping the City*, New York: Continuum.

Mills, S. (2008) American Theme Parks and the Landscapes of Mass Culture, *American Studies Today*, available at http://www.americansc.org.uk/Online/disney.htm.

Mitchell, W.J. (1996), *City of Bits: Space, Place and the Infobahn*, Cambridge, MA: MIT Press.

Mitchell, W.J. (1999), *E-Topia: Urban Life, Jim – But Not As We Know it*, Cambridge, MA: MIT Press.

Mitchell, W.J. (2002), 'City Past and future', *Urban Design Quarterly*, 81: 18–21.

Montgomery, J. (1998), 'Making a City: Urbanity, Vitality and Urban Design', *Journal of Urban Design*, 3: 93–116.

Moughtin, J.C., Oc, T. and Tiesdell, S.A. (1995), *Urban Design: Ornament and Decoration*, Oxford: Butterworth-Heinemann.

Mumford, L. (1961), *The Culture of Cities*, New York: Harcourt Brace.

MVRDV (2002), *The Regionmaker: Rheinruhrcity*, Ruit: Hatje Cantz.

Nasar, J.L. (1998), *The Evaluative Image of the City*, Thousand Oaks, CA: Sage Publications.

Neil, W.J.V. (2004), *Urban planning and cultural identity*, New York: Routledge.

Nemeth, C. (2004), *Human Factors Methods for Design*, New York: CRC Press.

Nijkamp, P. and Perrels, A.H. (1994), *Sustainable Cities in Europe*, London: Earthscan.

Norberg-Schulz, C. (1971), *Existence, Space and Architecture*, London: Studio Vista.

Norberg-Schulz, C. (1980), *Genius Loci*, New York: Rizzoli.

Ohnmacht, T., Maksim, H. and Bergman, M. (2009), *Mobilities and Inequality*, London: Ashgate.

Oc, T. and Tiesdell, S. (1997), *Safer City Centres: Reviving the Public Realm*, London: Paul Chapman Publishing.

Oc, T. and Tiesdell, S. (2000), 'Urban design approaches to safer city centres: The fortress, the panoptic, the regulatory and the animated'. In J.R. Gold and G. Revill (eds), *Landscaper of Defence*, Harlow: Prentice Hall, 118–208.

Oncu, A. and Weyland, P. (1997), *Space, Culture, and Power: New Identities in Globalizing Cities*, London and New Jersey: Zed Books.

Orum, A.M. and Chen, X. (2003), *City and places*, Oxford: Blackwell.

Moughtin, C., Oc, T. and Tiesdell, S. (1999), *Urban Design: Ornament and Decoration*, Oxford: Architectural Press.

Pantelic, J. (undated), *Issues in Reconstruction Following Earthquakes: Opportunities for reducing risks of future disasters and enhancing the development process*, National Centre for Earthquake Research. Available at: http://www.ceprode.org.sv/staticpages/pdf/eng/doc255/doc255-contenido.pdf.

Patton, J.W. (2000), 'Protecting privacy in public? Surveillance technologies and the value of public places', *Ethics and Information Technology*, 2: 181–187.

Pellegrino, P. (2000), *Le Sens de L'Espace. Livre II, La Dynamique Urbaine*, Paris: Anthropos.

Penn, A. and Turner, A. (2002), 'Space Syntax Based Agent Simulation'. In M. Schreckenberg and S.D. Sharma (eds), *Pedestrian and Evacuation Dynamics*, Berlin: Springer-Verlag.

Penn, A. *et al.* (1998), 'Configurational modelling of urban movement networks', *Environment and Planning B: Planning & Design*, 25: 59–84.

Perec, G. (1997), *Species of Spaces and Other Pieces*, London: Penguin.

Pergola, C. (1997), La città dei sensi, Firenze: Alinea.

Porteous, J.D. (1977), *Environment and Behavior: Planning and Everyday Urban Life*, Reading, MA: Addison-Wesley.

Porteous, J.D. (1985), 'Smellscape', *Progress in Human Geography*, 9(3): 356–378.

Porteous, J.D. (1990), *Landscapes of the mind,* Toronto: University of Toronto Press.

Porteous, J.D. (1996), *Environmental Aesthetics: Ideas, politics and planning*, London: Routledge.

Porteous, J.D. and Mastin, J.F. (1985), 'Soundscape', *Journal of Architectural and Planning Research*, 2(3), 169–186.

Project for Public Spaces (2001), *How to Turn a Place Around: A Handbook for Creating Successful Public Spaces*, New York: Project for Public Places.

Proshansky, H.M., Fabian, A.K. and Kaminoff, R. (1983), 'Place-Identity: Physical World Socialization of the Self', *Journal of Environmental Psychology*, 3: 57–83.

Rapoport, A. (1977), *Human Aspects of Urban Form: Towards a Man-Environment Approach to Urban Form and Design*, Oxford: Pergamon Press.

Ratti, C., Sevtsuk, A., Huang, S. and Pailer, R. (2005), 'Mobile Landscapes: Graz in Real Time', Proc. of *3rd Symposium on LBS & TeleCartography*, Vienna.

Relph, E., 1976, *Place and Placelessness*, London: Pion.

Reynoso, E. (2012), *Bringing Back Broadway: The Effect of Revitalization on the Broadway Theater District*. Available at www.seniorsequence.net.

Rheingold, H. (2002), *Smart Mobs: The next social revolution*, Cambridge, MA: Perseus.

Rodaway, P. (1994), *Sensuous Geographies: Body, Sense and Place,* London: Routledge.

Rose, G. (1995), 'Place and identity: a sense of place'. In D. Massey and P. Jess (eds), *A Place in the world? Place, Cultures and Globalization*, Oxford: Open University/Oxford University Press.

Rossi, A. (1984), *The Architecture of the City*, Cambridge, MA: MIT Press.

Rowe, C. and Koetter, K. (1978), *Collage City*, Cambridge, MA: MIT Press.

Russ, T.H. (2002), *Site Planning and Design Handbook*, New York: McGraw Hill.

Saetnan, A.R., Lomell, H.M. and Wiecek, C. (2004), 'Controlling CCTV in Public Spaces: Reflections on Norwegian and Danish observations', *Surveillance & Society*, 2(2/3): 396–414.

Sandercock, L. (1997), *Towards Cosmopolis*, London: Academy Editions.

Scott, A.J. and Soja, E. (1996) (eds), *The City: Los Angeles and Urban Theory at the End of the Twentieth Century*, Los Angeles: University of California Press, 426–462.

Secchi, B. (2000), *Prima lezione di urbanistica*, Roma-Bari: Editori Laterza.

References

Sepe, M. (2004), 'Complexity and sustainability: relief and representation of the new urban identity', *Proceedings of Sustainable City 2004*, Southampton: WIT Press, 211–221.

Sepe, M. (2005a), 'The Sensitive Relief method and the identity of a place', *Architektura & Urbanizmus*, 39(1–2): 65–80.

Sepe, M. (2005b), 'New housing demands: an ecological approach to the contemporary dynamics', *Proceedings of Sustainable Building 2005 – Tokyo*, 3568–3571.

Sepe, M. (2005c), 'The PlaceMaker: a flexible and interactive tool to support the sustainable city construction and transformation,' *Proceedings of Sustainable Planning 2005*, Southampton: WIT Press, 1525–1534.

Sepe M. (2006a), 'Contemporary territories: methods of analysis and tools of representation', *Urbanistica*, 129: 117-122.

Sepe, M. (2006b), 'Complex Analysis for the Sustainable Planning and Construction of the Place Identity: the Sensitive Relief Method', *International Journal of Sustainable Development and Planning*, 1: 14–31.

Sepe, M. (2006c), 'PlaceMaker: supporting sustainable urban planning', *Planning Practice & Research,* 21(3): 349–366.

Sepe, M. (2006d), 'Planning with PlaceMaker: complex indices for sustainable projects', *Proceedings of Sustainable City 2006*, Southampton: WIT Press, 137–146.

Sepe, M., (2007a), *Il Rilievo Sensibile: Rappresentare l'identità per promuovere il Patrimonio Culturale in Campania*, Milano: Franco Angeli.

Sepe, M. (2007b), 'Creating Sustainable Urban Landscape: Mapping with PlaceMaker', *International Journal of Sustainable Development and Planning*, 2(2): 184–204.

Sepe, M. (2007c), 'Urban landscape, place identity and their components: a new software tool for supporting the sustainable urban planning and design', *Aeihoros*, 6(1): 72–85.

Sepe, M. (2009a), 'Creative urban regeneration between innovation, identity and sustainability', *International Journal of Sustainable Development*, 12(2-3-4): 144–159, Special issue, L. Fusco, Girard, P. Lombardi and P. Nijkamp (eds), 'Creative Urban Design and Development'.

Sepe, M. (2009b), 'PlaceMaker method: planning walkability by mapping place identity', *Journal of Urban Design*, 14(4): 463–487.

Sepe, M. (2010a), 'Requalifying historic places for sustainable use: a complex-sensitive method', *HBRC Housing and Building Research Center Journal*, 4.

Sepe, M. (2010b), 'Liveability, quality and place identity in the contemporary city: how to monitor and mitigate the impact of globalization on urban spaces', *Journal of Place Management and Development*, 3(3): 221–246.

Sepe, M. (2010c), 'Place identity and PlaceMaker: planning the urban sustainability', *Journal of Urban Planning and Development*, 136(2): 139–146, Special issue, 'Best Practices on Land Management Strategies'.

Sepe, M. (2010d), 'A dynamic approach to the monitoring of the mass tourism impact on place identity: the PlaceMaker method', Special issue, *Rivista di Scienze del Turismo Ambiente, Cultura, Diritto Economia*, 2: 151–162.

Sepe, M. (2010e), 'Anthropic risk and place identity: a method of analysis and a case study", *Journal of Urbanism. International Research on Placemaking and Urban Sustainability*, 3(1): 95–121.

Sepe, M. (2011), 'Beauty and place identity: A method to investigate, interpret and design the demand for beauty of the city', *Proceedings of EURAU*, Napoli.

Sepe, M. (2012a), 'Contemporary urban dynamics and multimedia mapping: a complex-sensitive approach', *Journal of Urban Design and Planning*, Special Issue, 'The use of Geographical Information and ICT in Urban Design and Planning'.

Sepe, M. (2012b), 'A dynamic method and interactive software to monitor and design place identity'. In G. Borruso, S. Bertazzon, A. Favretto, B. Murgante and C. M. Torre, *Geographic Information Analysis for Sustainable Development and Economic Planning: New Technologies*, Hershey: IGI Global, 295–312.

Sepe, M. (2012c), 'Principles for place identity enhancement: a sustainable challenge for changes to the contemporary city', *Proceedings of Sustainable City 2012*, Ashurst Lodge, Ashurst, Southampton: WIT Press, 993–1004.

Sepe, M. (2012d) 'Places in transformation: Designing the urban identity reinterpreting the new needs', *Proc. of International Conference EAAE/ARCC Cities in transformation: Research and Design*, Milano, 33–34.

Sinai, T. (2008), 'Urban Housing Demand'. In S. Durlauf and L. Blume (eds), *The New Palgrave Dictionary of Economics*, New York: Palgrave MacMillan.

Sinai, T. and Waldfogel, J. (2004), 'Geography and the Internet: is the internet a substitute or complement for cities?', *Journal of Urban Economics*, 56: 1–24.

Sircus, J. (2001), 'Invented Places', *Prospect*, 81(Sept/Oct): 30–35.

Smith, M.A. and Kollock, P. (1999), *Communities in Cyberspace*, London: Routledge.

Soja, E. (1989), *Postmodern geographies. The Reassertion of Space in Critical Social Theory*, London: Verson.

Soja, E. (1996), *Thirdspace – Journeys to Los Angeles and Other Real-and-imagined Place*, Malden and Oxford: Blackwell Publishing.

Sorkin, M. (ed.) (1999), *Variations on a Theme Park: The New American City and the End of Public Space*, New York: Hill & Wang.

Southworth, M. (1969), 'The sonic environment of cities', *Environment and Behavior*, 1: 49–70.

Southworth and Ruggeri (2010), 'Beyond Placelessness, Place Identity and the global city'. In T. Banerjee and A. Loukaitou-Sideris (eds), *Companion to urban design*, London and New York: Routledge.

Stanek, L. (2011), *Henri Lefebvre on Space: Architecture, Urban Research, and the Production of Theory*, Minneapolis: University of Minnesota Press.

Stokols, D. and Shumaker, S.A. (1981), 'People in places: A transactional view of setting'. In J. Harvey (ed.), *Cognition, Social Behavior, and the Environment*, Hillsdale, NJ: Lawrence Erlbaum.

Swyngedouw, E. (1993), 'Communication, mobility and the struggle for power over space'. In G. Giannopoulos and A. Gillespie (eds), *Transport and Communications in the New Europe*, London: Belhaven.

Thackara, J. and Maas, W. (2003), 'Strumenti per costruire città', *Domus*, 861: 88–93.

Thrift, N. (1995), 'A hyperactive world'. In R. Johnston, P. Taylor and M. Watts (eds), *Geographies of global change*, Oxford: Blackwell, 18–35.

Tiesdell, S., Oc, T. and Heath, T. (1996), *Revitalising Historic Urban quarters*, Oxford: Butterworths.

Torres, M. (2000), *Luoghi magnetici: Spazi pubblici nella città moderna e contemporanea*, Milano: FrancoAngeli.

Towers, G. (2005), *Introduction to Urban Housing Design: At Home in the City*, Oxford: Architectural Press.

References

Turner, A. and Penn, A. (2002), 'Encoding natural movement as an agent-based system: an investigation into human pedestrian behaviour in the built environment', *Environment and Planning B: Planning and Design*, 29: 473–490.

Urban Design Group (2002), *Urban Design Guidance, Urban Frameworks: Development Briefs and Master Plans*, London: Thomas Telford Publishing.

Urry, J. (1995), *Consuming places*, London and New York: Routledge.

Vale, L.J. and Warner, S.B. jr (eds) (2001), *Imaging the City*, New Jersey: Centre for Urban Policy Research.

Venturi, R. (1966), *Complexity and Contradiction in Architecture*, New York: MoMA.

Venturi, R., Scott Brown, D. and Izenour, S. (1972), *Learning from Las Vegas: The Forgotten Symbolism of Architectural Form*, Cambridge, MA: MIT Press.

Viganò, P. (1999), *La città elementare*, Milano: Skira Editore.

Watson, G.B. and Bentley, I. (2007), *Identity by Design*, Oxford: Architectural Press.

Weitz, R. (1986), *New Roads to Development*, New York: Greenwood Press.

Whitehand, J.W.R. and Larkham, P.J. (1992), *Urban Landscape*, London and New York: Routledge.

Whyte, W.H. (1980), *The Social Life of Small Public Space*, Washington DC: Conservation Foundation.

Wolch, J. and Dear, M. (eds) (1989), *The Power of Geography: how territory shapes social life*, Boston: Unwin Hyman.

Zelinka, A. and Brennan, D. (2001), *Safescape, Creating Safer, More Livable Communities Though Planning and Design*, Chicago: Planner Press APA.

Zukin, S. (1991), *Landscape of Power: from Detroit to Disney World*, Berkeley: University of California Press.

Zukin, S. (1995), *The Cultures of Cities*, Oxford: Basil Blackwell.

Zukin, S. (2010), *Naked City: The Death and Life of Authentic Urban Places*, New York: Oxford University Press, Inc.

Websites

Gehl, J. (2002), *Public space and public life: City of Adelaide 2002*, http://www.adelaidecitycouncil.com

Puliti L. (2001), *Gregoire+Petetin*. Timezone, http://architettura.it/models/20010619/index.htm

Space Syntax (2005), *General Practice Brochure*, http://www.spacesyntax.com/downloads/books-brochures/

http://senseable.mit.edu

http://www.bringingbackbroadway.com

http://www.british-history.ac.uk

http://www.bettermarketstreetsf.org

http://www.laconservancy.org

http://www.maps.google.com

http://www.multiplicity.it

http://www.pps.org

http://www.spacesyntax.com/projects-clients-partners/

http://www.vr.ucl.ac.uk/depthmap

Index